MW01415444

World War II and American Racial Politics

This book examines the heterogeneous consequences of World War II for white racial attitudes and the executive branch response to civil rights advocacy. Contrary to conventional wisdom, analysis of the available survey evidence finds that the white mass public's racial policy attitudes largely did not liberalize during the war against Nazi Germany. In this context, advocates turned their attention increasingly to the possibility of unilateral action by the president, which led them to emphasize war-specific measures where the president had some discretion – discrimination in the defense industry and segregation in the armed forces – combined with support for the president's foreign policy initiatives, strategic decisions that had important implications for twentieth-century racial politics. Along with offering a reinterpretation of this critical period in American political development, this book also has implications for the theoretical relationship between war and the inclusion of marginalized groups in democratic societies more generally.

Steven White is an assistant professor of political science in the Maxwell School of Citizenship and Public Affairs at Syracuse University. His research examines race and American political development, particularly the complicated relationship between war and the inclusion of marginalized groups. His research has been published or is forthcoming in *Studies in American Political Development*, *American Politics Research*, and *Social Science Quarterly*. He has also written for more popular outlets, including *The Monkey Cage* and the *Los Angeles Review of Books*.

World War II and American Racial Politics

Public Opinion, the Presidency, and Civil Rights Advocacy

STEVEN WHITE
Syracuse University, New York

CAMBRIDGE
UNIVERSITY PRESS

CAMBRIDGE
UNIVERSITY PRESS

University Printing House, Cambridge CB2 8BS, United Kingdom

One Liberty Plaza, 20th Floor, New York, NY 10006, USA

477 Williamstown Road, Port Melbourne, VIC 3207, Australia

314–321, 3rd Floor, Plot 3, Splendor Forum, Jasola District Centre, New Delhi – 110025, India

79 Anson Road, #06–04/06, Singapore 079906

Cambridge University Press is part of the University of Cambridge.

It furthers the University's mission by disseminating knowledge in the pursuit of education, learning, and research at the highest international levels of excellence.

www.cambridge.org
Information on this title: www.cambridge.org/9781108427630
DOI: 10.1017/9781108596756

© Steven White 2019

This publication is in copyright. Subject to statutory exception and to the provisions of relevant collective licensing agreements, no reproduction of any part may take place without the written permission of Cambridge University Press.

First published 2019

Printed and bound in Great Britain by TJ International Ltd, Padstow

A catalogue record for this publication is available from the British Library.

Library of Congress Cataloging-in-Publication Data
Names: White, Steven, 1986– author.
Title: World War II and American racial politics : public opinion, the presidency, and civil rights advocacy / Steven White, Syracuse University, New York.
Description: Cambridge, United Kingdom ; New York, NY : Cambridge University Press, [2019] | Includes bibliographical references and index.
Identifiers: LCCN 2019008524 | ISBN 9781108427630 (alk. paper)
Subjects: LCSH: World War, 1939–1945 – African Americans. | World War, 1939–1945 – Social aspects – United States. | African Americans – Civil rights – History – 20th century. | United States – Race relations – History – 20th century. | World War, 1939–1945 – Influence. | Whites – United States – Attitudes – History – 20th century. | United States – Armed Forces – African Americans – History – 20th century. | United States – Race relations – Public opinion – History – 20th century. | Social surveys – United States – History – 20th century. | Public opinion – United States – History – 20th century.
Classification: LCC D810.N4 W47 2019 | DDC 940.53/7308996073–dc23
LC record available at https://lccn.loc.gov/2019008524

ISBN 978-1-108-42763-0 Hardback

Cambridge University Press has no responsibility for the persistence or accuracy of URLs for external or third-party internet websites referred to in this publication and does not guarantee that any content on such websites is, or will remain, accurate or appropriate.

Contents

List of Figures	*page* vi
List of Tables	vii
Acknowledgments	viii
1 Introduction	1
2 White Racial Attitudes, 1937–1950	29
3 White Veterans and Racial Attitudes, 1946–1961	67
4 The Roosevelt Administration and Civil Rights During World War II	95
5 The Truman Administration, Military Service, and Postwar Civil Rights	128
6 War, Race, and American Political Development	157
Appendix	172
Bibliography	187
Index	200

Figures

2.1	Support for federal antilynching legislation, 1937–1950	page 50
2.2	Regional support for federal antilynching legislation, 1937–1950	50
2.3	Opposition to federal antilynching legislation, 1937–1950	51
2.4	Regional opposition to federal antilynching legislation, 1937–1950	52
2.5	Support for abolishing the poll tax, 1940–1949	55
2.6	Regional support for abolishing the poll tax, 1940–1949	56
3.1	Antiblack prejudice, 1946 (marginal effects)	77
3.2	Antiblack prejudice, 1946 (marginal effects), continued	77
3.3	Military segregation, 1948 (marginal effects)	80
3.4	Lynching, 1948 (marginal effects)	81
3.5	Voting rights and sit-ins, 1961 (OLS)	86
3.6	Segregation and anti-integration protests, 1961 (OLS)	86
A1	Support for federal antilynching legislation by question wording	179
A2	Opposition to federal antilynching legislation by question wording	180

Tables

2.1	Antiblack prejudice, 1943–1946	*page* 44
2.2	Military segregation, 1942–1948	58
3.1	Antiblack prejudice, 1946 (veterans vs. nonveterans)	76
3.2	Military segregation, 1948 (veterans vs. nonveterans)	80
3.3	Lynching, 1948 (veterans vs. nonveterans)	81
3.4	Voting rights, segregation, and sit-ins, 1961 (veterans vs. nonveterans)	85
B1	1961 veterans analysis (OLS, no education controls)	185
B2	1961 veterans analysis (ordered probit models)	185
B3	Black friend, 1961 (veterans vs. nonveterans)	186

Acknowledgments

American political development (APD) scholars are perhaps overly inclined to think in terms of path dependence, but this project certainly would have turned out differently had I not been fortunate enough to be advised by Ira Katznelson, Robert Shapiro, and Robert Lieberman during my time as a graduate student at Columbia University. Thanks also to Kimberley Johnson, Jeff Lax, Justin Phillips, and Dorian Warren for their support and advice. I am particularly appreciative of Bob Shapiro and Kim Johnson for their help in turning the seemingly opaque process of publishing a book into something a bit more manageable.

This project has benefited from presentations at several conferences and workshops along the way, including meetings of the American Political Science Association and Midwest Political Science Association; the American Politics Workshop at Columbia University; the Politics and Protest Workshop at the CUNY Graduate Center (organized by James Jasper and John Krinsky); the Historical Political Economy working group (organized by Alexandra Cirone and Scott Abramson); the Penn Program on Democracy, Citizenship, and Constitutionalism Graduate Workshop; the Institutions in Context workshop at the University of Tampere (organized by Katri Sieberg); and job talks both successful and unsuccessful. With apologies to anyone I might have neglected, I am appreciative of suggestions and critiques from Paul Frymer, Karen Hult, Penny Lewis, Robert Mickey, Julie Novkov, Andrew Polsky, and Rogers Smith. I'm also grateful to Eric Schickler, who kindly shared data and answered questions at various points along the way.

My archival research was funded by the Harry S. Truman Library Institute and the Columbia University Department of Political Science. I'm thankful to all of the archivists at the Roosevelt and Truman presidential libraries, the Library of Congress, and Columbia University. I also want to thank Kay Hartman at the Higher Ground Hotel in Independence, Missouri, who kindly drove me and another researcher to the Truman Library one surprisingly cold and rainy April morning.

Graduate school was made far more enjoyable by the friends I made along the way. Jon Blake and Mike Smith made the first two years, especially the countless hours of methods homework completed in the windowless basement of the Lehman Library, much more bearable. Much of my dissertation was written on the seventh floor of the International Affairs Building and in cafes throughout Brooklyn, often working alongside Jon, Mike, Al Fang, Michelle Chun, Noah Buckley, and Andy Guess. My work benefited greatly from their company and ideas. Thanks also to Sara Moller, especially for hosting me during my research at the Library of Congress, as well as Joe Brown, Tony Daniel, Kevin Elliott, Alissa Stollwerk, and many other friends and colleagues I met at Columbia.

I was immensely fortunate to become an assistant professor at Syracuse University in Fall 2017, which was a wonderful place to finish this book. From the questions raised at my job talk to more informal advice once I started working there, I'm very thankful to all those working in the Department of Political Science for their support, especially Keith Bybee, Elizabeth Cohen, Chris Faricy, Shana Gadarian, Seth Jolly, Tom Keck, Sarah Pralle, Grant Reeher, and Brian Taylor. During the revision stage, feedback from the Moynihan Research Workshop for junior faculty provided helpful advice on how to reframe parts of the manuscript. I appreciate the suggestions from Brian Brege, Dimitar Gueorguiev, Tessa Murphy, Danielle Thomsen, Emily Thorson, and others in attendance (and thanks to Tessa and Katherine Michelmore for organizing it). I'm also extremely appreciative of all the work of Jacquie Meyer, Sally Greenfield, and Candy Brooks in the department office, as well as Sunju Raybeck and Kelley Coleman at the Campbell Public Affairs Institute.

The book publishing process felt like an impossible mystery to me when I began, but I'm thankful to Sara Doskow at Cambridge University Press for being supportive and helpful at every step along the way. I also appreciate the work of three anonymous reviewers, whose detailed suggestions made for a stronger final product. Portions of Chapters 2 and 3 also appear in my article, "Civil Rights, World War II, and U.S. Public Opinion," *Studies in American Political Development* 30(1), 2016, 38–61. This material is reprinted (and expanded on) here with permission from Cambridge University Press.

My sensibilities as a political scientist were inevitably shaped by the intellectual freedom given to me as a student at Hampshire College. I'm appreciative of the support and guidance provided by Eric Schocket, Susan Tracy, and Wilson Valentín-Escobar. I also benefited immensely from coursework and conversations with Howard Gold at Smith College, without whom I might never have decided to get a PhD in political science.

I appreciate the support of my parents, Peggy Ray and Mike White, my grandparents George and Lois Bentley and Elmer and Wanda White, and my brother, Nick Helton. They probably didn't want me to move 800 miles away when I graduated from high school, but they have always been supportive. I also want to thank my partner, Caroline Wazer, whose empathy and humor kept me grounded during even the most frustrating moments of grad school. Graciously, she even continued to support me as I meandered through what turned out to be a rather prolonged academic job search and, at long last, finished this book. All errors, of course, are the responsibility of our cat, Carlos.

1

Introduction

In the middle of American participation in World War II, racial violence broke out in Detroit. June 20, 1943, was a hot summer day, and many of Detroit's residents, black and white alike, went to Belle Isle, an island park in the Detroit River. Problems began with a few unrelated scuffles, but as tensions increased, rumors of a riot started to spread. By 11 PM, thousands were brawling on the bridge between the city and the island, leading to what one historian described as "a festival of violence against African Americans." By early morning, the police had arrested forty-seven people, and the unrest temporarily subsided. The riot, however, was further propelled by rumors that quickly spread around the city. In Paradise Valley, a predominantly black neighborhood, a rumor spread that a white mob had thrown a black woman and her child over the bridge. Some residents responded by attempting to travel to Belle Isle, only to find access to the bridge barricaded. Angered but without the expected outlet to vent their frustrations, they returned to Paradise Valley and began destroying many of the white-owned businesses. As police began moving into Paradise Valley, another rumor spread among white crowds gathered along Woodward Avenue. This time the rumor was that black men at Belle Isle had raped several white women. A white mob began attacking black residents; police did little to stop it. It would take another twenty hours before the mayor of Detroit and the governor of Michigan went on the radio to proclaim a state of emergency; it would take even longer before federal troops were brought in to bring the riot to a close. In the end, thirty-four people were killed – the largest number of them black men shot by police – and more than 700 were injured. Adjusted for inflation, property damage reached $28 million. War production in Detroit, the core of what President

Franklin Roosevelt had called "the arsenal of democracy," came to a halt.¹

Ten days after the riot, an editorial in *The Nation* linked the riot and the racial divisions it represented to the ideological logic of World War II. "The Axis is losing battles in Europe and the Pacific," the editorial began, "but it can console itself with victories recently won in the United States." The language only grew stronger from there. "It is time for us to clear our minds and hearts of the contradictions that are rotting our moral position and undermining our purpose," it read. "We cannot fight fascism abroad while turning a blind eye to fascism at home. We cannot inscribe our banners 'For democracy and a caste system.' We cannot liberate oppressed peoples while maintaining the right to oppress our own minorities." Remaining passive in the face of such racial inequities, the article declared in conclusion, meant Americans "have no right to say complacently: 'We are not as these Herrenvolk'."²

Such sentiments were not unusual during World War II. A year later, in 1944, the Swedish economist Gunnar Myrdal published his mammoth opus on American race relations, *An American Dilemma: The Negro Problem and Modern Democracy*. Over the course of nearly 1,500 pages, Myrdal made the contradiction between the aims of war and Jim Crow clear. This war, he wrote, "is an ideological war fought in defense of democracy." The nature of the totalitarian dictatorships the Allied forces were fighting "made the ideological issue much sharper in this War than it was in the First World War." Further, since Nazism is "based on a racial superiority dogma," American democratic principles "had to be applied more explicitly to race." The implication of this, to Myrdal, was clear. "In fighting fascism and nazism," he wrote, "America had to stand before the whole world in favor of racial tolerance and the inalienable human freedoms."³ Myrdal's book was,

---

¹ For an overview of the "Detroit race riot," as it came to be known, see Harvard Sitkoff, *Toward Freedom Land: The Long Struggle for Racial Equality in America*, (Lexington: The University Press of Kentucky, 2010), 43–64. For the "festival of violence" quote, see Kenneth Robert Janken, *White: The Biography of Walter White, Mr. NAACP*, (New York: The New Press, 2003), 275.

² "Defeat at Detroit," *The Nation*, July 3, 1943, 4. A typographical error in the print magazine excluded a quotation mark, which is edited in here for clarity. Partially cited, among other places, in Maria Hohn, "'We Will Never Go Back to the Old Way Again': Germany in the African-American Debate on Civil Rights," *Central European History* 41, 2008, 616.

³ Gunnar Myrdal, *An American Dilemma: The Negro Problem and Modern Democracy*, (New York: Harper & Brothers Publishers: 1944), 1004.

according to Alan Brinkley, a "major factor in drawing white liberal attention to problems of race – precisely because Myrdal himself discussed racial injustice as a rebuke to the nation's increasingly vocal claim to be the defender of democracy and personal freedom in a world menaced by totalitarianism."[4] Although it received some scattered criticism, the nature of the book – its social scientific language, nonpartisan sponsorship, massive length, Myrdal's European-ness – led it to seem like a "definitive analysis" of the American race problem in elite discourse.[5]

These arguments by white liberals complemented the wartime rhetoric of civil rights organizations and black newspapers, who advocated what came to be called the "Double-V campaign" for victory at home *and* abroad.[6] Civil rights leaders like Walter White of the National Association for the Advancement of Colored People (NAACP) and A. Philip Randolph of the Brotherhood of Sleeping Car Porters used the wartime context to reshape the nature of their arguments and the structure of their policy agenda. Fighting white supremacy abroad, they thought, might finally give them the tools needed to make a real dent in white supremacy at home.

Others, however, were not so sure. The southern journalist John Temple Graves was among them. Black civil rights leaders, Graves wrote in 1942, had made "plain beyond question an intent to use the war for settling overnight the whole, long, complicated, infinitely delicate racial problem." He was no fan of the Double-V campaign. "So little are they concerned by the fact that their all-embracive crusade means a domestic war while their country is making supreme war abroad that they have

---

[4] Alan Brinkley, *The End of Reform: New Deal Liberalism in Recession and War*, (New York: Vintage Books, 1995), 168–169.

[5] Ibid., 169–170; for criticism, see, e.g., Leo P. Crespi, "Is Gunnar Myrdal on the Right Track?" *Public Opinion Quarterly* 9(2), 1945, 201–212. Ralph Ellison also penned a notable critique that the *Antioch Review* declined to publish at the time. Fortunately, this was later published in a collected volume of Ellison's writing. See Ralph Ellison, *Shadow and Act*, (New York: Vintage Books, 1995), 303–317. Of course, Myrdal was not the only person writing on this topic. Countless books and articles were published linking the war to racial equality. Another important contribution was Carey McWilliams, *Brothers Under the Skin*, (Boston: Little, Brown and Company, 1943).

[6] For a discussion of the Double-V campaign, see Harvard Sitkoff, "Racial Militancy and Interracial Violence in the Second World War," *Journal of American History* 58(3), 1971, 668–681; Neil A. Wynn, *The Afro-American and the Second World War: Revised Edition*, (New York: Holmes & Meier, 1993 [1976]); Jonathan Rosenberg, *How Far the Promised Land?: World Affairs and the American Civil Rights Movement from the First World War to Vietnam*, (Princeton: Princeton University Press, 2005).

invited their followers to think in terms of a Double V-for-Victory – victory in battle with Hitler and victory in battle at home," Graves wrote. "Victory, unhappily, doesn't work that way." Later in the same article, while detailing improvements in the conditions of black southerners during the war, he noted the decline of lynchings, but warned, "Unhappily the number may increase now as a result of the agitations of the white man against the black and the black against the white." For Graves, war meant putting domestic debates aside and doubling down on the war abroad. "This war must be won," Graves wrote. "And the black man in the South, where most black men live, must get on with the white man in the South, no matter what Washington orders or New York demands."[7]

Some white southern voices were less constrained. On the floor of the US Senate, Mississippi's James Eastland declared southern soldiers – presumably he meant the white ones – wanted to return home "to see the integrity of the social institutions of the South unimpaired" and "white supremacy maintained." According to Eastland, that was the real point of fighting the fascist menace. "Those boys are fighting to maintain the rights of the States," Eastland declared. "Those boys are fighting to maintain white supremacy."[8]

These stories are not just interesting historical anecdotes, but rather reflective of the ambiguities of academic scholarship on World War II's effect on racial politics in America. Political scientists Philip Klinkner and Rogers Smith argue "it is hard to escape the conclusion that it was... the emergence of fascism and Nazism in the 1930s that most set the stage for

---

[7] John Temple Graves, "The Southern Negro and the War Crisis," *Virginia Quarterly Review* 18(4), 1942, 501, 514, 516.

[8] Ira Katznelson, *Fear Itself: The New Deal and the Origins of Our Time*, (New York: Liveright Publishing Corporation, 2013), 206. Jason Morgan Ward describes the broader rhetoric of this sort that emerged in the white South. In comparison to civil rights advocates' Double-V campaign, Morgan Ward writes, "defenders of segregation articulated their own vision of Double Victory. Championing white supremacy and demanding freedom from outside interference, Southern conservatives deemed civil rights agitation and federal encroachment to be as dangerous as an Axis invasion. The white South, like African Americans, had entered the war fighting on two fronts." He later describes this effort as "[m]ore than an elite rhetorical strategy but less than an authentic grassroots rebellion." Jason Morgan Ward, "'A War for States' Rights': The White Supremacist Vision of Double Victory," in *Fog of War: The Second World War and the Civil Rights Movement*, ed. Kevin M. Kruse and Stephen Tuck, (New York: Oxford University Press, 2012), 127, 140. See also Jason Morgan Ward, *Defending White Democracy: The Making of a Segregationist Movement & the Remaking of Racial Politics, 1936–1965*, (Chapel Hill: University of North Carolina Press, 2011).

Introduction 5

real transformations" on civil rights.[9] Many historians, too, have been inclined to take a positive view of the war. Pete Daniel argues World War II "unleashed new expectations and, among many whites, taught tolerance." Taking it a step further, Daniel goes so far as to argue "the war in many ways made the civil rights movement possible."[10] Among historians, this view was initially developed in the 1960s by scholars who saw the World War II era as the "forgotten years of the Negro revolution."[11]

Historians, however, have increasingly taken a more critical perspective on the war's relationship with civil rights. "If historians search for the roots of the civil rights movement in the wartime struggle, they will doubtlessly find something in the discordant record resembling the evidence they seek," Kevin Kruse and Stephen Tuck write. While acknowledging "the turmoil and rhetoric and bloodshed of war did indeed provide a far-reaching challenge to Southern, national and global systems of race," they argue it "did not push racial systems in a single direction, and certainly not one moving inexorably toward greater equality."[12] More cynical perspectives can also be found in the work of some political scientists. Daniel Kryder, for example, highlights the correlation between war and instances of racial crowd violence, especially during World War II, while Ronald Krebs demonstrates the limits of military service as a tool for black civil rights gains more generally, particularly in comparison to other cases.[13]

Both perspectives contain kernels of truth. The logic of a war against Nazi racism gave civil rights groups a compelling rhetorical framework and made it intellectually more difficult to justify domestic Jim Crow. Yet the war also coincided with significant incidents of racial

---

[9] Philip A. Klinkner and Rogers M. Smith, *The Unsteady March: The Rise and Decline of Racial Equality in America*, (Chicago: University of Chicago Press, 2002), 137.

[10] Pete Daniel, "Going Among Strangers: Southern Reactions to World War II," *Journal of American History* 77 (3), 1990, 910.

[11] Richard M. Dalfiume, "The 'Forgotten Years' of the Negro Revolution," *Journal of American History* 55(1), 1968, 90–106.

[12] Kevin M. Kruse and Stephen Tuck, "Introduction: The Second World War and the Civil Rights Movement," in *Fog of War: The Second World War and the Civil Rights Movement*, ed. Kevin M. Kruse and Stephen Tuck, (New York: Oxford University Press: 2012), 11–12. They further note that the historian Harvard Sitkoff actually became somewhat more cynical about the war and civil rights as well. Ibid., 5, 13f6.

[13] Daniel Kryder, *Divided Arsenal: Race and the American State During World War II*, (New York: Cambridge University Press: 2002), 251; Ronald R. Krebs, *Fighting for Rights: Military Service and the Politics of Citizenship*, (Ithaca: Cornell University Press, 2006).

violence, many concentrated near military bases. Some black veterans returned home only to be beaten by white mobs, which sometimes included law enforcement. And as the writing of John Temple Graves suggests, there was no shortage of whites who found the attempt by civil rights activists to use the war's antifascist logic to be troubling. Not everyone was so convinced that, to use a phrase from *The Nation*'s editorial page, the war could not be fought against fascism abroad while also maintaining elements of fascism at home. For many white Americans, the war was fought to defend the status quo, white supremacy and all.

Taking note of the discrepancies between these contradictory narratives, this book examines the potentially heterogeneous consequences of World War II for American racial politics. In particular, I focus on trends in white racial attitudes and the executive branch response to black civil rights advocacy.[14] Stated in its most extreme form, I am interested in what this response might look like in a world with no World War II. Perhaps more realistically, I hope to at least provide a theoretically and empirically grounded assessment of the specific ways in which the war influenced the politics of civil rights in its aftermath, as distinct from – although almost certainly interacting with – the New Deal and its resultant coalitional and ideological pressures.[15]

Perhaps the most novel contribution of this book is a historically grounded assessment of the war's effects on white racial attitudes. Until recently, American political development scholars rarely engaged with

---

[14] While acknowledging the complexity of American racial politics during the wartime period – which I discuss in more detail in the concluding chapter – I argue that the focus on black civil rights is still merited. In 1940, African Americans represented 10 percent of the population overall, and 24 percent of the population in the South. In some states, they approached a majority. In Mississippi, to take the closest example, 49 percent of residents were African Americans (this was a slight decrease from the 1930 Census, when Mississippi had more black residents than white residents). Residents of "Hispanic origin (of any race)," by contrast, constituted only one percent of the national population, while residents who identified as "Asian and Pacific Islander" represented just 0.2 percent. In 1940, even Texas had more African American residents than Hispanic residents. Campbell Gibson and Kay Jung, "Historical Census Statistics on Population Totals by Race, 1790 to 1990, and by Hispanic Origin, 1970 to 1990, for the United States, Regions, Divisions, and States," Working Paper No. 56, Census Population Division. As such, black civil rights advocacy drew more national political attention than the rights claims of other marginalized groups, meaning there was more focus on this issue in the executive branch and more public opinion polls that asked questions about it.

[15] As noted later in this chapter, I define the World War II era somewhat more broadly than just the period of US participation in warfare.

public opinion data, focusing instead on the elite institutions that make up the American state. This is particularly true of scholarly accounts of World War II. Did the war lead white Americans – civilians and veterans alike – to liberalized views on race relations and civil rights in its aftermath? Or were white Americans able to maintain an acceptance of – and in some cases a commitment to – white supremacy despite the experience of the war against Nazism? Relying on rarely used survey data from the 1930s and 1940s, I find that the war's effects on white racial attitudes were more limited than is widely assumed. While there is some evidence of declining racial prejudice, white attitudes towards antilynching legislation actually seem to have moved in the racially conservative direction. While there are fewer available surveys that asked about wartime issues, I also demonstrate that whites were overwhelmingly opposed to integrating the armed forces and extending job discrimination protections in the postwar period. I follow this analysis of aggregate white opinion with an analysis of white veterans, relative to their nonveteran counterparts. While veterans were not widely liberalized on racial issues as a result of their service, I do find some intriguing exceptions from this general trend.

After demonstrating far less change in white racial attitudes during the war than many have assumed, I turn my attention to the presidency.[16] In the context of a war against Nazism abroad, wartime civil rights activists emphasized the possibility of unilateral executive action as a means for achieving their policy goals, which were often framed as pertaining directly to the war effort. Did this wartime advocacy lead the Roosevelt and Truman administrations to address civil rights differently and earlier than when they would have otherwise? Relying on a wide range of archival evidence, I demonstrate how wartime activism succeeded in pressuring Roosevelt to issue an executive order combatting discrimination in the defense industry, but failed to convince him to act on segregation in the military. I then describe how the military integration movement continued into the Truman presidency, eventually succeeding in beginning the process of integration the nation's armed forces in the postwar period. Along the way, I highlight the ways in which the wartime context both helped and hindered the goals of the movement. While the probability of any change at all occurring was likely higher as a result of the war, advocates were also incentivized to focus on these war-specific

---

[16] Later in this chapter, I offer a more detailed justification of my focus on the executive branch rather than other national political institutions.

measures and frame their demands as consistent with the foreign policy goals of the president.

In this introductory chapter, I begin with a discussion of the relationship between war and rights claims in general, and World War II and black civil rights claims in particular. I also provide historical background on the "long" civil rights movement and offer a critical overview of existing scholarly accounts of the place of World War II in the study of race and American political development. I then discuss several definitional issues, including the temporal boundaries and scope of the project, as well as how I unpack "World War II" as an explanatory variable. I conclude with a roadmap of the chapters that follow.

WAR, RIGHTS CLAIMS, AND AMERICAN POLITICS

There is a long intellectual lineage behind the idea that war might be related to the incorporation of marginalized groups. For some, the reason is that war is a time of upheaval, which might carry over to domestic politics as well, as such disruptions can provide opportunities for groups to make rights claims in new ways. For others, the reason relates more to rights claims associated with military service, an idea that has a long tradition in republican political thought. Historically, this existed as least as early as ancient Rome.[17] In the High Roman Empire, for example, the distinction between legionaries and auxiliaries in the army was partly based on citizenship. Citizenship was required as a condition of joining the legionaries, while auxiliary soldiers were generally not citizens upon enrollment, but were instead granted citizenship after twenty-five years of service.[18] The historian Otto Hintze has noted more generally that there exists a common notion that one who serves in a nation's military "must logically and fairly be granted the regular rights of citizenship."[19]

This theoretical linkage between war and military service and rights claims is part of the American political tradition as well, dating back to the American Revolution. Thousands of black soldiers served in the military during the Revolutionary War, some of whom received freedom in exchange for their service. For many others held in slavery, the war

---

[17] Krebs, *Fighting for Rights*, 17
[18] Mark Hassall, "The Army," in *The Cambridge Ancient History*, ed. Alan K. Bowman et al., Vol. 11, (New York: Cambridge University Press, 2000), 336.
[19] Otto Hintze, "Military Organization and the Organization of the State," in *The State: Critical Concepts*, ed. John A. Hall, (New York: Routledge, 1994), 200. Cited in Krebs, *Fighting for Rights*, 17.

presented an opportunity to flee to freedom. It is estimated that as many as 20 percent of the enslaved population could have gained freedom during the war. In the war's aftermath, states in New England started to ban slavery. Vermont led the way, but a handful of other states followed suit. Some states even extended suffrage rights to black men, although in many cases this was later restricted.[20]

Of all the wars in American history, the Civil War was most clearly linked to the rights of African Americans. The eleven Confederate states attempted to secede to preserve slavery, and emancipation eventually came to be seen as a military necessity for the Union forces. The period of Reconstruction that followed was, in the words of Eric Foner, a "massive experiment in interracial democracy without precedent in the history of this or any other country that abolished slavery in the nineteenth century."[21] During Reconstruction, black freedmen voted and held elected office and progressive taxation was implemented to fund social expenditures, all protected by national oversight.[22] Ultimately, however, white southern "Redeemers" succeeded in winning back control of state governments, eventually leading to the rise of Jim Crow.[23]

Civil rights advocates were initially optimistic that World War I might offer an opportunity to break down these postemancipation barriers, particularly if African Americans served honorably in the armed forces. Warning that "the German power" posed a significant threat to African

---

[20] Numbers drawn from Klinkner and Smith, *The Unsteady March*, 19–20. For fuller historical accounts, see Thomas J. Davis, "Emancipation Rhetoric, Natural Rights, and Revolutionary New England: A Note on Four Black Petitions in Massachusetts, 1773–1777," *New England Quarterly* 62(2), 1989, 248–263; James Oliver Horton and Lois E. Horton, *In Hope of Liberty: Culture, Community and Protest Among Northern Free Blacks, 1700–1860*, (New York: Oxford University Press, 1998); Joanne Pope Melish, *Disowning Slavery: Gradual Emancipation and 'Race' in New England, 1780–1860*, (Ithaca: Cornell University Press, 2000); Lois E. Horton, "From Class to Race in Early America: Northern Post-Emancipation Racial Reconstruction," *Journal of the Early Republic* 19(4), 1999, 629–649. Along with the rewards-for-service framework, it is also possible that other factors, like revolutionary ideas of natural rights, played a role for at least some. For an examination of state-level variation in nineteenth-century black suffrage rights, see David A. Bateman, *Disenfranchising Democracy Constructing the Electorate in the United States, the United Kingdom, and France*, (New York: Cambridge University Press, 2018).

[21] Eric Foner, *Reconstruction: America's Unfinished Revolution, 1863–1877*, (New York: Harper & Row, 1988), xxv.

[22] Ibid.; W. E. B. Du Bois, *Black Reconstruction*, (New York: Harcourt, Brace and Company, 1935).

[23] C. Vann Woodward, *The Strange Career of Jim Crow*, (New York: Oxford University Press, 1955).

Americans and other racial minorities, W. E. B. Du Bois called for African Americans to enthusiastically support the war effort. "Let us not hesitate," he told his readers. "Let us, while this war lasts, forget our special grievances and close our ranks shoulder to shoulder with our own white fellow citizens and the allied nations that are fighting for democracy."[24] Despite the hopes of civil rights advocates, however, World War I did not prove to be a fruitful period for racial inclusion. Indeed, racial violence increased in the war's aftermath, most notably in the "Red Summer" of 1919.[25]

World War II, by contrast, is often thought of as the exemplar of the good war, both in terms of its justification and its linkage to minority incorporation. Despite their disappointments with World War I, civil rights advocates again supported the war effort. This time, they hoped, their rights claims would be more successful. If any war were to be a positive force for black civil rights advocates, World War II – a war waged in part against a racist regime, regularly justified in broadly egalitarian rhetoric – is an extremely likely candidate. Insomuch as I want to complicate this notion and highlight the diverse, even contradictory effects of this particular war on American racial politics, this project has implications for broader scholarly debates about the extent to which wars are, to simplify matters somewhat, "good" or "bad" for marginalized groups. But before turning more directly to the case of World War II, the next section provides historical background information on civil rights politics in the first half of the twentieth century. By examining this historical lead-in, the role of World War II can be more readily gleaned.

HISTORICAL BACKGROUND

Although popular accounts of the American civil rights movement focus on the 1950s and 1960s, historians have increasingly emphasized the importance of earlier periods of civil rights organizing.[26] The Niagara

---

[24] W. E. B. Du Bois, "Close Ranks," *The Crisis*, July 1918. For a discussion of historical debates regarding Du Bois' editorial, see William Jordan, "'The Damnable Dilemma': African-American Accommodation and Protest During World War I," *Journal of American History* 81(4), 1995, 1562–1583

[25] Chad L. Williams, *Torchbearers of Democracy: African American Soldiers in the World War I Era*, (Chapel Hill: University of North Carolina Press, 2010), 225. See also Chad Williams, "World War I in the Historical Imagination of W. E. B. Du Bois," *Modern American History* 1(1), 2018, 3–22.

[26] Robert Korstad and Nelson Lichtenstein, "Opportunities Found and Lost: Labor, Radicals, and the Early Civil Rights Movement," *Journal of American History* 75(3), 1988,

Movement, founded in 1905 and led by Du Bois and William Monroe Trotter, was perhaps the most prominent example of a new form of civil rights politics that repudiated the accommodationist approach of other figures like Booker T. Washington. While the Niagara Movement only lasted for a few years, the NAACP was formed its wake by Du Bois and a number of other civil rights advocates. During the first few decades of its existence, the NAACP became especially associated with the fight against lynching. After realizing that a public awareness campaign would be insufficient for bringing an end to lynching, the NAACP began lobbying for policy change in national governmental institutions. Victories like the Supreme Court case *Moore* v. *Dempsey* coexisted alongside defeats like the filibuster against antilynching legislation in the Senate.[27]

The New Deal era opened up new possibilities for civil rights politics. While Franklin Roosevelt was too concerned with maintaining the support of white southerners to actively support civil rights policies, he nonetheless received a majority of the black vote in the 1936 election. This was the first time black voters had gone Democratic, a voting shift that would persist throughout Roosevelt's presidency.[28] While a large part of this was due to the fact that the New Deal's economic programs had benefited working people of all races, if unevenly, there were also important forms of symbolic outreach that would help maintain black support for Roosevelt's programs. Some white liberals inside the White House like Eleanor Roosevelt and Harold Ickes were known to be sympathetic to civil rights. Ickes, for example, helped organize a 1939 performance by Marian Anderson at the Lincoln Memorial after she was denied access to Constitution Hall by the Daughters of the American Revolution.[29] Roosevelt's small group of black advisors – often referred to as the "Black Cabinet" – likewise symbolized

---

786–811; Jacquelyn Dowd Hall, "The Long Civil Rights Movement and the Political Uses of the Past," *Journal of American History* 91(4), 2005, 1233–1263; Glenda Elizabeth Gilmore, *Defying Dixie: The Radical Roots of Civil Rights, 1919–1950*, (New York W. W. Norton & Company, 2008).

[27] Megan Ming Francis, *Civil Rights and the Making of the Modern American State*, (New York: Cambridge University Press, 2014).

[28] Nancy J. Weiss, *Farewell to the Party of Lincoln: Black Politics in the Age of FDR*, (Princeton: Princeton University Press, 1983), xiii.

[29] John B. Kirby, *Black Americans in the Roosevelt Era: Liberalism and Race*, (Knoxville: University of Tennessee Press, 1980), 21. Raymond Arsenault, *The Sound of Freedom: Marian Anderson, the Lincoln Memorial, and the Concert That Awakened America*, (New York: Bloomsbury Press, 2009).

at least slightly more access than previous Democratic presidents had offered to African Americans.[30] Important changes to civil rights advocacy were also afoot. By the early 1940s, the NAACP had formed an important new alliance with the Congress of Industrial Organizations (CIO), which would gradually transform the very meaning of American liberalism.[31]

The 1940s were a critical period in the transformation of civil rights politics, so civil rights advocacy could hardly be unaffected by the war effort. An enemy more explicitly racist than Nazi Germany is difficult to imagine, and in this sense World War II provided a unique set of opportunities for the 1940s civil rights movement. "Unlike the aftermath of World War I," Kimberley Johnson writes, "nearly two decades of organizational activity and institution building prior to World War II provided a means of translating the rhetoric, limited reforms, and slim political openings created by a war for democracy into action."[32]

But what form would such action take? There has never been a singular civil rights agenda, and the wartime period was no different. *What the Negro Wants* – a 1944 volume collecting conservative, liberal, and radical perspectives – exemplifies this.[33] Some authors advanced only a relatively limited set of rights claims, while others emphasized the importance of issues like interracial marriage that would not be protected by the federal government until decades later.[34]

---

[30] Jane R. Motz, "The Black Cabinet: Negroes in the Administration of Franklin D. Roosevelt," (M.A. thesis, University of Delaware, 1964); Thomas Lee Green, "Black Cabinet Members in the Franklin Delano Roosevelt Administration," (PhD dissertation, University of Colorado, 1981); Weiss, *Farewell to the Party of Lincoln*, 136–156.

[31] Eric Schickler, *Racial Realignment: The Transformation of American Liberalism, 1932–1965*, (Princeton: Princeton University Press, 2016). See also Hall's "story of a 'long civil rights movement' that took root in the liberal and radical milieu of the late 1930s." Hall, "The Long Civil Rights Movement and the Political Uses of the Past," 1235.

[32] Kimberley Johnson, *Reforming Jim Crow: Southern Politics and State in the Age Before Brown* (New York: Oxford University Press, 2010), 99.

[33] Rayford W. Logan, ed., *What the Negro Wants*, (Chapel Hill: University of North Carolina Press, 1944).

[34] Du Bois, for instance, was clear in his chapter that moderation would not suffice. "By 'Freedom' for Negroes, I meant and still mean, *full economic, political and social equality with American citizens, in thought, expression, and action, with no discrimination based on race or color*," he wrote. W. E. B. Du Bois, "My Evolving Program for Negro Freedom," in *What the Negro Wants*, 65. Emphasis in original.

While acknowledging this ideological diversity, this book focuses on the national agenda promoted by the NAACP (especially its leader, Walter White) in conjunction with labor leaders (especially A. Philip Randolph).[35] White led the NAACP from the early 1930s until his death in 1955. He personified the NAACP's strategy of top-down leadership, emphasizing the cultivation of elite contacts in Congress and the White House to create alliances in favor of civil rights. White also, especially during the war years, came to be well known for his newspaper columns and books, particularly *A Rising Wind* (1945), which described his tours of military bases in Europe with an eye towards racial segregation. He often reported on these tours to the executive branch, always advocating for at least gradual moves towards integration of the armed forces. Randolph was a prominent black labor organizer who led the Brotherhood of Sleeping Car Porters. Whereas White advocated an elite-driven strategy, Randolph's labor background made him much more inclined towards bottom-up pressure, including mass protests. Despite their differences, Randolph and White nonetheless allied on a number of causes, particularly wartime issues like defense industry discrimination and military segregation.

THE WARTIME CIVIL RIGHTS AGENDA

I use the alliance between the NAACP and Randolph as a proxy for the mainstream "civil rights agenda" of the era. I do this not to downplay the very real disagreements some more radical activists had with the national NAACP in the era, but rather to highlight the sorts of civil rights claims national political actors were hearing.[36] While an elite organization, the NAACP saw substantial growth in membership during the war – one source suggests it increased nearly tenfold – which increased its mass

---

[35] Christopher Baylor describes how 1940 marked a turning point in the NAACP's advocacy. While the organization had been skeptical of labor unions in the past – in large part due to very real racial discrimination in many unions – they nonetheless allied themselves with the CIO just before the war. Christopher A. Baylor, "First to the Party: The Group Origins of the Partisan Transformation on Civil Rights," *Studies in American Political Development* 27(2), 2013. See also Christopher Baylor, *First to the Party: The Group Origins of Political Transformation*, (Philadelphia: University of Pennsylvania Press, 2017).

[36] For an analysis of local NAACP strategies that diverged at times from the national movement, see Beth Tompkins Bates, "A New Crowd Challenges the Agenda of the Old Guard in the NAACP, 1933–1941," *American Historical Review* 102(2), 1997, 340–377.

base beyond the prewar years.[37] It also forged this new alliance with labor on the eve of US entry into the war. This led NAACP leaders like White to collaborate with labor leaders like Randolph on a number of areas.

The wartime civil rights agenda can be broken down into two sets of policy goals: those that existed prewar and those that were formulated in the context of the war itself. The first set were goals like antilynching and anti–poll tax legislation, which carried over from unsuccessful efforts in the 1930s. Although sometimes framed in novel ways that drew on wartime rhetoric, the issues themselves were not new. The second set of goals consisted of more war-specific measures, particularly calls for "fair employment" in the defense industry and the integration of the armed forces. While concerns with job discrimination and segregation had always been on the civil rights agenda, US entry into World War II brought these issues to the fore of the civil rights agenda in a way that marked a departure from the 1930s. The wartime civil rights agenda could be a double-edged sword, however, as the war-specific nature of the claims both helped and hindered the movement. While increasing the odds of any change at all occurring, it also constrained the scope of the agenda to war-specific measures (discrimination *in the defense industry* and segregation *in the armed forces*) and helped forge a complex alliance between the domestic goals of civil rights advocates and the foreign policy goals of Democratic presidents that would limit the more radical voices of the movement.

This wartime agenda can also be viewed in light of the citizenship rights that it demanded.[38] In the wartime period, advocates highlighted

---

[37] Harvard Sitkoff, "Racial Militancy and Interracial Violence in the Second World War," *Journal of American History* 58(3), 1971, 663. See also Simon Topping, "'Supporting Our Friends and Defeating Our Enemies': Militancy and Nonpartisanship in the NAACP, 1936–1948," *Journal of African American History* 89(1), 2004, 17.

[38] "Citizenship," wrote T. H. Marshall, "is a status bestowed on those who are full members of a community." The concept "speak[s] of respect, of rights, of dignity," in the phrasing of Nancy Fraser and Linda Gordon. T. H. Marshall, *Citizenship and Social Class: And Other Essays*, (New York: Cambridge University Press, 1950), 28; Nancy Fraser and Linda Gordon, "Civil Citizenship Against Social Citizenship? On the Ideology of Contract-Versus-Charity," in *The Condition of Citizenship*, ed. Bart van Steenbergen, (Thousand Oaks: SAGE, 1994), 90. See also Evelyn Nakano Glenn, *Unequal Freedom: How Race and Gender Shaped American Citizenship and Labor*, (Cambridge: Harvard University Press, 2004), 19. The Marshallian tradition of civil, political, and social citizenship offers a useful theoretical framework for thinking about African Americans rights claims in the World War II era, although it requires certain

several types of rights. Perhaps most straightforward were the civil rights to be protected from a lynch mob and to have access to employment free from discrimination. Lynching was perhaps the most fundamental violation of the right to liberty of the person, and the ease with which white mobs evaded punishment evinced a clear absence of the right to justice for black southerners. The fight against discrimination in the defense industry, too, emphasized an important right associated with civil citizenship. "In the economic field," T. H. Marshall wrote, "the basic civil right is the right to work, that is to say the right to follow the occupation of one's choice in the place of one's choice, subject only to legitimate demands for preliminary technical training."[39] While such civil rights claims predominated the discourse of the era, early efforts at achieving the political rights of citizenship are also evident. The poll tax was more subtle than lynching, but its disenfranchising effect for black southerners (and many poor white southerners alike) was clearly designed to limit political rights to a chosen subset of citizens.

In contrast to the other three major issues, the right to serve in the military is more difficult to categorize, as military service is often understood more as an obligation of citizenship than as a right. Rights and obligations are connected, however, particularly when fulfilling one's obligations is seen as a prerequisite for receiving one's rights.[40] As Margot Canaday notes, "[t]he right to serve in the military" is better understood as "the right to fulfill the obligation to serve in the military," which in turn provides access to the republican exchange for greater

---

revisions to fit this historical context. Citizenship rights for black southerners were actually initially expanded during Reconstruction but were retracted during the Redemption and Jim Crow eras, only to expand again over the course of the twentieth century. In Marshall's original analysis, which is focused on white men in England, civil citizenship emerged in the eighteenth century, political citizenship in the nineteenth century, and social citizenship in the twentieth century. For a discussion of how this differed for black southerners, see Johnson, *Reforming Jim Crow*; and Michael B. Katz, *The Price of Citizenship: Redefining the American Welfare State: Updated Edition*, (Philadelphia: University of Pennsylvania Press, 2008), 345–346. During the era examined in this book, black southerners "had virtually no civil rights" and overwhelmingly lacked political rights but did have "limited social citizenship," particularly in the form of education, although educational opportunities were of course separate and deeply unequal. Johnson, *Reforming Jim Crow*, 13, 15. This historically specific context shaped the rights demanded by wartime advocates.

[39] Marshall, *Citizenship and Social Class*, 15–16.
[40] For a discussion of rights and obligations with respect to military service and full citizenship rights, see Linda K. Kerber, *No Constitutional Right to Be Ladies: Women and the Obligations of Citizenship*, (New York: Hill and Wang, 1998), especially Chapter 4.

citizenship rights.[41] For those who could not – or would not – serve in the military, this pathway to rights was foreclosed. To the extent that the right to serve in the military became an important – and, for some, the most important – part of the rights agenda, it inevitably privileged the rights of some more than the rights of others. Perhaps most obviously, the right to fight at this time was largely a gendered rights claim that opened up opportunities to men rather than women. It was also a rights claim that privileged those in agreement with their country's foreign policy goals, something that was less controversial during World War II but would lead to major tensions in the Cold War era and during the Vietnam War.

WORLD WAR II, RACE, AND AMERICAN POLITICAL DEVELOPMENT

Trying to piece together a broad picture of the effects of World War II on American racial politics from existing literature would result in an uneven, often contradictory, and occasionally even empty patchwork of analyses. While many Americanist political scientists have tended to ignore international factors in their work, those who have not have varied in the care of their argumentation. Most obviously open to revision are common assumptions about the war's effects that, when the footnotes are carefully analyzed, are largely reducible to arguments about plausibility rather than any particular empirical evidence.[42]

Consider, for example, the extent to which World War II liberalized white racial attitudes by bringing into relief an ideological tension between a war against Nazism abroad and the maintenance of Jim Crow at home. Philip Klinkner and Rogers Smith's *The Unsteady March*, perhaps the most influential text in American politics on the role of war in motivating civil rights advances, makes several striking off-handed comments about the relationship between the war and white attitudes. The authors do so, however, without offering any original analyses of public opinion data that might be used to substantiate such claims. Klinkner

---

[41] Margot Canaday, *The Straight State: Sexuality and Citizenship in Twentieth Century America*, (Princeton: Princeton University Press, 2009), 9f27. On the way in which military service can be traded for the reward of certain rights, see Yahil Levy, "Convertible Sacrifice – A Conceptual Proposition," *Sociological Perspectives* 56(3), 2013, 440.

[42] I focus here on arguments about public opinion, but this is also true of arguments about the Supreme Court. I discuss this more in the concluding chapter.

and Smith claim, for example, that the "Nazi menace forced at least some white Americans to begin to reexamine the racial inequalities in their midst."[43] This is a very clear claim, but not verified with analysis of the available survey data. Later, they fill in the causal processes. "[T]he ideological demands of fighting an enemy who espoused racial hierarchies made more white Americans sensitive to the presence of racial discrimination in America," they argue. "The vision of blacks marching to claim their rights contradicted the image of America as the defender of democracy."[44] Klinkner and Smith do offer some willingness to concede that white opinion in the South did not liberalize, and perhaps even hardened in its white supremacist resolve.[45] But in general, their claim about a shift in white attitudes is fairly strong. This claim about public opinion affects not only their assessment of the public, but also normative assessments of other actors like President Roosevelt. "Roosevelt's unwillingness to take a stronger stand on racial issues was, in hindsight, regrettable and costly," they argue. "True, white Southerners were becoming more restive, but it seems clear that in the context of the war, nationally public attitudes on race had shifted enough that he could have been more outspoken for reform."[46]

While a close analysis of the available survey evidence can offer an important empirical corrective to these arguments about the war's effects on white racial attitudes, other areas of inquiry require a bit more nuance. The debate about the war's effects on the presidency and executive branch is the clearest example. Why did Roosevelt, a New Yorker associated in the popular imagination with the party's liberal wing, act as little as he did? Why did Truman, a native Missourian prone to racial slurs, act as much as he did? And to what extent, if any, did World War II shape these varied responses to civil rights advocacy?

---

[43] Klinkner and Smith, *The Unsteady March*, 137.
[44] Ibid., 160.
[45] Ibid., 168.
[46] Ibid., 199. Although Klinkner and Smith's research is not centrally concerned with public opinion, it has had the effect of strengthening the view that World War II liberalized white racial attitudes. Saldin, for example, refers to Klinkner and Smith as an authority in asserting an "undeniable growth of racial liberalism link[ed] to World War II." Robert P. Saldin, *War, the American State, and Politics Since 1898*, (New York: Cambridge University Press, 2010), 114. Elsewhere, Saldin is somewhat more nuanced than Klinkner and Smith in his assumptions about public opinion. See ibid., 114–115. Daniel Kryder likewise makes assumptions about the white public, albeit somewhat more negatively than Klinkner and Smith. See Kryder, *Divided Arsenal*, 10.

Historians and sociologists have increasingly emphasized international factors but focused more on pressures related to the Cold War than World War II.[47] In rethinking traditional structuralist accounts of the American civil rights movement, sociologists of contentious politics have been influenced by such work. Doug McAdam, for example, points to the Cold War as the important difference-maker for the civil rights records of Roosevelt and Truman. In his words, "the otherwise puzzling contrast between Truman's actions and FDR's inaction becomes entirely comprehensible when placed in the very different international contexts in which they occurred."[48] Despite his interest in extending the timeline of the civil rights movement backwards in history – and his growing attention to international factors in doing so – McAdam seems to actively downplay any importance of World War II. Indeed, this focus is inherent in McAdam's description of the case as the "American civil rights movement of the *post-World War II period*."[49] This shorthand use of "postwar" to define time boundaries inherently leaves out the wartime period itself as a relevant era for analysis, effectively biasing studies away from considering World War II's effects on racial politics.

Among political scientists, the most prominent account of war's effects on racial politics is offered by Klinkner and Smith. According to their model, progress on civil rights happens when there is a war requiring mobilization of African Americans, the nature of the enemy requires

---

[47] Historians like Mary Dudziak first emphasized the strategic incentives State Department officials faced in trying to win over "third world" audiences who were also being engaged by the Soviet Union. White supremacy in America, they discovered, proved a hindrance in convincing such audiences of the American government's sincerity. Mary L. Dudziak, *Cold War Civil Rights: Race and the Image of American Democracy*, (Princeton: Princeton University Press, 2000).

[48] Doug McAdam, *Political Process and the Development of Black Insurgency 1930–1970: Second Edition*, (Chicago: University of Chicago Press, 1999 [1982]), xxi. Other sociologists have been less sure of any effect of Cold War politics. See Joshua Bloom, "The Dynamics of Opportunity and Insurgent Practice: How Black Anti-Colonialists Compelled Truman to Advocate Civil Rights," *American Sociological Review* 80(2), 2015, 391–415.

[49] McAdam, *Political Process and the Development of Black Insurgency*, viii. My italics. Later, in urging social movement scholars to look back further than the Montgomery bus boycotts, McAdam writes that "the broader civil rights episode began early in the postwar period and certainly by the time of the Dixiecrat revolt in 1948." Ibid., xxvii. At another point, he argues "our models of social movements need to be as attuned to, and predictive of, the crucial period of institutionalized conflict over federal racial policies which *followed* World War II as they have previously been to the events of 1955–56 in Montgomery." Ibid., xxxi, my emphasis.

leaders to justify the war using egalitarian rhetoric, and protest movements are able to pressure the government to at least partially live up to this rhetoric.[50] The case of World War II, they argue, fits this model very well. They point to Roosevelt's executive order on fair employment in the defense industry as one major example of this.[51] They also place substantial emphasis on the role of postwar violence against black veterans in motivating Truman's executive orders in the later part of the decade.[52]

There are also more skeptical political science accounts. Kryder emphasizes the executive branch response to racial politics during World War II as being primarily about maintaining social order amidst racial conflict in order to more effectively use military power. Such policies "may have appeared progressive, but other purposes – the full mobilization of industrial production and the maintenance of the party coalition – outweighed in importance the principle and the goal of egalitarian social reform."[53] This more negative language used by Kryder to describe seeming wartime advances is consistent with his skepticism about the white mass public.[54] Krebs offers another, more critical analysis. While "often portrayed as indicative of blacks' conditional loyalty," he argues the Double-V campaign instead "channeled mass anger in safe directions."[55] Such rhetorical constraints, Krebs argues, continued in the postwar era. Since activists were "wary of being painted as Communists, they concentrated their energies on formal civil and political rights, setting aside the deep political economy of race." The country, he argues, "is still coping with the implications of that choice."[56]

In contrast to plausible conjectures about the war's effects on mass white attitudes, these accounts of the response to civil rights advocacy by the executive branch are deeply grounded in various forms of evidence. Yet while they share certain similarities, they also present points of tension and disagreement. To what extent should we understand the 1940s'

[50] Klinkner and Smith, *The Unsteady March*, 3–4.
[51] For their analysis of how this case fits into their theoretical framework, see ibid., 160.
[52] See ibid., 204–205, for a discussion of how the Truman era fits into their theoretical framework.
[53] Kryder, *Divided Arsenal*, 4.
[54] Kryder suggests Americans were "less familiar with the aims of the war and their relationship to democratic ideals than Myrdal believed." Ibid., 10
[55] Krebs, *Fighting for Rights*, 151. This is similar to Finkle's account, which Krebs cites. Lee Finkle, "The Conservative Aims of Militant Rhetoric: Black Protest During World War II," *Journal of American History* 60(3), 1973, 692–713.
[56] Krebs, *Fighting for Rights*, 153–54.

relatively military-centric civil rights advances as "limited" in some way, particularly by comparison to the 1960s civil rights landmarks or other counterfactual World War II–era trajectories? Or were these outcomes "like the dog that could dance – that he did so poorly is far less significant than the fact that he did it at all"?[57] Assessing how the wartime context both helped and hindered – as well as placing this debate about the executive branch in the era's larger attitudinal context – can help to make sense of this.

TEMPORAL BOUNDARIES

Writing about the World War II era requires a definition of the war's temporal boundaries. Although this might seem straightforward, it turns out to be a bit more complicated than some might expect. Wars contain different stages, generally following a sequence that begins with the emergence of a threat, followed by mobilization and eventually actual warfare, with each stage of the sequence possibly having different implications for domestic politics.[58] In the United States, the experience of World War II began with a perception of a growing Axis threat. A period of neutrality gave way to mobilization, which included the Lend-Lease program and the emergence of an extensive defense industry. The Japanese attack on Pearl Harbor marked the beginning of the third stage, where the United States would formally engage in warfare against the Axis powers.

There are at least two broad ways to think about defining the temporal boundaries of the war. Quantitative political scientists tend to define US participation in World War II as extending from December 7, 1941, to August 14, 1945: that is, from the Japanese bombing of Pearl Harbor to the signing of a formal peace treaty.[59] This approach has several benefits: it fits with conventional textbook understandings of the war and, for quantitative work, allows for a clear beginning and end to the analysis.

---

[57] Philip A. Klinkner, "Review of *Divided Arsenal: Race and the American State*," *American Political Science Review* 95(3), 2001, 735.
[58] Elizabeth Kier and Ronald R. Krebs, "Introduction: War and Democracy in Comparative Perspective," in *In War's Wake: International Conflict and the Fate of Liberal Democracy*, ed. Elizabeth Kier and Ronald R. Krebs, (New York: Cambridge University Press, 2010), 6–7.
[59] William G. Howell, Saul P. Jackman, and Jon C. Rogowski, *The Wartime President: Executive Influence and the Nationalizing Politics of Threat*, (Chicago: University of Chicago Press, 2013), 65–66.

Mary Dudziak, by contrast, argues that the definition of World War II is "fuzzier around the edges than we usually imagine."[60] Rather than viewing the starting line as the Japanese attack on Pearl Harbor, Dudziak quotes the historian Waldo Henrichs as writing that the war instead "crept up, stage by stage, over many years." She notes that Truman did not declare a cessation of hostilities until the end of 1946, at which time he noted that a "state of war still exists." It wasn't until 1951 that Truman formally called for an end of a state of war against Germany, but the United States remained an occupying force there.[61]

Dudziak's assessment highlights several deficiencies in traditional accounts of World War II that define different moments in time as simply war or not-war. American politicians (and at least some members of the American public) were attuned to events overseas, and the possibility of US engagement in the war, prior to Pearl Harbor. Similarly, the wartime era did not cleanly end with the dropping of atomic bombs in Hiroshima and Nagasaki in 1945. Even if the fighting overseas came to an end for US troops, the immediate postwar era was marked by several politically important incidents of racial violence against returning black veterans of the war, as well as continued pressures to change the racial policies of the US military. In this way, the clear temporal boundaries favored by quantitative researchers examining this era might be too limited.[62]

This book examines what might be considered the "long" World War II era. The 1941–1945 period of direct American engagement in the war might comprise the most direct wartime period, but the lead-up to war – and the postwar milieu that followed, leading into the eventual Cold War era – are critical for properly understanding the role of World War II in race and American political development. As such, this book discusses the 1930s civil rights agenda of lynching and the poll tax, notes the creeping up of war and the response of civil rights actors who reshaped the agenda in strategic ways, then considers the postwar period as a relevant feature of the World War II era, interpreting Truman's military integration actions as occurring in the borderland between the World

---

[60] Mary L. Dudziak, *War Time: An Idea, Its History, Its Consequences*, (New York: Oxford University Press, 2012), 62.
[61] Ibid., 37–38, 40.
[62] "Most of the civil rights advancements that built upon Roosevelt's wartime actions occurred during times of peace," including "the 1948 desegregation of the military," Howell et al. write. Defining Truman's military desegregation order as a peacetime outcome, however, is technical to a fault and misses relevant features of the postwar milieu that are different from peacetime. Howell et al., *The Wartime President*, 2.

War II and Cold War eras (with their origins clearly being in the political and structural context of World War II rather than appearing out of thin air in the late 1940s as a response to changing international incentives).[63]

UNPACKING "WORLD WAR II" AS AN EXPLANATORY VARIABLE

What, though, does it mean to treat something as big and seemingly amorphous as "World War II" as an explanatory variable? Particular characteristics of a given war are often thought to be relevant for explaining its effects. One common approach is to focus on scale, with many accounts suggesting that large conflicts – particularly "total wars" – tend to have more transformative effects than smaller conflicts.[64] In the history of American warfare, World War II stands out for both its extensive reach into everyday life on the home front and the massive number of casualties on battlegrounds abroad. More than 16 million Americans served in the war (more than in any other) and nearly 300,000 died in battle around the world.[65] Domestically, rationing measures and the boom in war production meant that the war was felt even by those who did not serve.[66]

But even if the war's scale suggests it is likely to have domestic political consequences, the underlying mechanisms remain underspecified. To be more useful as an analytical concept, "the war" can be further unpacked into its constitutive elements, each of which have different compelling and constraining logics. I focus here on three aspects of World War II: (1) the ideological justification of the war; (2) the actual material undertaking of mobilization and warfare; and (3) the manner in which war can displace "normal" domestic politics.

---

[63] The only seeming exception is my analysis in Chapter 3 of a survey fielded in 1961. While this is much later than my time frame, this survey provides another vantage point for assessing correlations between World War II era military service and racial attitudes.

[64] Arthur Marwick, *War and Social Change in the Twentieth Century: A Comparative Study of Britain, France, Germany, Russia and the United States*, (London: Macmillan, 1974); Arthur Marwick, ed., *Total War and Social Change*, (New York: St. Martin's Press, 1988). For an overview of scholarly refinements to the role of scale, see Kier and Krebs, "Introduction," 8–12.

[65] US Department of Veterans Affairs, "America's Wars Fact Sheet," www.va.gov/opa/publications/factsheets/fs_americas_wars.pdf

[66] Mark H. Leff, "The Politics of Sacrifice on the American Home Front in World War II," *Journal of American History* 77(4), 1991, 1296–1318.

The war against the Axis forces was justified ideologically as a war to protect liberal democratic values. Taking this general framing as a starting point, civil rights advocates strategically highlighted the antiracist logic of a war against Nazism in particular as a way of linking domestic civil rights politics to the broader international goals of the war. Within academic work, this line of thinking has its origins in Myrdal's book, which emphasized the contradiction between American ideals of democracy and the realities of American racism, a contradiction that many found especially salient when mobilizing for war against Nazi Germany.[67] Arguments about the war's potential effects on white racial attitudes tend to emphasize this aspect of the war, but it was also used by civil rights advocates in their rhetorical appeals to political elites.

Mobilization and warfare also required a massive material undertaking.[68] During the mobilization period, an industrial job surplus meant black workers were more in demand, in turn opening possibilities and points of leverage for the civil rights movement on job discrimination issues. During the warfare period especially, manpower needs meant that questions of racial segregation in the armed forces became especially prominent on the civil rights agenda.

Finally, the mobilization and warfare of World War II could also serve to displace "normal" domestic politics because focusing on the war effort was seen as a more urgent need than issues like civil rights legislation. War was often used as a hammer against civil rights organizations, with some claiming that their advocacy might be disruptive to morale. This logic was particularly common in the War Department, which often pushed back against the "social experimentation" of integration in the armed forces. It is also possible that many whites in the mass public felt this way, viewing the war as an inappropriate time for domestic political advocacy.

Attention to these different elements of "war" illustrates the ways in which the war both helped and hindered civil rights advocacy. This can be seen not simply in the difference between the various elements – the ways in which liberal interpretations of the war's ideology compelled and

---

[67] Klinkner and Smith offer a more modern articulation of this argument when they emphasize the importance of enemies that require the US government to frame the conflict in egalitarian terms.

[68] Paul A. C. Koistinen, *Arsenal of World War II: The Political Economy of American Warfare, 1940–1945*, (Lawrence: University Press of Kansas, 2004).

the exigencies of military strategy constrained – but also in the differences within each category. Even within the seemingly more positive ideological sense of the war, there was important variation. Some rights claims took the form of liberal calls for greater democratic inclusion across all of society. Others, by contrast, took a more republican form, emphasizing the military service of black men and the limited sets of rights this service "earned" them, such as serving in an integrated military or being free from racial violence upon their return (Truman, in particular, found this to be a compelling argument). Many white Americans, by contrast, simply viewed the war as being fought in defense of America's place in the world, with its internal federalist system of strong states' rights intact. As different actors battled out, even seemingly liberating aspects of the war could be used in defense of maintaining racial hierarchies instead.[69]

This political struggle took place in multiple political arenas, and, as such, treating World War II as an explanatory variable in this way requires distinguishing between these different arenas. Such distinctions are important because, as Giovanni Capoccia and R. Daniel Kelemen write, "a historical moment that constitutes a critical juncture with respect to one institution may not constitute a critical juncture with respect to another." One cannot "identify relatively brief periods of momentous political, social, or economic upheaval and assert that these are critical junctures in a general sense."[70] This fits with Stephen Skowronek's view of politics as "structured by persistent incongruities and frictions among institutional orders."[71] Distinguishing different political arenas – and allowing that some might be more, less, or even not at all affected by a particular juncture like the war – is thus a key part of this book's theoretical framework.

While motivated by an interest in American political development writ large, this book focuses on two political arenas: public opinion measured

---

[69] For a broader discussion of liberalism, republicanism, and ascriptivism, see Rogers Smith, *Civic Ideals*. For a discussion of the extent to which liberalism and ascriptivism, in particular, can coexist, see Ira Katznelson, "*Review of Civic Ideals: Conflicting Visions of Citizenship in U.S. History,*" Political Theory 27(4), 1999, 565–570. For a discussion of how some southern whites reinterpreted the war's logic, see Ward, "'A War for States' Rights': The White Supremacist Vision of Double Victory."

[70] Giovanni Capoccia and R. Daniel Kelemen, "The Study of Critical Junctures: Theory, Narrative, and Counterfactuals in Historical Institutionalism," World Politics 59(3), 2007, 349.

[71] Cited in ibid., 350. Stephen Skowronek, "Order and Change," Polity 28(1), 1995, 95.

by surveys rather than American culture in a more multifaceted sense; and the executive branch, rather than other national political institutions like the legislative and judicial branches. The focus on white racial attitudes is easier to justify, as the topic has been the subject of largely unsubstantiated assumptions and an analysis of the available survey evidence can provide a helpful correction.

The focus on the executive branch at the expense of other political institutions, however, merits additional justification. Since the NAACP's founding, Congress had failed to act on civil rights legislation, and the war was an insufficient juncture for moving congressional inaction past institutional limits like the southern filibuster.[72] If the war had been a liberalizing force for white racial attitudes, congressional inaction might be surprising, as Congress is the national political institution most closely linked to shifts in aggregate public opinion.[73] In the absence of such attitudinal shifts, however, it makes sense that political change on controversial issues like civil rights took place in the executive branch, where elite actions were less constrained by public sentiments and able to be worked out more behind the scenes.[74] This is especially true during times of war, when executive discretion grows. This growth in wartime executive power presented new opportunities for civil rights activism, particularly when rights claims could be tied directly to the war effort.

---

[72] While Congress is a useful site for preference expression, it is a less useful site if the object of inquiry is actual public policy outcomes, at least for the study of civil rights in the 1940s. Recent scholarship by Julian Zelizer supports this interpretation. "In certain respects, World War II had a transformative effect on the United States," he writes. Congress, though, "was difficult to change." Julian E. Zelizer, "Confronting the Roadblock: Congress, Civil Rights, and World War II," in *Fog of War: The Second World War and the Civil Rights Movement*, ed. Kevin M. Kruse and Stephen Tuck, (New York: Oxford University Press, 2012), 32. The war, Zelizer writes, "did not bring progress on the legislative front." Ibid., 3. For an examination of how congressional behavior can illustrate emerging differences between northern and southern Democrats, relative to northern Republicans, see Eric Schickler, Kathryn Pearson, and Brian D. Feinstein, "Congressional Parties and Civil Rights Politics from 1933 to 1972," *Journal of Politics* 72(3), 2010, 672–689.

[73] Even with a greater liberalizing trend in public opinion, countermajoritarian features of the Senate like the filibuster made Congress a difficult avenue for change.

[74] While recent scholarship has suggested far less policy responsiveness than an earlier era of research indicated, even earlier arguments about "dynamic representation" distinguished between different branches of the national government with respect to how much representation was expected. James A. Stimson, Michael B. Mackuen, and Robert S. Erikson, "Dynamic Representation," *American Political Science Review* 89(3), 1995, 543–565.

Because of this shift in focus to the executive branch by civil rights leaders during the war, I emphasize this political arena rather than others.[75]

Finally, if the war can be said to have altered American racial politics in some way, it is important to distinguish between different ways in which this might occur. The war could have merely been an interruption, in which case it temporarily disrupted an ongoing domestic process, but in the war's aftermath the process resumed unchanged. The war could also have been a catalyzing force, accelerating the pace of an ongoing domestic process but leaving its contours basically unchanged. Another possibility is that the war could have been transformative, serving as a critical juncture that fundamentally altered the trajectory of domestic politics. If this were the case, the presence of the war means that the domestic outcome of interest is substantively different in some way, relative to the counterfactual where the war did not occur.[76] After presenting the evidence in the following chapters, the conclusion returns to this question to offer the best possible empirical assessment of the ways in which World War II did – and, in other ways, did not – alter the response to black civil rights advocacy.

ROADMAP

World War II was a theoretically important juncture for American racial politics, but the extent to which it was a "critical" one should be open to inquiry, and potentially variable by institutional arena. This framework – which locates this study clearly in the purview of historical institutionalist approaches to the study of politics – leads to a set of questions that can be applied to different political arenas.

I present my findings in two parts, starting with white racial attitudes. Public opinion provides one constraint on the strategies of elites.[77] If white racial attitudes liberalized over the course of the war, politicians would have faced a more favorable context for the introduction of

---

[75] This project, then, offers a more complete assessment of the war's heterogeneous effects on race and American political development by both filling obvious gaps in the literature in some areas (e.g., public opinion) as well as adjudicating between points of tension and disagreement in others (e.g., the presidency). I discuss potential ways that future research might reassess the Court's role in the concluding chapter.

[76] Kier and Krebs, "Introduction," 14–15.

[77] Even in the Jim Crow South, public opinion provided some constraint, at least white public opinion. See Devin Caughey, *The Unsolid South: Mass Politics and National Representation in a One-Party Enclave*, (Princeton: Princeton University Press, 2018).

racially liberal policies. If white racial attitudes did not liberalize, however – or if they became more conservative – politicians would have been more incentivized to ignore civil rights advocacy. In Chapter 2, I describe and assess the racial liberalization hypothesis, a clearly stated articulation of an argument popularized by Myrdal and adhered to by many historical institutional accounts today: the notion that World War II had a liberalizing impact on white racial attitudes. Contrary to the Myrdalian account, however, I use rarely utilized survey evidence to demonstrate that there is much less evidence for the racial liberalization hypothesis than is often assumed, particularly when the focus is on measures of policy rather than prejudice. Although there is some evidence that the war coincided with decreases in antiblack prejudice (e.g., whether black blood is biologically distinct from white blood), I demonstrate that white attitudes toward civil rights policies – particularly federal intervention in state lynching cases – did not liberalize over the course of the war. If anything, white opposition to antilynching legislation actually seems to have increased. While the available evidence is more limited, I also demonstrate that whites were largely opposed to wartime civil rights demands like integration of the armed forces.

In Chapter 3, I analyze those whites who actually served in the war and ask to what extent their military service had racially liberalizing effects on them relative to similarly situated nonveterans. For veterans, the results are somewhat more mixed. White veterans were indistinguishable from nonveteran whites on many measures of racial prejudice, and they were equally committed to segregation both in the armed services and in society more broadly. They were, however, more supportive of federal antilynching legislation in the war's immediate aftermath, and southern white veterans were more supportive of black voting rights in the early 1960s. Relying on archival materials related to small-scale experiments in the military, I also consider the counterfactual where Roosevelt had moved to integrate the armed forces during or prior to US entry into World War II, highlighting the potential consequences for white racial attitudes of FDR's refusal to integrate the armed forces during the war.

The lack of major attitudinal shifts necessitated a move by advocacy organizations away from Congress to policy options less directly connected to majoritarianism. In Chapter 4, I examine the Roosevelt administration's record on civil rights in the context of World War II. Relying on internal executive branch documents as well as attempts by black newspapers to get the administration to comment on the Double-V campaign, I demonstrate the White House's familiarity with the Double-V rhetoric of civil rights activists and frame this as part of a larger debate within the Roosevelt administration about whether to maintain a New Deal focus on social policy or focus almost entirely on the military aspects of World War II. I then examine how wartime activism compelled Roosevelt to issue an executive order to combat defense industry discrimination, while similar efforts to integrate the armed forces proved unsuccessful.

In Chapter 5, I examine the effects of the war and its aftermath on the Truman administration's civil rights actions. In conjunction with broader political pressures and electoral incentives, I point to Truman's belief in the republican virtues of military service as a variable that can mediate between his personal racism and relatively more extensive civil rights program. I show how civil rights advocates – particularly by highlighting incidences of violence against returning black veterans in the immediate postwar period – convinced Truman to issue an executive order establishing the President's Committee on Civil Rights. I then discuss his executive order calling for equality of opportunity and treatment in the armed forces, issued after congressional inaction on his civil rights committee's proposals, which eventually led to the desegregation of the US military. This was not without its challenges, however, particularly from the Army, which frequently pushed back against the committee tasked with implementing the order.

Chapter 6 gathers the evidence from the preceding chapters to offer a refinement of the more general theoretical relationship between war and the inclusion of marginalized groups. I then discuss questions that remain open for future scholarship, particularly possibilities that might arise from expanding the scope of the analysis to other political institutions and other marginalized groups. I conclude with a discussion of the importance of studying war to better understand the outcomes of not just civil rights politics but domestic political processes more generally.

2

White Racial Attitudes, 1937–1950

It is often assumed that fighting a war against Nazism led to an increase in white support for black civil rights. Activists, journalists, academics, and others during World War II regularly claimed that when shown "the gross discrepancy between our ideals and our practices," as one contemporaneous observer described it, white Americans would be forced to confront their own racial prejudices and legacies of discrimination, resulting in a major step forward for racial progress.[1] Indeed, claims about the impact of World War II on white racial attitudes can be found in sources ranging from contemporaneous accounts to present-day historical institutionalist scholarship and scattered other sources like constitutional law books.[2]

Common assumptions about the war's liberalizing effect on white racial attitudes largely derive from popular interpretations of Gunnar Myrdal's massive text, *An American Dilemma: The Negro Problem and*

---

[1] Margaret C. McCulloch, "What Should the American Negro Reasonably Expect as the Outcome of a Real Peace?," *Journal of Negro Education* 12(3), 1943, 565.

[2] For contemporaneous accounts, see Gunnar Myrdal, *An American Dilemma: The Negro Problem and Modern Democracy*, (New York: Harper & Brothers Publishers, 1944); Charles Wallace Collins, *Whither Solid South? A Study in Politics and Race Relations*, (New Orleans, Pelican Publishing Company, 1947); Howard W. Odum, "Social Change in the South," *Journal of Politics* 10(2), 1948, 242–258. For examples from historical institutionalist scholarship, see Philip A. Klinkner and Rogers M. Smith, *The Unsteady March: The Rise and Decline of Racial Equality in America*, (Chicago: University of Chicago Press, 1999); Daniel Kryder, *Divided Arsenal: Race and the American State During World War II*, (New York: Cambridge University Press, 2000); Robert P. Saldin, *War, the American State, and Politics Since 1898*, (New York: Cambridge University Press, 2010). For an example in legal scholarship, see Alfred H. Kelly, "The School Desegregation Case," in *Quarrels That Have Shaped the Constitution*, ed. John A. Garraty, (New York: Harper & Row Publishers, 1987 [1962]).

Modern Democracy. Myrdal interpreted white racism as a deviation from the American Creed. The ideological logic of the war, he argued, would lead Americans to bring themselves closer to the Creed's egalitarian values, resulting in greater racial egalitarianism in the war's wake.[3] Although Myrdal's work was more prospective than empirical, it has likely been the most influential account of the war's relationship with American racial politics, with more recent scholarly overviews of the period frequently strengthening the influence of the Myrdalian account.[4] The extent to which these claims are consistent with the available survey evidence, however, remains to be properly assessed.

I begin this chapter with a discussion of survey research from the World War II era, with attention to its historical emergence and methodological issues that arise when using older datasets. I next discuss the conditions under which white racial attitudes are likely to change, comparing the World War II era to the more commonly studied civil rights organizing that took place in the late 1950s and early 1960s. I then offer a clear statement of the conventional view of how World War II affected white racial attitudes, which I call the racial liberalization hypothesis. The remainder of the chapter then assesses this hypothesis with respect to a wide range of survey questions related to racial prejudice and racial policy attitudes.

Based on an analysis of the available survey evidence from the era, I argue the war's impact on white racial attitudes is actually more limited than has been widely assumed. While there is some evidence that white racial prejudice decreased during the war, this is generally not true for attitudes toward racially egalitarian policies. White opposition to federal antilynching legislation seems to have actually increased during the war. While the available survey evidence is more limited for attitudes toward war-specific civil rights issues, I provide evidence that both integration of the military and job discrimination protections were highly unpopular with whites in the immediate postwar period. Along with offering an important empirical corrective, the findings in this chapter are helpful

---

[3] Myrdal, *An American Dilemma*.

[4] See, in particular, Klinkner and Smith, *The Unsteady March*. As noted in Chapter 1, Klinkner and Smith make several claims about the nature of white public opinion. They argue it is "hard to escape the conclusion" that the "Nazi menace forced at least some white Americans to begin to reexamine the racial inequalities in their midst" and "the ideological demands of fighting an enemy who espoused racial hierarchies made more white Americans sensitive to the presence of racial discrimination in America." Ibid., 137, 160.

for understanding why the wartime civil rights movement proceeded as it did: turning away from Congress – the branch most constrained by mass attitudes – toward the possibility of unilateral action by the president, particularly when domestic advocacy could be tied directly to the war effort.

SURVEY RESEARCH IN THE WORLD WAR II ERA

Scholars often conjecture about what "the public" thought about some political issue for every period of American history. The New Deal era, however, is a unique period in American political development in that it coincides with the emergence of social scientific tools that could actually measure the political attitudes of ordinary citizens in a relatively generalizable way.[5] On September 10, 1935, interviewers with the Gallup Organization went into the field for six days to ask around 1,500 Americans two questions: (1) "Do you think expenditures by the Government for relief and recovery are too little, too great, or just about right?"; and (2) "As a general principle, would you favor limiting the power of the Supreme Court to declare acts of Congress unconstitutional?" The organization reported back that majorities felt expenditures were too high and that the Supreme Court's power should not be limited.[6]

Although the organization never made it a focal point, Gallup surveys did sporadically address issues related to race and civil rights when they rose to national prominence. Gallup inquired about Justice Hugo Black's involvement with the Ku Klux Klan and federal intervention in state lynching cases as early as 1936 and 1937, respectively. In 1939,

---

[5] For a discussion of how social and political historians have used other means of examining "public opinion," see Lawrence R. Jacobs and Robert Y. Shapiro, "Public Opinion and the New Social History: Some Lessons for the Study of Public Opinion and Democratic Policy Making," *Social Science History* 13, 1989, 1–24.

[6] This information from "Gallup Poll, Sep, 1935" is available from the iPoll Databank, http://ropercenter.cornell.edu/ipoll-database/. The next year, Gallup predicted that Roosevelt would win his 1936 reelection bid against Republican Alf Landon with around 56 percent of the vote. This prediction contradicted that of *The Literary Digest*, a popular magazine that had correctly predicted the winner of many earlier presidential contests. Polling literally millions of Americans drawn from lists of its own subscribers, automobile registrations, and telephone users, *The Literary Digest* predicted that Landon would win with around 57 percent of the vote. Roosevelt in fact got almost 61 percent of the vote, beating Landon by over ten million votes and winning every state except Maine and Vermont. *The Literary Digest* released its final issue in 1938, while George Gallup and his brand of public opinion polling became an integral part of the modern American political landscape.

it asked respondents about the Daughters of the American Revolution's decision to prevent "a well-known Negro singer" – Marian Anderson – from performing in one of their music halls.[7] Other organizations followed in Gallup's footsteps. By the time of US entry into the war, the National Opinion Research Center (NORC) had taken the lead in asking probing questions about racial prejudice and civil rights, significantly expanding the scope of questions being asked. NORC was founded in 1941 at the University of Denver as the first academic survey institute. Although now based at the University of Chicago and best known for their General Social Survey, much of their early work focused on aiding the Office of War Information with fact-finding missions about public morale and attitudes toward wartime issues. They also completed "the first national measurement of racial attitudes."[8]

President Franklin Roosevelt was enthusiastic about the new tools and became the first president to use private polling, although he did not hire a private White House pollster. Rather, Hadley Cantril "secretly worked as an unpaid, unofficial public opinion advisor for the FDR White House."[9] Cantril, in collaboration with Mildred Strunk, would later edit the largest published volume of topline survey results from this period in 1951.[10] Several government institutions were drawn to survey research during the Roosevelt presidency. In 1943, the Office of War Information surveyed black opinion in five cities, concluding, somewhat bluntly, that "Negroes feel bad about many things."[11]

The emergence of public opinion polling in general – and polling on questions about racial issues in particular – during this time period is important, as it means scholarship on World War II can measure white racial attitudes in a manner not possible for earlier conflicts.

---

[7] Also in 1939, Roper, in association with *Fortune* magazine, fielded a series of questions delving into specific issues of racial prejudice, asking questions about residential segregation, black intelligence, and the "ultimate outcome of the Negro problem in this country."

[8] National Opinion Research Center, *Social Science Research in Action*, (Chicago, 2011), 4, 42.

[9] Robert M. Eisinger, *The Evolution of Presidential Polling*, (New York: Cambridge University Press, 2003), 3.

[10] Hadley Cantril and Mildred Strunk, *Public Opinion 1935–1946*, (Princeton: Princeton University Press, 1951).

[11] Memorandum, "The Negroes' Role in the War: A Study of White and Colored Opinion," July 8, 1943, Folder: Race Tension – Jonathan Daniels File – Minority Problems, 1942–1945, Box 27, Philleo Nash Papers (hereafter Nash Papers), Harry S. Truman Library, Independence, Missouri (hereafter HSTL). This quote is the title of the first section of the report. See p. 1.

Until recently, however, these surveys were rarely used by contemporary researchers.[12] One reason is that these datasets were previously quite difficult to access.[13] A second concern is the extent to which the "quota sampling" procedure employed at the time created a biased view of "the public."

Before proceeding, the methodological issues raised by quota sampling merit further discussion. Modern surveys use probability sampling methods.[14] The quota sampling procedure employed by organizations like Gallup and NORC prior to the early 1950s differed in several ways from these methods. For quota samples, researchers determined in advance what proportions of the sample would come from what segments of the population, dividing the population into "mutually exclusive subpopulations (or strata) thought to capture politically relevant divisions," particularly region and gender.[15] Each strata was then given a certain size in the sample by the researchers. Although there was some slight variation in how different survey organizations implemented quotas, quota sampling techniques were similar overall.

This sampling method led to two key differences from population characteristics as measured by the US Census. Strata were inherently nonrepresentative due to the lack of random sampling. Even within the

---

[12] Some early exceptions that did utilize surveys from this era include Robert S. Erikson, "The Relationship Between Public Opinion and State Policy: A New Look Based on Some Forgotten Data," *American Journal of Political Science* 20(1), 1976, 25–36; Gregory A. Caldeira, "Public Opinion and the U.S. Supreme Court: FDR's Court-Packing Plan," *American Political Science Review* 81(4), 1987, 139–153; Benjamin I. Page and Robert Y. Shapiro, *The Rational Public: Fifty Years of Trends in Americans' Policy Preferences*, (Chicago: The University of Chicago Press, 1992); Stephen M. Weatherford and Boris Sergeyev, "Thinking About Economic Interests: Class and Recession in the New Deal," *Political Behavior* 22(4), 2000, 311–339; Matthew A. Baum and Samuel Kernell, "Economic Class and Popular Support for Franklin Roosevelt in War and Peace," *Public Opinion Quarterly* 65, 2001, 198–229.

[13] Fortunately, the iPoll Database from the Roper Center for Public Opinion Research at Cornell University (formerly the University of Connecticut) now makes many of these datasets more easily obtainable. While the datasets are often in rather messy form and require some significant cleaning before analysis can be done, this offers many new potential research paths.

[14] There are two main versions of this. The American National Election Studies and General Social Survey datasets are generated using a multistage area probability design that results in a representative sample of national opinion. Other studies, like the National Annenberg Election Survey, use random digit dialing telephone interviews, thereby generating a random sample of telephone owners.

[15] Adam J. Berinsky, "American Public Opinion in the 1930s and 1940s: The Analysis of Quota-Controlled Sample Survey Data," *Public Opinion Quarterly* 70(4), 2006, 502.

bounds of how the quota was allocated, however, interviewers were given sufficient discretion in the field, leading to "nonrandom selection within strata."[16] Put more concretely, within a strata defined by region and gender, interviewers might have chosen to interview people who seemed more approachable, often resulting in a class bias. The earliest surveys also interviewed more men than women, but this began to be corrected in the 1940s, with women and men coming to be roughly equal in their share of the sample.

Fortunately, these problems are not prohibitive. Adam Berinsky and Eric Schickler advocate a weighting procedure to correct for the known biases of these datasets.[17] Weighting allows researchers to create an estimate of aggregate opinion that adjusts for such demographic categories that were undersampled. The percentages reported in this chapter are weighted to account for undersampling related to region, gender, and social class.[18] This means that in cases where, for example, women were undersampled relative to men, the aggregate estimates of white opinion described in the text are adjusted to correct for this. While no methodological technique is perfect, these survey questions are the most representative source for analyzing broad trends in white attitudes

---

[16] Ibid., 507–508.

[17] Ibid.; Adam Berinsky and Eric Schickler, "Gallup Data, 1936–1945: Guide to Coding & Weighting," Unpublished Manuscript, Massachusetts Institute of Technology and University of California, Berkeley, 2011.

[18] Several weighting protocols are available depending on what information the surveys contain that can be matched to census figures. Corrections for region and gender biases are always used (and since I am focused on white racial attitudes, race is held constant for my purposes here). Class, however, is a more amorphous concept, and the measurements surveys provide that can be matched to census information were not consistent over time. The best approximation available is educational attainment. With this information, one can construct what Berinsky and Eric Schickler call an "eduWhites" weight, which is appropriate "if one is seeking to investigate white opinion, either nationally or with respect to regional differences." Educational attainment, however, was often not asked in the prewar period. In these earlier surveys, the best approximations are whether the respondent works in a "professional" industry or not and telephone ownership. A "profWhites" weighting procedure is identical to "eduWhites" but uses a dummy variable for professional in place of educational attainment. A modified version of Berinsky and Schickler's "phoneBlack" weight is likewise identical, except a dummy variable for phone ownership is used rather than professional status or educational attainment. For cross-tabulations, I use the best possible weight available given the nature of the dataset. The rank order of preference is (1) eduWhites, (2) profWhites, and (3) modified phoneBlack. While identical weighting would be preferred if the data allowed for it, a comparison of the raw cross-tabulations suggests the weights do not actually make a substantial difference when it comes to interpretation. For more details on how weights are calculated, see the appendix. For a more extensive discussion, see Berinsky and Schickler, "Gallup Data, 1936–1945: Guide to Coding & Weighting."

during this time period, especially when weighted in accordance with the Berinsky and Schickler protocol.[19]

HOW DO WHITE RACIAL ATTITUDES CHANGE?

The case of white racial attitudes during World War II has implications for a broader question as well: whether changes in attitudes generally – and white racial attitudes in particular – are event-driven or stem largely from less contingent, more structural sources.[20] While scholars have offered a range of explanations for variation in attitudes, explaining attitudinal change is somewhat more difficult. For example, early "Michigan School" research on partisan identification emphasized the influence of factors like childhood socialization.[21] Such variables, while useful in explaining attitudes at a given point in time, are unlikely to explain changes in attitudes over the course of individuals' lives. Instead, they imply – often accurately – that attitudes, once formed, are sticky. As Kellstedt notes, this was long believed by many to be true of racial attitudes, "apparently a function of childhood socialization and education," and thus stable in a similar manner as the Michigan School scholars believed to be true of partisan identification.[22]

Attitudes do sometimes change, though, so what variables might help explain such changes? Many scholars of trends in public opinion point to the role of the media as a catalyst for change in white racial attitudes, particularly during the 1950s/1960s civil rights era. Howard Schuman et al., for example, refer to "many Northern whites who witnessed, through television and other media, the brutality of Bull Connor and other white supremacists." They note that public opinion trends fit with historical

---

[19] For another analysis using these techniques, see Eric Schickler, *Racial Realignment: The Transformation of American Liberalism, 1932–1965*, (Princeton: Princeton University Press, 2016). "While opinion polls conducted in the 1930s and 1940s have numerous problems that have limited their use by scholars," Schickler writes, "the National Science Foundation has funded an extensive collaborative effort to make the data suitable for analysis." Ibid., 102.

[20] For example, Adam Berinsky argues wartime attitudes largely reflect peacetime patterns, suggesting an event like World War II should not necessarily drive white racial attitudes. Adam J. Berinsky, *In Time of War: Understanding American Public Opinion from World War II to Iraq*, (Chicago: University of Chicago Press, 2009). Paul Kellstedt's analysis of white racial attitude change in the 1950s and 1960s similarly suggests change is slower and more structural. Paul Kellstedt, *The Mass Media and the Dynamics of American Racial Attitudes*, (New York: Cambridge University Press, 2003)

[21] Angus Campbell, Philip Converse, Warren Miller, and Donald Stokes, *The American Voter*, (New York: Wiley, 1960).

[22] Kellstedt, *The Mass Media and the Dynamics of American Racial Attitudes*, 10.

accounts that "speak of the rethinking and searching of conscience that were prompted by the events of 1963."[23]

Benjamin Page and Robert Shapiro also note this "pro-civil rights opinion trend" and likewise suggest that "[a] good many events of the late 1950s and early 1960s, heavily covered by the mass media, surely played a part."[24] Although they acknowledge "the general hostility of Americans to protests and demonstrations," they argue "televised images of Southern policemen beating peaceful black demonstrators and setting dogs upon them galvanized the nation. There can be little doubt that the civil rights movement and Southern whites' highly visible 'massive resistance' to it had a major impact on public opinion."[25] Media coverage – especially of violent white resistance to protesters – is seen as key by both of these major accounts of attitudinal trends.

Paul Kellstedt offers the most systematic study of the relationship between aggregate racial attitude change and the quantity and tenor of media coverage. He shows how the quantity of stories in *Newsweek* spiked beginning in 1963, when there were 152 stories about race and civil rights. This continued for several years during the height of the 1960s civil rights movement. Kellstedt also points to the tenor of the coverage, demonstrating how this era saw media coverage that framed the debate in egalitarian rather than individualistic messages.[26] This, he argues, was a hospitable environment for the growth of racial liberalism in aggregate public opinion. The role of the media is absolutely central for Kellstedt. Fitting with Schuman et al. and Page and Shapiro, he notes, "Most of the key events of the movement, after all – desegregation battles in Little Rock and elsewhere, bus boycotts, freedom rides – took place in communities that few non-southerners would have known about were it not for the national press."[27] Even in this hospitable environment, however, white racial attitude change was relatively gradual.[28]

---

[23] Howard Schuman, Charlotte Steeh, Lawrence Bobo, and Maria Krysan, *Racial Attitudes in America: Trends and Interpretations: Revised Edition*, (Cambridge: Harvard University Press, 1997), 27–28.

[24] Page and Shapiro, *The Rational Public*, 76.

[25] Ibid., 77. See also James P. Winter and Chaim H. Eyal, "Agenda Setting for the Civil Rights Issue," *Public Opinion Quarterly* 45(3), 1981, 376–383. They argue the place of civil rights on the public agenda correlates with coverage of civil rights on the front page of the *New York Times* in the period 1954–1976.

[26] Kellstedt, *The Mass Media and the Dynamics of American Racial Attitudes*, 31–37.

[27] Ibid., 5.

[28] Kellstedt calls such shifts "*glacial*, in the sense that they are slow-moving, stable in the short term but never stable in the long term." Ibid., 131. Page and Shapiro also find

The 1960s civil rights era is a useful comparison to the World War II era because it highlights important historical differences, one of which is the variable role of the media. In the World War II era, the idea of a singular national media was still emerging.[29] There were also important technological differences. In an era before television news, newspapers were the dominant form of media.[30] Radio became widespread during this period, with its prevalence rising from 46 percent of households in 1930 to 82 percent of households in 1940. With the exception of World War II battles, however, there was little news content on radio at this point.[31] Importantly for comparing the World War II era to the civil rights era of the late 1950s and early 1960s, the former is situated just before the rise of television. While almost every household had a television set by the end of the 1950s, almost no households had them at the end of the 1940s.[32] This means that the powerful audiovisual images seen by audiences in the late 1950s and early 1960s were not even technologically possible during the World War II era.

Even if they were possible, compared to the mid-1960s, national and local media aimed at a white audience largely did not discuss racial issues in this era.[33] This was quite different from coverage in the late 1950s

---

that, even in the 1960s, attitudinal shifts on race were gradual. For a visualization of trends in racial attitudes over many decades, see Page and Shapiro, *The Rational Public*, 70–78.

[29] David Greenberg, "The Idea of 'the Liberal Media' and Its Roots in the Civil Rights Movement," *The Sixties: A Journal of History, Politics and Culture* 1(2), 2008, 170.

[30] Newspaper circulation reached 40 million by the 1930s. As fewer cities had multiple papers, the development of modern professional norms of journalism began to emerge, including the use of more concrete evidence and the growing dominance of the "inverted pyramid" style of writing familiar to modern readers. Jonathan M. Ladd, *Why Americans Hate the Media and How It Matters*, (Princeton: Princeton University Press, 2011), 47–49.

[31] Ibid., 49; Darrell West, *The Rise and Fall of the Media Establishment*, (Boston: Bedford/St. Martin's, 2001), 56.

[32] In 1949, just 2 percent of households had television sets, a number that rose to 55 percent by 1955 and 87 percent by 1959. Ladd, *Why Americans Hate the Media and How It Matters*, 50. See also Markus Prior, *Post-Broadcast Democracy: How Media Choice Increases Inequality in Political Involvement and Polarizes Elections*, (New York: Cambridge University Press, 2007). Most movie theaters showed a newsreel, generally about ten minutes in length, particularly in the 1930s and 1940s, but with the exception of foreign affairs, there was relatively little attention to politics. Michael Emery, Edwin Emery, and Nancy L. Roberts, *The Press and America: An Interpretive History of the Mass Media*, ninth Edition, (Boston: Allyn & Bacon, 2000), 329.

[33] This is of course quite the opposite of black newspapers, which regularly highlighted the tensions between a war for democracy and racism on the home front. Whites, however, were not attuned to this coverage. For a discussion of black newspapers and

and early 1960s, when veteran journalists who "hadn't always grasped the gravity of the racial issue" began to be replaced with a younger generation who more "instinctively appreciated the revolutionary nature of the struggle," according to David Greenberg.[34] As such, any theoretical tensions between American ideals of egalitarianism and the reality of Jim Crow racism were not primed for most white Americans. Thus, while it is possible the ideological logic of the war led to a rethinking of racial attitudes, it is also possible that this tension was perceived more by elites than the white mass public more generally. Accounts of the war's relationship with civil rights have tended to emphasize the plausibility of the ideological logic argument, rather than thinking through the extent to which the broader white public even considered the content of such arguments or not.[35]

THE RACIAL LIBERALIZATION HYPOTHESIS

The rest of this chapter analyzes what I call the racial liberalization hypothesis:

Racial Liberalization Hypothesis: World War II led to liberal shifts in white attitudes toward race and civil rights.

By "liberalization," I mean a trend toward lower levels of racial prejudice or greater support of policy interventions to address racial inequities. An aggregate increase in the view that black and white Americans have the

---

protest movements generally, see Charlotte G. O'Kelly, "Black Newspapers and the Black Protest Movement: Their Historical Relationship, 1827–1945," *Phylon* 43(1), 1982, 1–14. For a more recent, book-length treatment, see Fred Carroll, *Race News: Black Journalists and the Fight for Racial Justice in the Twentieth Century*, (Urbana, Chicago, and Springfield: University of Illinois Press, 2017). There were of course some exceptions – discussion of the FEPC and the Detroit race riot being two examples that were discussed by white newspapers – but these were not the norm, nor did they fit into the egalitarian tenor emphasized by Kellstedt as an important ingredient for the growth of racial liberalism.

[34] Greenberg, "The Idea of 'the Liberal Media' and Its Roots in the Civil Rights Movement," 175. For a more in-depth narrative of these civil rights sympathizers in the media during Kellstedt's era of interest, see Gene Robert and Hank Klibanoff, *The Race Beat: The Press, the Civil Rights Struggle, and the Awakening of a Nation*, (New York: Alfred A. Knopf, 2006).

[35] While Kellstedt's theoretical framework is in some ways similar to Myrdal's argument about the American Creed, it goes further in specifying a particular mechanism through which tensions might come about for ordinary citizens. When considered in this theoretical framework, however, it is not obvious that the war should have necessarily led to a more racially liberal mass public.

same innate abilities would be considered evidence of liberalization, as would an increase in the view that the government should intervene to stop lynchings. Of course, the first example is illustrative of racial *prejudice*, while the second example is illustrative of racial *policy attitudes*. Throughout the chapter, I note the extent to which there are different trends for the two types of questions.

The racial liberalization hypothesis is simply an explicitly stated version of the common view. Not everyone believes this – Kryder's book suggests it is likely incorrect – but it is intellectually predominant.[36] It is also entirely plausible. If the racial liberalization hypothesis is correct, the most likely mechanism linking the war to white racial attitudes is the ideological logic of a war against Nazi racism undermining elite justifications of Jim Crow. Certainly civil rights activists – advocating as they did a Double-V campaign for victory at home and abroad – found this logic compelling. When *The Nation*'s editorial pages declared, in the aftermath of the 1943 Detroit race riot, that Americans "cannot fight fascism abroad while turning a blind eye to fascism at home," this is what they meant.[37] It is often assumed that many ordinary white Americans saw this connection as well. Beyond the historical institutionalist accounts already noted, this extends to such varied sources as constitutional law books. Writing of World War II, Alfred H. Kelly asserts, "[T]he egalitarian ideology of American war propaganda, which presented the United States as a champion of democracy engaged in a death struggle with the German racists, created in the minds and hearts of most white people a new and intense awareness of the shocking contrast between the country's too comfortable image of itself and the cold realities of American racial segregation."[38] This claim is simply presented as background to a discussion of *Brown* v. *Board*; it is indicative of a widespread belief that the racial liberalization hypothesis is accurate in popular understandings of the war.

There are, however, reasons to be skeptical and to expect a null or even negative result. The relative dearth of national media coverage related to race and civil rights politics would imply a framework like that of Kellstedt's would not apply as well to the World War II period. While the ingredients for an egalitarian media framing were there, the national

---

[36] For Kryder's skeptical perspective, see Kryder, *Divided Arsenal*, 10.
[37] Cited in Maria Hohn, "'We Will Never Go Back to the Old Way Again': Germany in the African-American Debate on Civil Rights," *Central European History* 41, 2008, 616.
[38] Alfred H. Kelly, "The School Desegregation Case," 312.

media chose not to put them together. Many whites, therefore, simply might not have connected the dots. As such, a null result would be theoretically consistent with Kellstedt's media-centric model.

There is also the possibility of a backlash effect. If southern whites in particular were committed to the maintenance of segregation especially, any perception that the war was being used as a force against Jim Crow by civil rights advocates might have caused them to double down. When the southern newspaper columnist John Temple Graves wrote of the Double-V campaign that "[v]ictory, unhappily, doesn't work that way" and warned of a potential increase in lynchings, this is what he was predicting.[39] Contrary to the more positive account of the war's effects on white attitudes associated with Myrdal, it is entirely possible to imagine southern whites fearing the Double-V campaign was being persuasive, and thus doubling down on their white supremacist resolve.

What, then, does the available evidence suggest? To assess the racial liberalization hypothesis, I turn to rarely used public opinion surveys from 1937 to 1950.[40] I examine measures of prejudice and policy preferences that are repeated at multiple time points. I begin with six questions dealing with racial prejudice. I then consider questions about the two primary civil rights policy issues of the 1930s and early 1940s: federal antilynching legislation and abolition of the poll tax.[41] Although data sources are more limited, I also examine white attitudes on the wartime civil rights issues that came to dominate the agenda in the 1940s: segregation of the armed forces and discrimination in the defense industry, as well the question of whether black soldiers from the southern states should receive ballots as part of proposed congressional soldier voting legislation. I discuss the question wordings in the relevant sections.

---

[39] John Temple Graves, "The Southern Negro and the War Crisis," *Virginia Quarterly Review* 18(4), 1942, 501.

[40] These datasets were obtained from the iPoll Databank, http://ropercenter.cornell.edu/ipoll-database/. I provide more details as they are introduced throughout the chapter.

[41] One limitation to these two policy questions is that they are sectional in nature, primarily referencing racial politics in the southern states. For an analysis of legislative action on these and other civil rights issues of the era, see Jeffrey A. Jenkins and Justin Peck, "Building Toward Major Policy Change: Congressional Action on Civil Rights, 1941–1950," *Law and History Review* 31(1), 2013, 139–198. For a discussion of northern white liberals and tensions between their support for government action in the southern states but reticence to take on segregation in the northern states, see Schickler, *Racial Realignment*, 118.

If World War II led to a liberalization of white racial attitudes in the aggregate, we should see a liberal shift in racial attitudes, both prejudice and policy. Such a trend would be interpreted as support for the racial liberalization hypothesis. If, however, there is no change or even a conservative shift, this will be interpreted as evidence against the racial liberalization hypothesis. I also examine subgroup variation related to region and size of place to further assess the contours of these aggregate trends.[42]

RACIAL PREJUDICE

In May 1944, NORC administered a national study called "Attitudes Toward Negroes."[43] The sample consisted of 2,521 white adults who were interviewed face to face.[44] While other surveys asked a question here and there about race in the midst of other inquiries, this survey is

---

[42] Studying regional variation raises the complicated question of how to define the South. Following Berinsky and Schickler, I define the South here as the eleven states of the former Confederacy plus Kentucky and Oklahoma. See, for instance, Eric Schickler, "New Deal Liberalism and Racial Liberalism in the Mass Public, 1937–1968," *Perspectives on Politics* 11(1), 2013, 92f22. This is slightly more expansive than the traditional eleven-state definition advocated by V. O. Key and slightly less expansive than the broader definition advocated by Ira Katznelson and colleagues. For the original justification of an eleven-state South, see V. O. Key, Jr., *Southern Politics in State and Nation*, (Knoxville: University of Tennessee Press, 2006 [1949]), 11. For contemporary examples following in this tradition, see Earl Black and Merle Black, *Politics and Society in the South*, (Cambridge: Harvard University Press, 1987); Seth C. McKee and Melanie J. Springer, "A Tale of 'Two Souths': White Voting Behavior in Contemporary Southern Elections," *Social Science Quarterly* 96(2), 2015, 588–607; Robert Mickey, *Paths Out of Dixie: The Democratization of Authoritarian Enclaves in America's Deep South, 1944–1972*, (Princeton: Princeton University Press, 2015); Steven White, "The Heterogeneity of Southern White Distinctiveness," *American Politics Research* 42(4), 2014, 551–578. For a justification of a more expansive definition, see Sean Farhang and Ira Katznelson, "The Southern Imposition: Congress and Labor in the New Deal and Fair Deal," *Studies in American Political Development* 19, 2005, 1–30; Melanie Springer, "Defining 'the South' (Is Not a Straightforward Matter)," (paper presented at the 2011 meeting of the State Politics and Policy Conference, Hanover, NH); David A. Bateman, Ira Katznelson, and John Lapinski, "*Southern Politics* Revisited: On V. O. Key's 'South in the House,'" *Studies in American Political Development* 29(2), 2015, 154–184.

[43] This dataset ("USNORC1944-0225: Attitudes Toward Negroes") was obtained from the iPoll Databank, http://ropercenter.cornell.edu/ipoll-database/.

[44] The 2,521 respondents include 1,180 men and 1,341 women. While women were frequently undersampled in the 1930s, this practice seems to have declined in the 1940s (and in this case, there are actually more women than men in the sample). A 32-category eduWhites weight, following Berinsky and Schickler's protocol, is created to match the sample to census statistics for gender, education, and region.

entirely about race. The results provide a unique look at white attitudes in the middle of World War II.[45] This particular survey made a number of people uncomfortable. In December 1944, a confidential report summarizing the results was sent to seventy-five people asking for comments on how the data might be used in a constructive manner and whether it would be advisable to release the numbers into general distribution. Later the results were in the process of being prepared for publication by the American Council on Race Relations, but the council was concerned about a preliminary release. "The danger of publishing such figures, without due caution and interpretation," they argued, "lies in the fact that many persons reading the results of the poll would mistake figures published for actual facts."[46]

Six of the questions from this survey were repeated on a single occasion. This section compares the aggregate and regional numbers between t_1 and t_2 to offer some assessment of change over time. A good living question ("Do you think Negroes have the same chance as white people to make a good living in this country?") was previously asked in November 1943.[47] This survey interviewed 2,560 national adults face to face. Five other questions were repeated in May 1946.[48] This survey interviewed 2,589 national adults face to face. There were questions about fair treatment ("Do you think most Negroes in the United States are being treated fairly or unfairly?"), jobs ("Do you think Negroes

---

[45] The timing coincided with interesting developments. By the beginning of 1944, magazines were beginning to cover Myrdal's *An American Dilemma*. See chapter 4 of David W. Southern, *Gunnar Myrdal and Black-White Relations: The Use and Abuse of an American Dilemma, 1944–1969*, (Baton Rouge: Louisiana State University Press, 1987). The *Smith* v. *Allwright* Supreme Court case was argued in January and decided in April of that year. While the numbers should be interpreted in this context, it is unlikely that a large number of white Americans had ever heard of the name Gunnar Myrdal, and the consequences of *Smith* were yet to be seen in many places by May 1944.

[46] Jean Converse, *Survey Research in the United States: Roots and Emergence 1890–1960*, (Berkeley: University of California Press, 1987), 312–313. The survey results also made their way into the White House. In July 1944, Philleo Nash (then Assistant Deputy Director of the Office of War Information) sent FDR administrative assistant Jonathan Daniels "an advance tabulation on the Denver Opinion Research Center's most recent Negro study." Memorandum, Philleo Nash to Jonathan Daniels, July 21, 1944, Folder: Race Tension – Jonathan Daniels File – Minority Problems, 1942–1945, Box 27, Nash Papers, HSTL.

[47] This dataset ("USNORC1943-0217: Postwar Problems, Old Age Pension, Public Schools and Free Speech") was obtained from the iPoll Databank, http://ropercenter.cornell.edu/ipoll-database/.

[48] This dataset ("USNORC1946-0241: Minorities; United Nations") was obtained from the iPoll Databank, http://ropercenter.cornell.edu/ipoll-database/.

should have as good a chance as white people to get any kind of job, or do you think white people should have the first chance at any kind of job?"), blood ("As far as you know, is Negro blood the same as white blood, or is it different in some way?"), intelligence ("In general, do you think Negroes are as intelligent as white people – that is, can they learn just as well if they are given the same education?"), and having a black nurse ("If you were sick in a hospital, would it be all right with you if you had a Negro nurse, or wouldn't you like it?"). The blood question might seem strange at first, but it actually relates quite directly to the war effort: the Red Cross at this time segregated donations – storing black blood separately from white blood – even during total war.[49]

Table 2.1 presents the weighted percentages for each survey question.[50] These questions provide different vantage points on attitudinal change during the war. The first four questions (jobs, intelligence, blood, and having a black nurse) tap into general prejudice. The blood question, in particular, is an extreme case that taps into a form of biological racism common in the day. For these questions, an increase in affirmative answers should be taken as evidence of growing liberalism. The good living and fair treatment questions, by contrast, involve respondents making an assessment of conditions, which leaves their empirical meaning a bit more ambiguous. The objective answer is "no," but increases in the "yes" answer during the war might reflect a perception that things are getting better, if not equitable. As such, these two questions are not ideal for testing the racial liberalization hypothesis but are discussed here because they are of general historical interest. Results should be interpreted with care, since it is not possible to look at the average of multiple polls, but simply two data points. As such, these results should be seen as suggestive rather than definitive.

---

[49] Thomas A. Guglielmo, "'Red Cross, Double Cross': Race and America's World War II-Era Blood Donor Service," *Journal of American History* 91(1), 2010, 63–90.

[50] To maintain consistency across years, I omit the extraneous volunteered responses collected by NORC to simply look at "yes," "no," and "don't know" (or similar) responses. In situations where a significant percentage of respondents volunteered a different response, I note this in a footnote and describe how the weighted percentages would change if all categories are kept in the analysis. Weights were constructed following Berinsky and Schickler's approach. I calculate a 32-category eduWhites weight for the 1943 dataset. I am only able to calculate a 24-category eduWhites weight for the 1946 dataset, however, since I am unable to distinguish between whites who attended high school and whites who actually graduated (these two groups are thus lumped together).

TABLE 2.1: *Antiblack prejudice, 1943–1946*

Question Wording	1943	1944	1946
"Do you think Negroes should have **as good a chance** as white people to get any kind of job, or do you think white people should have the first chance at any kind of job?"		40%	47%
"In general, do you think Negroes **are as intelligent** as white people – that is, can they learn just as well if they are given the same education?"		46%	55%
"As far as you know, is Negro blood **the same** as white blood, or is it different in some way?"		31%	40%
"If you were sick in a hospital, would it be **all right with you** if you had a Negro nurse, or wouldn't you like it?"		53%	47%
"Do you think most Negroes in the United States **are being treated fairly** or unfairly?"		66%	66%
"Do you think Negroes **have the same chance** as white people to make a good living in this country?"	51%	58%	

Note: Percentages refer to the percent of whites answering with the option in bold. The first four questions measure white racial prejudice, while the final two questions measure white perceptions of conditions for African Americans.

Three prejudice measures are consistent with the racial liberalization hypothesis. Whites became more likely to say African Americans should have the same chance at a job, rising from 40 percent to 47 percent (outside of the South, support for equal opportunity increased from 47 percent to 52 percent, while southern support increased from 15 percent to 25 percent).[51] Whites also became more likely to say black blood was the same as white blood, with the number increasing from 31 percent to 40 percent (in the North, whites moved from 34 percent to 42 percent saying it was the same, while in the South, whites moved from only

---

[51] NORC asked a similarly worded question in April 1947. While documentation exists that indicates the question was asked, the iPoll website indicates that "[n]o data is available" for that particular survey's questions about race. The topline numbers provided by the website suggest the results are not much different from the 1946 survey (52 percent of all respondents said black workers should have as good a chance as white workers, but this number is likely based on both white and black respondents).

20 percent saying it was the same to 32 percent saying so).[52] Finally, whites became more likely – moving from 46 to 55 percent – to say black people were as intelligent as white people. In contrast to the other two examples, this shift is almost entirely nonsouthern. In the South, 30 percent of whites said yes in 1944 compared to 31 percent in 1946. In the North, however, this number increased from 50 percent in 1944 to 62 percent in 1946.[53]

One prejudice measure, however, is not consistent with the racial liberalization hypothesis. The question about having a black nurse actually saw a decrease in support, from 53 percent of whites saying they would be okay with this in 1944 to 47 percent in 1946.[54] This seems primarily driven by northern whites, where support dropped from 58 percent to 52 percent, while moving only from 34 percent to 31 percent in the South.

Finally, while the questions asking for assessments of social conditions do not measure prejudice in the same way, they still provide a revealing look at white racial attitudes from another vantage point. The percentage of whites who said they thought African Americans had the same chance as whites to make a good living actually increased from 51 percent in

---

[52] Nationally, the number saying it was different was effectively constant, moving from 34 percent to 33 percent. "Don't know" responses, however, dropped from 35 percent to 28 percent.

[53] A question about black intelligence was also asked by Roper in 1939, although the question was worded differently. Respondents were first asked whether they "think negroes now generally have higher intelligence than white people, lower, or about the same." Those who responded "lower" were then asked if they thought this was because "[t]hey have lacked opportunities," "[t]hey are born less intelligent," or both. Overall, just 21 percent of whites said black people were as intelligent as white people in 1939, with 78 percent saying they had lower intelligence. Among those whites who picked the lower intelligence option, however, 33 percent agreed that it was because "[t]hey have lacked opportunities," while 45 percent said it was because "[t]hey are born less intelligent" (another 22 percent said it was a combination of both). Given this follow-up, for a better comparison to the 1944 NORC question (which asked whether respondents think " Negroes are as intelligent as white people – that is, can they learn just as well if they are given the same education"), it is more probably more accurate to say that 47 percent of whites either said black people were equally intelligent as whites *or* were only less intelligent because they lacked such opportunities – a number that is nearly identical to the 46 percent that said black people were as innately intelligent as white in 1944.

[54] In the 1944 dataset, 3 percent of respondents volunteered that they would be okay with having a black nurse, but only if no white nurse were available. If the extraneous responses are kept in, the estimate of white opinion would be that 51 percent of whites were willing to have a black nurse. In 1946, just 1 percent of white respondents volunteered this response. Keeping extraneous responses in the 1946 dataset would not change the estimate of white public opinion. In that sense, dropping the extraneous responses increases the decline by two percentage points.

1943 to 58 percent in 1944.[55] In the nonsouthern states, whites moved from 48 to 55 percent, while in the South, whites moved from 64 to 69 percent. White assessments of whether African Americans were being treated fairly remained constant from 1944 to 1946, at 66 percent in both years.[56] Outside the South, the number was 63 percent in 1944 and 62 percent in 1946. In the South, the same numbers were 79 percent and 77 percent.

While regional breakdowns are probably the most common way to look at subgroup variation in white racial attitudes, differences between rural and urban residents provide another useful perspective.[57] Here, I briefly analyze trends in the attitudes of rural southerners (a group that is likely to be especially racially conservative) and urban residents in the Northeast (a group that is likely to be especially racially liberal).[58] In many cases, the decreases in racial prejudice seem to reflect rural southern whites going from "extremely prejudiced" to "slightly less prejudiced." For example, while only 10 percent of whites in the most rural areas of the South expressed support for equal job opportunities in 1944, by 1946 this number had risen to 25 percent – a sizable increase percentage-wise, albeit still a minority viewpoint. Similarly, notions among this group of white southerners that black blood is biologically the same as white blood increased from 19 percent in 1944 to 39 percent in 1946. The

---

[55] If all extraneous responses are kept in the dataset, the shift is smaller (51 percent to 54 percent). One problem with comparing these two datasets is that, while the question wording is identical, the 1943 survey did not record volunteered extraneous responses, while the 1944 dataset did. The more direct comparison would compare the "yes," "no," and "don't know" responses as I do in the main text, but this does involve ignoring the 4 percent of whites in the 1944 dataset who gave responses that NORC categorized into an extraneous "No, because of laziness, don't want to; Yes, but won't work; yes, if they want to; become undesirable, arrogant" category.

[56] The number is 62 percent if all volunteered responses are kept in the dataset. In 1944, 4 percent of respondents volunteered extraneous responses that NORC categorized into a "Yes, too good, more than they deserve, Should be put back in their place, too fairly" category. In 1946, 4 percent once again volunteered similar extraneous responses.

[57] "Urban voters may have been particularly aware of the changing composition of the party coalition and thus were quick to respond to it," Schickler suggests. Schickler, *Racial Realignment*, 126. More generally, Schickler finds that urban residence tends to be especially predictive of civil rights liberalism among whites in this era, relative to other demographic characteristics.

[58] I define "rural" as farming communities and towns with fewer than 2,500 residents. I define "urban" as metropolitan communities with populations over 500,000 people. While I occasionally use "the North" as shorthand for the non-South throughout this book, when I refer to the "Northeast" specifically I mean the New England and Mid-Atlantic regions.

changes in the urban Northeast were generally much smaller (58 percent in both years for the job opportunities question, and from 36 percent to 44 percent for the blood question).

Overall, there is some evidence for the racial liberalization hypothesis with respect to the racial prejudice measures, although there was a conservative shift on the nurse question. There are, however, clear limitations to this analysis. First, given the importance of black military service in this era, it would be informative to see trends in attitudes toward black veterans. Unfortunately, the survey did not ask about black military service, although a snapshot of attitudes toward giving black soldiers ballots will be described later in this chapter. Second, two data points are less than ideal, especially since there is no available prewar question. Fortunately, the two policy issues that follow are better in this regard.

ANTILYNCHING LEGISLATION

I next turn to an assessment of changing white attitudes on federal intervention in state lynching cases. Lynching was raised as a national political issue by civil rights organizations like the NAACP.[59] As William Hastie and Thurgood Marshall argued during the war, "[t]he recent outbreaks of mob violence again emphasize the fact that only Federal action will free us from lynchings and the threat of lynching."[60] Federal antilynching legislation was often proposed but never successfully passed in the Senate (although it did pass in the House of Representatives). Such legislation was a challenge to Roosevelt's congressional New Deal alliance. Roosevelt and his congressional supporters "tailored New Deal legislation to southern preferences," according to Ira Katznelson et al., trading maintenance of southern Jim Crow for southern support for New Deal economic legislation. This meant that not even "the most heinous aspects of regional repression, such as lynching, [could be] be brought under the rule of law."[61] Yet for many politicians outside the South, black migration meant "black political power was becoming an unavoidable

---

[59] Megan Ming Francis, *Civil Rights and the Making of the Modern American State*, (New York: Cambridge University Press, 2014).

[60] William H. Hastie and Thurgood Marshall, "Negro Discrimination and the Need for Federal Action," *Law Guild Review* 2(6), 1942, 21.

[61] Ira Katznelson, Kim Geiger, and Daniel Kryder, "Limiting Liberalism: The Southern Veto in Congress, 1933–1950," *Political Science Quarterly* 108(2), 1993, 297.

reality."[62] Antilynching legislation soon became more than the sum of its parts, effectively serving as a symbol for racial conservatives of the meddling of northern liberals in the white South's affairs.

To assess white attitudes towards federal antilynching legislation, I use Gallup questions about federal intervention in state lynching cases, which were asked before and after – although, interestingly, not during – the war.[63] I divide opinion in each survey into "support," "opposition," and "don't know."[64] I use the best possible survey weight to correct for the biases of the sampling procedure.[65]

A word of caution is in order regarding question wordings. While the analysis presented here is consistent with evidence regarding the poll tax (which provides a useful robustness check, as there is no substantial variation in question wording there), Gallup's questions about lynching are indicative of some of the weaknesses of early survey research. The questions can be roughly divided into four groups. The first three questions, all from 1937, asked quite simply whether Congress should pass a law making lynching a federal crime. The next three questions, asked between 1937 and 1940, asked whether the federal government should have the authority to punish local authorities who do not protect against a lynching mob. (The first of these is vague about the punishment, while the next two are explicit about fining or imprisoning them.) In the postwar period, from 1947 to 1950, Gallup returned to a more general question, asking, with only very slight variations, a question along the lines of, "At present, state governments deal with most crimes committed in their own state. In

---

[62] George C. Rable, "The South and the Politics of Antilynching Legislation, 1920–1940," *Journal of Southern History* 51, 1958, 209.

[63] These datasets were obtained from the iPoll Databank, http://ropercenter.cornell.edu/ipoll-database/. For a full list of survey titles and question wordings, see the appendix.

[64] While Schickler discards the "don't know" responses to create dichotomous response categories in his analysis of the prewar lynching questions, I leave the "don't know" responses in to allow for a valid third category of uncertainty. As will be discussed momentarily, this helps to assess prewar and postwar shifts in the opposition category.

[65] For the postwar questions, this means calculating the eduWhites weight. The prewar surveys are more limited. Making the best of the available information, I use profWhites weights for the January 1937, November 1937, and January 1940 datasets; I use phoneBlack weights for the August 1937, October/November 1937, and December 1937 datasets. Weights for the prewar questions were previously computed by Schickler. I calculate the postwar weights myself. Differences in weights are necessitated by differences in available information in surveys from different time periods. It is unlikely this has a sizable effect, however. While the weighted figures are technically more accurate than unweighted ones, the substantive difference between them is generally small.

the case of a lynching do you think the Federal Government should have the right to step in and deal with the crime – or do you think this should be left entirely to the state government?" There is one outlier in the question wording, however. The 1947 question asks whether the federal government should be able to step in only "if the State Government doesn't deal with it justly." This concluding qualifier ("justly") leaves much more room for interpretation and possibly suggests a less all-encompassing policy. I consider this question a third category, and the remaining 1948–1950 questions without the qualifier as the fourth category.

Because of these differences in question wording, caution is needed in analyzing over-time trends. While the first (1937) and fourth (1948–1950) groups of questions share some similarities (they both ask whether the federal government should have authority over state lynching cases, without making reference to specific penalties), the 1937 questions do not refer directly to state action. And while the 1947 question is similar to the 1948–1950 questions in many ways, the ending to the question is much more ambiguous, perhaps suggesting a weaker policy (in turn opening up the possibility of more expressed support). This sort of limitation, however, is an inherent part of the data and reflects the difficulties of working with surveys from this era.[66]

Figure 2.1 plots trends in national white support, while Figure 2.2 plots southern and nonsouthern whites separately. For the first three data points in 1937, national white support for federal intervention ranges from 58 to 61 percent (the numbers are 59 to 68 percent in the North, compared to 43 to 54 percent in the South). For the next three, when phrasing about punishing local officials is introduced from November 1937 to January 1940, support begins at 60 percent with the version of the question where the exact nature of the punishment is not specified, with very little regional variation. For the question wordings that include the language about fining and imprisoning local officials, the numbers drop to 42 to 46 percent nationally, including 46 to 51 percent outside the South and 26 to 29 percent in the southern states. Postwar support is generally lower, except in the 1947 survey where the question wording used the concluding qualifier that suggested a less definitive federal role.[67] For the five surveys fielded between February 1948 and January 1950, however, national white support for federal intervention ranges

---

[66] To better highlight variation in wording, a version of the graphs where I use different markers in the figures for different categories of questions can be found in the appendix.

[67] In that survey, 67 percent expressed support.

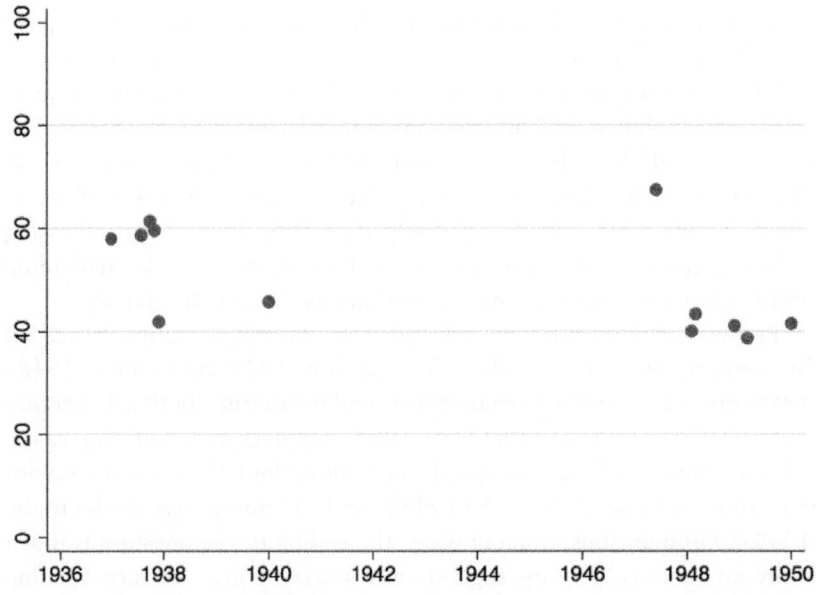

FIGURE 2.1: Support for federal antilynching legislation, 1937–1950

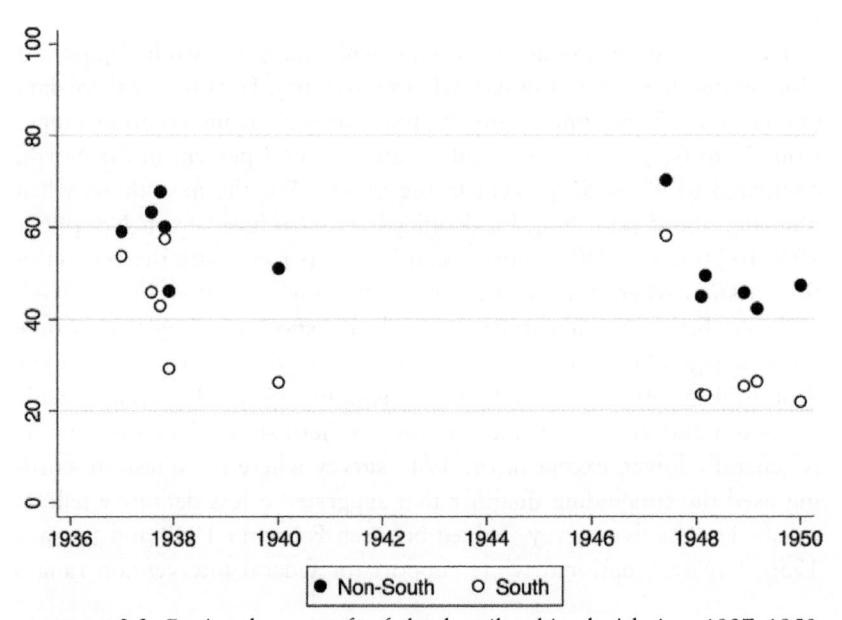

FIGURE 2.2: Regional support for federal antilynching legislation, 1937–1950

Antilynching Legislation

from 39 to 43 percent (42 to 49 percent in the North, compared to 22 to 26 percent in the South).

Precise causal inference is impossible to draw from such data, but a few general statements seem consistent with the results. The polling evidence certainly provides no support for the idea that the war led to an increase in support for federal intervention in state lynching cases. It is possible there was simply no effect of the war (the apparent trend could be random fluctuations, question wording effects, etc.). If anything, there seems to have been an increase in racially conservative opposition.

To better visualize trends in opposition, Figures 2.3 and 2.4 plot the percentage of whites that opposed federal intervention from 1937 until 1950, first overall and then separating out southern and nonsouthern whites. Before the war, opposition never rose above 46 percent overall, 41 percent in the North, and 64 percent in the South. Notably, these prewar heights of opposition coincide with the more extreme question wording about fining or imprisoning local officials, which was dropped in the postwar period. For the prewar questions that did not specify these punishments, opposition was never above 26 percent overall (and never above 39 percent in the South). By January 1950, however, opposition to federal intervention was up to 51 percent overall – a majority – and a

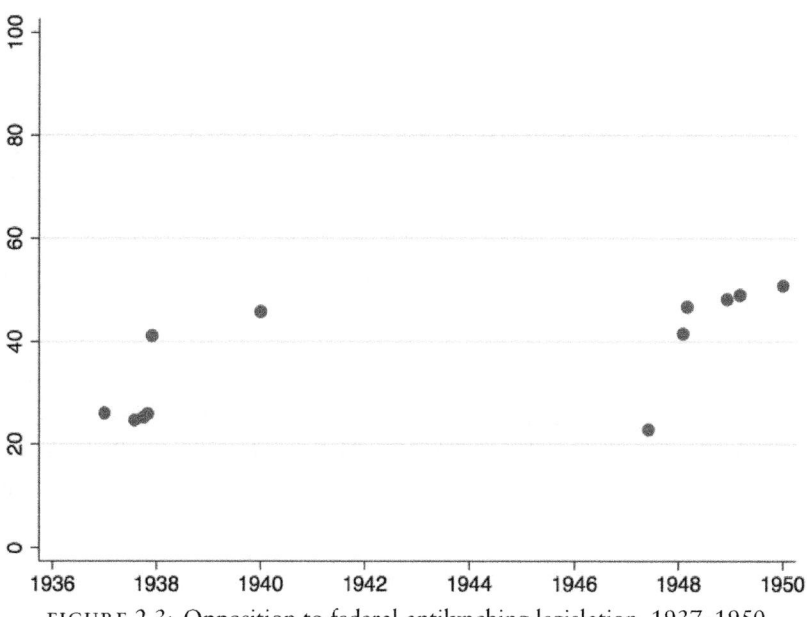

FIGURE 2.3: Opposition to federal antilynching legislation, 1937–1950

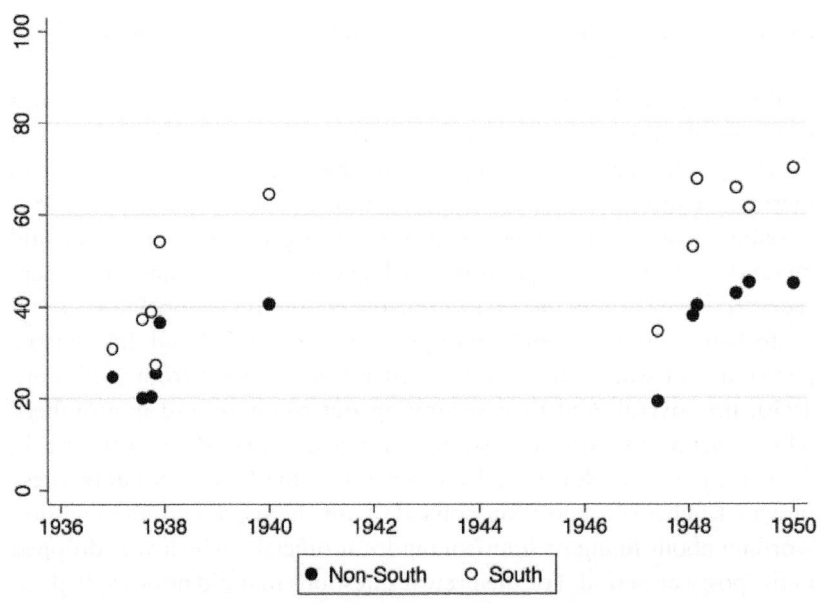

FIGURE 2.4: Regional opposition to federal antilynching legislation, 1937–1950

new height of 70 percent in the South. This seems to have been partly the result of white indecision evolving into a hardened states' rights position and partly a decline in active support for federal intervention as well.[68]

Comparing southerners in the most rural areas to northeastern residents in the most urban ones is again revealing, but in a slightly different manner than it was for measures of racial prejudice. In January 1940, 65 percent of whites in the most populous urban areas in the Northeast expressed support for a congressional antilynching bill. Between February 1948 and January 1950, support for federal intervention in these same areas ranged from 47 percent to 58 percent across five different surveys. For whites in the most rural southern areas, support stood at 22 percent in January 1940, then ranged from 11 percent to 19 percent in those same five postwar surveys. The decline in support, then, actually seems more concentrated in the urban Northeast, where support dropped from nearly two-thirds of whites to just a slight majority (and, in one case, only a plurality). There was, however, less room for a decrease in southern opinion, since it was already much more opposed.

---

[68] Before the war, "no opinion" responses averaged 14 percent, while in the postwar period, they averaged 11 percent.

This does not mean the urban Northeast was not more supportive of civil rights liberalism – it was. It does, however, highlight the extent to which liberalism was "limited" at this time by mass preferences. Rather than being a window where policy attitudes could become more accommodating, the war seems to have solidified the prospect of such measures and thus increased skepticism. Antilynching legislation was never enacted and eventually fell off the agenda.

So, what might be behind the apparent shift in attitudes? Several factors besides the war cannot be ruled out as possibilities. The number of lynchings had declined since the mid-1930s, which might have led more white respondents to think lynching would go away on its own without federal action, thereby decreasing the issue's salience for sympathetic whites.[69] Another possibility is that it might reflect the NAACP's changing policy focus. By the late 1940s, the organization's civil rights agenda included a wide range of issues beyond lynching, which might have led less supportive or uncertain white respondents to interpret the lynching question as representing something bigger than lynching per se. Respondents could have perceived that growths in black militancy during the war were increasing the prospect of other policy changes, with antilynching legislation serving as a precedent.[70] It is also possible that a genuine, if unmeasurable, wartime liberalization might have been reversed by developments in the latter half of the 1940s such as the Truman civil rights committee (established in December 1946 and report released in October 1947) or the Dixiecrat movement in 1948.[71]

---

[69] Robert L. Zangrando, *The NAACP Crusade Against Lynching, 1909–1950*, (Philadelphia: Temple University Press, 1980), 6–7. Social movement activity, particularly protests, can increase issue salience for members of a group directly affected by the issue. See Tony E. Carey, Jr., Regina P. Branton, and Valerie Martinez-Ebers, "The Influence of Social Protests on Issue Salience Among Latinos," *Political Research Quarterly* 67(3), 2014, 615–627. To the extent that media coverage is a proxy for issue salience, the lack of coverage of issues related to lynching by the white press might have made it a not particularly salient issue for whites. Lee Epstein and Jeffrey A. Segal, "Measuring Issue Salience," *American Journal of Political Science* 44(1), 2000, 66–83.

[70] Zangrando, *The NAACP Crusade Against Lynching*, 167.

[71] There do not seem to be any notable shifts related to the 1948 presidential campaign. If there was a decrease in support for federal antilynching legislation, it likely began earlier than this. The potentially confounding influence of the Truman civil rights committee is more difficult to assess, however. All of the postwar lynching questions discussed here were fielded after the committee's report was released. The only postwar lynching question fielded before the report – albeit well after the committee's establishment – was the June 1947 question that used the "justly" modifier in its phrasing. While expressed support for antilynching legislation was indeed higher here, it is not possible to assess

Another difficulty is properly disentangling the racial and federalism components of the question wording. In an ideal research design, trends in support for federal intervention in lynching could be compared to trends in support for a question about race that did not involve an obvious federalism component, as well as a question about federalism that did not involve an obvious racial component. Unfortunately, data limitations preclude such an analysis. That said, even if such an analysis were possible, the extent to which states' rights rhetoric was closely tied to southern opposition to civil rights might make it difficult to fully disentangle attitudes towards race and federalism in practice, particularly in the World War II era. Evidence about attitudes toward state-level antidiscrimination laws (presented later in this chapter) also suggests that even when federalism is not an issue, there is still clear aversion to policies to address racism.

Whatever the interpretation, the trends presented here can still serve as an important reference point for accounts of the war and racial attitudes. At the very least, while acknowledging a potentially more complicated story, the racial liberalization argument does not seem consistent with the lynching data.

ABOLITION OF THE POLL TAX

The second policy issue that was especially salient before the war was the poll tax. While the poll tax was less directly tied to race than lynching – a topic I return to momentarily – it was nonetheless an important part of the civil rights agenda in this time period. To assess shifts in white attitudes on the poll tax, I use Gallup questions about whether the tax should be abolished.[72] This question was asked once in 1940, then four more times in the late 1940s. Like the lynching questions, however, it was never asked during the war itself. The question wording, fortunately, was very similar over time. "Some Southern states require every voter to pay a poll tax amounting to about a dollar a year before they can vote," the question began. The respondent is then asked whether they think "these poll taxes" should be "abolished" or "done

---

whether this is related to the Truman committee, or merely the qualifier in the question wording resulting in higher levels of support.

[72] These datasets were obtained from the iPoll Databank, http://ropercenter.cornell.edu/ipoll-database/. For a full list of survey titles and question wordings, see the appendix.

away with" (the specific phrase at the end is the only part that varies over time).[73]

Figures 2.5 and 2.6 plot white support for abolishing the poll tax nationally as well as broken down by region. In December 1940 – a year before the United States entered World War II – national white attitudes stood at 61 percent wanting to abolish poll taxes, 27 percent wanting to keep them, and 12 percent not offering an opinion. In the South, 51 percent of whites supported getting rid of poll taxes, with 40 percent wanting to keep them and 9 percent not expressing an opinion. Jumping forward to the postwar questions, national white support for abolition of the poll tax ranged from 64 to 67 percent, and among white southerners

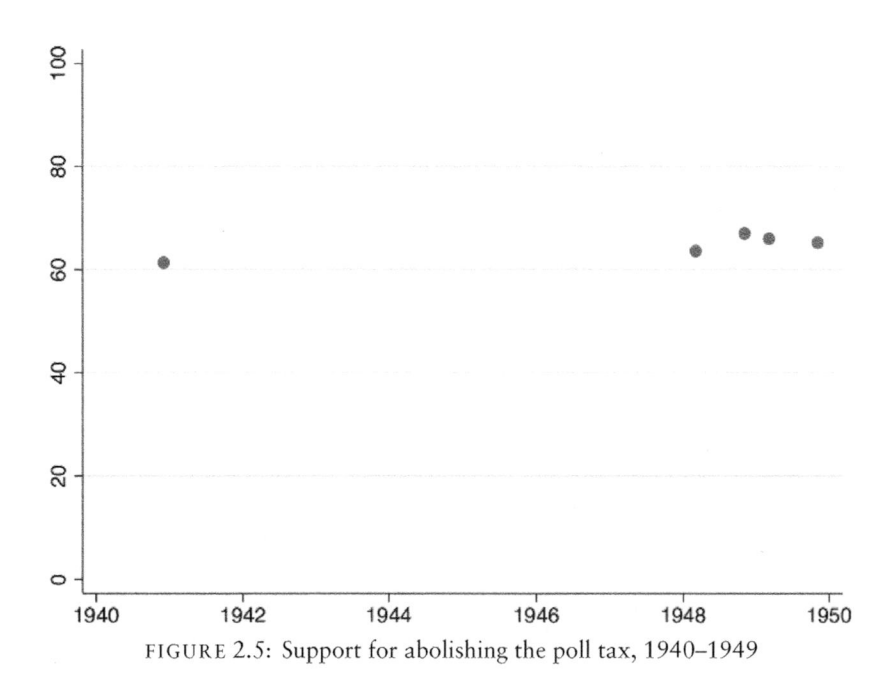

FIGURE 2.5: Support for abolishing the poll tax, 1940–1949

---

[73] The prewar survey allowed respondents to distinguish between "YES!" and "Yes" (also "NO!" and "No"), which is how they articulated preference intensity. The postwar surveys simply offered "Yes" and "No" responses, however, so I collapse the 1940 survey into simple "YES!"/"Yes" and "NO!"/"No" categories to allow for comparison. All surveys also allowed the respondents to declare "no opinion," which I again choose to keep in my analysis. The 1940 survey weights were constructed by Berinsky and Schickler, and I use their code to reproduce it (again altering their decision to drop respondents who offered no opinion on the poll tax question). For the postwar questions, I construct my own weights that correspond to Berinsky and Schickler's preferred education weights ("eduWhites") based on their method.

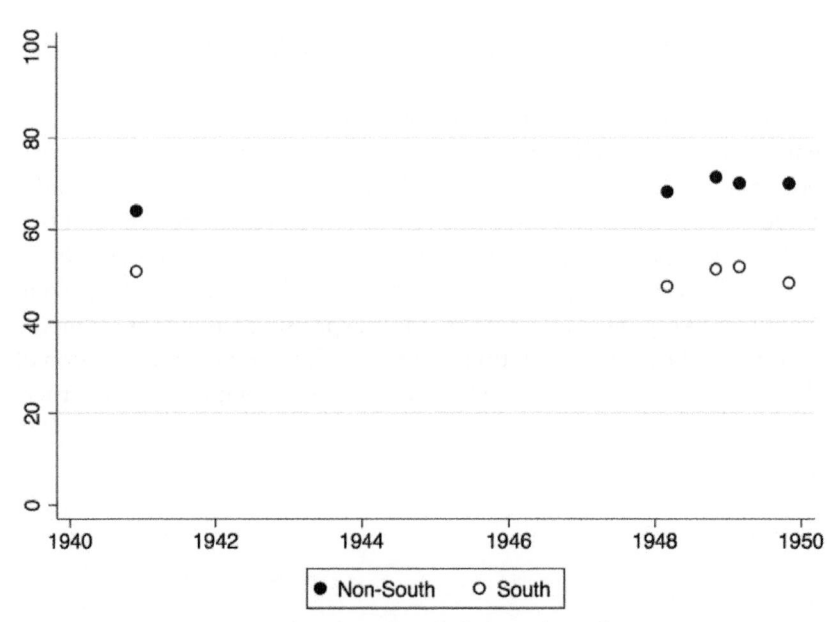

FIGURE 2.6: Regional support for abolishing the poll tax, 1940–1949

it ranged from 48 to 52 percent. The evidence, then, points to an increase in support of 3 to 6 percentage points in aggregate white opinion, with any change likely concentrated outside of the southern states.[74] This is a slight shift, although it is difficult to discern the extent to which it represents a small but real change rather than a slight fluctuation within the margin of sampling error.[75]

There are again some concerns regarding interpretation that merit consideration. The poll tax was a complicated issue in the context of 1940s racial politics. Poll tax opponents in the 1940s tried to frame the issue as a suffrage restriction that hurt poor whites. By focusing on the single issue of the poll tax, they hoped to separate the issue from the broader struggle for black voting rights. Roosevelt himself viewed reforming "Polltaxia" as part of his broader effort in the late 1930s to purge southern conservatives in his party, which was motivated by a range of issues beyond race. After the United States entered World War II, some advocates used the ideological logic of the war to compare the

---

[74] Outside of the southern states, white support for getting rid of the poll tax ranged from 64 percent in 1940 to 68–71 percent in the postwar period.

[75] Additional data points from the prewar era would help in making this determination, but unfortunately only one prewar survey exists.

poll tax's disenfranchisement with elections in fascist Europe. Insomuch as the poll tax was framed by political elites like Roosevelt and national advocacy organizations as a burden on poor whites, using it as a test of racial policy is a bit difficult.

The extent to which the poll tax was likely less explicitly racialized in the minds of most whites than lynching is perhaps also helpful in making sense of why its abolition was more widely supported, even in the southern states.[76] That said, it is certainly true that supporters of the poll tax in the South saw it as an important tool in maintaining white supremacy. Some nonsouthern liberal Democrats likewise described it in similar terms. Congressman Arthur Mitchell, for example, said abolishing the poll tax would "eventually aid in wiping out the disenfranchisement of Negroes... in the Southern states" (for him, a welcome development).[77]

Overall, it would be ill-advised to look only at the poll tax as a measure of racial policy liberalism. In conjunction with an analysis of antilynching legislation, which was always more explicitly racialized, looking at the relatively small shifts in attitudes toward the poll tax still helps to fill in the broader picture. The absence of major attitudinal change on the poll tax is not consistent with the racial liberalization argument, at least in its stronger forms, particularly in combination with the findings on antilynching attitudes. The possible slight growth in anti–poll-tax attitudes is, however, suggestive of the greater receptiveness of white Americans to rights claims that could be framed in nonracial terms (i.e., benefiting poorer whites, not just African Americans).

WARTIME CIVIL RIGHTS ISSUES

Compared to the survey questions regarding antilynching legislation and the abolition of the poll tax, the available survey evidence makes an examination of the racial liberalization hypothesis with respect to the new wartime civil rights issues much more difficult. The issue of military segregation, however, is a partial exception. A question about whether the armed services should be integrated was asked once during the war

---

[76] Kimberley Johnson describes how, in an effort to preserve Jim Crow but also respond to wartime democratization pressures, many southern whites sought to redefine "the poll tax issue as an issue of *white* democracy." Kimberley Johnson, *Reforming Jim Crow: Southern Politics and State in the Age Before Brown*, (New York: Oxford University Press, 2010), 99.

[77] Steven F. Lawson, *Black Ballots: Voting Rights in the South, 1944–1969*, (New York: Columbia University Press, 1976), 55–85.

TABLE 2.2: *Military segregation, 1942–1948*

Question Wording	1942	1948
"Should negro and white soldiers serve together in all branches of the armed forces?"	38%	
"It has been suggested that white and colored men serve together throughout the U.S. Armed Services – that is, live and work in the same units. Do you think this is a **good idea** or a poor idea?"		25%
"Would you **favor** or oppose having Negro and white troops throughout the U.S. Armed Services live and work together – or should they be separated as they are now?"		23%

Note: Percentages refer to the percent of whites answering "yes" or the percent of whites answering with the option in bold.

and once in the war's aftermath. Of course, this is not ideal from a methodological perspective. As with the racial prejudice questions, it would be better to have more than two data points, and, as with the lynching questions, the question wording is not entirely consistent. With these limitations taken into careful consideration, however, a comparison of these two survey questions still provides the best possible empirical basis for understanding how white Americans felt about military integration in the World War II era.

Table 2.2 presents the weighted percentages for each survey question. In June 1942, Gallup asked whether "negro and white soldiers" should "serve together in all branches of the armed forces."[78] In this survey, 54 percent of whites opposed military integration, with 38 percent supporting it and 8 percent offering no opinion.[79] In the South, 72 percent of whites opposed military integration, with 22 percent offering support and 7 percent expressing no opinion. Outside of the southern states, 50 percent of whites opposed military integration, with 42 percent supporting it and 8 percent offering no opinion.

Moving ahead to May 1948, Gallup asked about military integration again.[80] This time, they asked the question in two ways. When asked

---

[78] This dataset ("USAIPO1942-0270: Gallup Poll #270") was obtained from the iPoll Databank, http://ropercenter.cornell.edu/ipoll-database/.

[79] Unfortunately for weighting purposes, education was not asked in this survey, so I use a "profWhites" weight for the 1942 survey.

[80] This dataset ("USAIPO1948-0419: Gallup Poll #419") was obtained from the iPoll Databank, http://ropercenter.cornell.edu/ipoll-database/. This time, educational information was collected in the study, so I use an "eduWhites" weight.

whether it was a good or poor idea "that white and colored men serve together throughout the U.S. armed services – that is, live and work in the same units," 64 percent of whites said it was a poor idea, 5 percent said it was a fair idea, 25 percent said it was a good idea, and 6 percent offered no opinion.[81] In the South, 89 percent of whites said it was a poor idea, compared to 57 percent of nonsouthern whites.

When asked whether they would "favor or oppose having negro and white troops throughout the U.S. armed services live and work together – or should they be separated as they are now," 68 percent of whites said black and white troops should remain separated, 23 percent said they should be together, and 10 percent offered no opinion.[82] In the South, 91 percent of whites said that troops should remain separated, while 61 percent of nonsouthern whites agreed.[83]

The interpretation of these numbers is somewhat complicated. On the one hand, a simple comparison of the numbers is not consistent with the racial liberalization hypothesis. While 38 percent of whites offered support for integrating the armed forces in 1942, only 23 to 25 percent did so in 1948, depending on the question wording.[84] Similar to the pattern with attitudes towards federal antilynching legislation, it is possible that there was actually a growth in the racially conservative position. While 54 percent of whites said they opposed military integration in 1942, that number climbed to between 64 and 68 percent in 1948, depending on the question wording.

The extent to which the question wordings preclude a proper assessment of change over time is worthy of consideration, however. One important difference between the 1942 and 1948 question wordings is

---

[81] A small number of others volunteered responses, which were coded into categories "poor for negroes – no chance for advancement," "good if negro same as white, they can work together," "depends on individual," "not for southern troops," "fair, if handled rights," "theoretically, yes, practically no," and "miscellaneous." Leaving these in the dataset would not change the estimates, other than the no opinion category rounding down to 5 percent.

[82] Once again, a small number of others volunteered responses, which were coded into categories like "separated if they are treated the same," "leave it up to the soldiers," "work together but live separately," "this should be a very slow gradual mixing," "depends on class of people," "together if they can get along," and "miscellaneous." If these responses were kept in the dataset, the estimates would be 66 percent in favor of separation, 22 percent supportive of black and white troops living and working together, and 9 percent offering no opinion.

[83] In the most rural parts of the southern states, white opposition was nearly universal, with 98 percent of whites opposing integration.

[84] If the good idea and fair idea responses are added together, the 25 percent number in 1948 grows slightly to 30 percent.

that the former do not specify the prospect of black and white soldiers sharing housing. This additional detail might be sufficient to explain the lower levels of expressed support for integration in the 1948 survey.[85] Despite this very real limitation, however, the evidence at least suggests that white Americans were broadly opposed to military integration both before the war and in its aftermath. Even if change over time is difficult to isolate, the numbers still serve as an important empirical baseline.[86]

Other parts of the wartime civil rights agenda were not asked about at all before the war's formal conclusion. This reflects a broader problem with public opinion polls. Survey researchers only asked about questions after they became a part of elite discourse, which limits the possibility of analyzing change over time in many cases.[87] Fortunately, survey organizations did ask some questions about other wartime racial issues from time to time. While these questions cannot be used as data sources to assess the racial liberalization hypothesis – due to the fact that they were not asked at multiple points in time – they are nonetheless of interest in providing a more well-rounded portrait of the nature of white racial attitudes in the era. I focus here on two such policy issues: debates about a permanent FEPC in the war's aftermath and whether southern black soldiers should be given ballots during their overseas service.

Pollsters never asked about Roosevelt's executive order combatting discrimination in the defense industry specifically. In the war's aftermath, however, they did ask about fair employment legislation more generally, both at the state and national levels, as civil rights advocates pushed for a permanent, national FEPC. For example, a 1945 Gallup survey asked whether there should be a state law prohibiting discrimination

---

[85] It is also possible that in 1942, respondents perceived military integration as something that would happen overseas, whereas in 1948 they interpreted it as something that would happen on domestic bases.

[86] For an examination of variation in white attitudes on these issues with respect to partisanship and ideology, see Schickler, *Racial Realignment*, 112.

[87] Taeku Lee, *Mobilizing Public Opinion: Black Insurgency and Racial Attitudes in the Civil Rights Era*, (Chicago: University of Chicago Press, 2002). The sociologist and survey researcher Paul Lazarsfeld made a similar point in a 1950 essay where he described "the choice of specific topics in even the simplest opinion poll." "Even if we do not work for a specific client, do we not have a tendency to ask questions which will make interesting reading in tomorrow's newspapers?," he wrote. "Don't we overlook the fact that, in a way, the pollster writes contemporary history? Might not the 1984 historian reproach us for not having given enough thought to what he will want to know about 1950?" Paul F. Lazarsfeld, "The Obligations of the 1950 Pollster to the 1984 Historian," *Public Opinion Quarterly* 14(4), 1950–51, 617–618.

in employment.[88] One version of the question asked whether the state should have a law that would "require employers to hire a person if he is qualified for the job, regardless of his race or color." When phrased in a way that focused the law's impact on employers, 41 percent of whites favored the law, 47 percent opposed it, and 12 percent offered no opinion. Outside of the southern states, 47 percent of whites supported such a law, with 39 percent opposing it and 14 percent expressing no opinion. In the South, by contrast, 77 percent of whites opposed it, with just 16 percent supporting it and 7 percent offering no opinion.

The second version of the question asked whether the state should pass a law "which would require employees to work alongside persons of any race or color." The question wording difference seems to have had a notable effect on white responses. When phrased in a way that emphasized the law's impact on employees, only 31 percent of whites favored the law, while 61 percent opposed it and 8 percent offered no opinion. When faced with this question wording, nonsouthern white opinion shifted in the conservative direction, with 56 percent of nonsouthern whites opposing this law, 36 percent supporting it, and 8 percent offering no opinion.[89] In the South, 81 percent of whites expressed opposition to this version of the question, with 12 percent supporting it and 7 percent offering no opinion.

Along with providing evidence that most white Americans did not support laws designed to address racial discrimination in employment, these numbers are also interesting because they suggest that it was not merely federal intervention that was opposed by whites offering racially conservative survey responses. While the lynching questions from earlier in the chapter blend racial attitudes and attitudes toward federalism, these questions are explicitly about state laws rather than national laws. As such, any response is a more direct measurement of an individual's racial policy attitudes, not their attitudes toward federal intervention.[90]

---

[88] This dataset ("USAIPO1945-0349: Gallup Poll #349") was obtained from the iPoll Databank, http://ropercenter.cornell.edu/ipoll-database/. The numbers presented are based on the inclusion of an "eduWhites" weight.

[89] Even in the most urban parts of the Northeast, 49 percent opposed the law when the question was worded this way.

[90] For a more focused analysis on public opinion and the postwar effort to enact permanent FEPC legislation at the state level, see Anthony S. Chen, *The Fifth Freedom: Jobs, Politics, and Civil Rights in the United States, 1941–1972*, (Princeton: Princeton University Press, 2009).

Finally, pollsters asked one question about the wartime soldier voting legislation that was directly focused on black soldiers. From December 31, 1943, to January 4, 1944, NORC conducted "Survey #1944-0222: Soldier's Vote," a "spot-check" survey.[91] As the notes provided by the Roper Center describe it, "The cross-section of this spot-check survey consisted of a typical miniature of the population, with the proper proportion in each geographic section, of rich and poor, young and old, men and women, Democrats, Republicans, and non-voters."[92] Face-to-face interviews were conducted with 485 national adults, which is small but usable for certain types of analyses.[93] Along with a short series of other questions about soldiers and voting, the issue of black soldiers being given ballots is specifically addressed. Respondents were asked, "Do you think Negroes over 21 in the armed forces should be allowed to vote or not?" Whether soldiers – including black soldiers – should be given ballots during the tenure of their overseas service clearly drew together many of the key themes of this book. The congressional debate over soldier voting was controversial on numerous fronts, and it became a legislative instance where "a peculiar combination or cumulation of circumstances," as Key described it, led southern Democrats and Republicans to vote together against northern Democrats. "The Republicans did not want the soldiers to vote Democratic," Key writes. "The southern Democrats did not want colored soldiers to vote."[94] What, though, did white Americans in the mass public think of the issue?

White Americans as a whole supported giving black soldiers ballots by an 82 percent to 13 percent margin, with 5 percent saying they did not know. Overall, there was substantial support for allowing black soldiers to vote, with opposition coming almost entirely from southern whites. Outside the South, an overwhelming 92 percent of whites offered support for giving ballots to black soldiers, with only 5 percent opposed and 3 percent saying they did not know. In the South, however, only 48 percent

---

[91] This dataset ("USNORC1944-0222: Soldier's Vote") was obtained from the iPoll Databank, http://ropercenter.cornell.edu/ipoll-database/.

[92] National Opinion Research Center, *Should Soldiers Vote! A Special Report Based on a Spot-Check Survey*, (Denver, 1944).

[93] Unfortunately the dataset has other problems as well: the coding of the census regions variable is missing one of the nine categories, which obviously presents certainly difficulties with subnational analysis. As such, I create a variant on the eduWhites weight that treats region as a South/non-South distinction.

[94] Key, *Southern Politics in State and Nation*, 358–59.

of whites did so, while 41 percent opposed such a measure and 11 percent said they did not know. Despite this clear regional variation, however, a slight plurality of southern whites still offered support for the measure, which might seem surprising.

This quantitative analysis can be complemented by archival materials NORC left behind. Although transcriptions of comments by all respondents do not appear to be available, NORC did release 13 responses, divided between northerners and southerners, in their report on the results. I reproduce those here, with the statements in quotation marks and the descriptions of the anonymous respondents unchanged from how NORC referred to them.

Some did point to the wartime context. "Some people are prejudiced," a packing house clerk in Chicago said, "but if a man is good enough to fight for his country, he should be allowed to vote." Others, however, focused on intelligence and education as qualifications for voting. "They shouldn't be deprived of voting just because of their color," said a California fire chief. "It all depends upon their intelligence. That goes for white people, too. But there are more illiterate Negroes than whites." A Chicago machine operator distinguished between regions in this regard. "I don't know," he said. "The northern Negroes that go to our schools got sense enough to vote. Those from the South are such an ignorant class they don't really know for what they are voting." Some responses were pithier. "Yes," a female personnel worker in New York City said. "The 14th Amendment says 'No discrimination.'" "They pay taxes," said a clerk's wife in Pennsylvania. "[I]f they are allowed to vote in their own state," said a contractor's wife in Illinois. Not all the short responses were positive, however. "No," said a ship worker's wife in Pennsylvania. "I don't like them."[95]

Southern responses reflect the greater opposition in the region overall. The only clear positive response reflected that of the Chicago packing house clerk. "If they are good enough to fight they are good enough to vote," said a sales engineer's wife in Louisiana. But this response is clearly the odd one out. A retired army officer in Houston said, "Only if they are allowed to vote at home" – which, in the South, they were generally not. Others gave a range of reasons for their opposition to giving black soldiers ballots. "The Negro in my opinion is not intelligent enough to vote," said a chain store manager in Tennessee. "[T]hey

---

[95] National Opinion Research Center, *Should Soldiers Vote! A Special Report Based on a Spot-Check Survey.*

are too easily influenced," argued a farmer's wife in Mississippi. Others offered "just so" responses. "No – not down South," said a female drug store clerk in Alabama. A cabinet maker in Louisiana offered the most emphatic response. "No! Absolutely not!!," he said, apparently with sufficient feeling that the interviewer felt it necessary to include an additional exclamation mark when transcribing his remarks.[96]

What to make of the perhaps surprisingly positive white attitudes depends on one's perspective on the soldier voting legislation itself. Alexander Keyssar's history of voting rights in America considers the soldier voting legislation to be "an important step" in the advancement of civil rights.[97] In conjunction with other factors, this leads Keyssar to argue that the "equilibrium in voting laws was decisively disrupted by World War II."[98] David Mayhew approvingly cites this account in his argument about the centrality of wars to American politics.[99] From this perspective, white support might seem perplexing. Katznelson, by contrast, argues congressional acquiescence to southern preferences in the details of the legislation exposed "tensions between symbolic and sincere behavior with regard to civil rights." Further, and "[c]ontrary to Keyssar's canonical assessment," he argues the most notable aspects of the legislation were decisions not to standardize the ballot and not to give the federal government significant power to deal with uncooperative southern states.[100] This perspective on soldier voting is much easier to reconcile with the lack of staunch opposition by whites in the broader public.[101]

---

[96] Ibid.
[97] Alexander Keyssar, *The Right to Vote: The Contested History of Democracy in the United States*, (New York: Basic Books, 2000), 247.
[98] Ibid., 244
[99] David R. Mayhew, "Wars and American Politics," *Perspectives on Politics* 3, 2005, 479.
[100] Ira Katznelson, *Fear Itself: The New Deal and the Origins of Our Time*, (New York: Liveright Publishing Corporation, 2013), 202. For a more general – and more positive – assessment of local administrative control of elections in US history and how this relates to the *practice* of voting rights, see Alec C. Ewald, *The Way We Vote: The Local Dimension of American Suffrage*, (Nashville: Vanderbilt University Press, 2009). For a discussion of the soldier voting legislation specifically, and the Jim Crow era more generally, see ibid., 78; 123–124.
[101] Whatever one's prior analytical perspective, care should be taken in interpreting the survey results. The fact that this is the only survey evidence allowing researchers to assess public attitudes on the soldier voting issue makes it integral to any contemporary academic assessments. While one survey, particularly one with a small sample, naturally carries risks of error and uncertainty, arguments about the nature of a broader public response would benefit from engagement with this survey evidence, limited though it might be. The support is in some ways an interesting preview of southern white attitudes

Although voting rights would not be protected at the federal level until 1965, such debates offer an intriguing look at the connection between voting and citizenship claims in an earlier era. While the influence of black voters was substantially limited in the pre-Voting Rights Act period, the value of political rights extend beyond these more easily measurable characteristics. The ballot, Judith Shklar writes, "has always been a certificate of full membership in society, and its value depends primarily on its capacity to confer a minimum of social dignity." Rather than a "means to other ends," suffrage is "the characteristic, the identifying, feature of democratic citizenship."[102] While pollsters did not ask questions about black voting rights in general in the World War II era, the next chapter does examine the extent to which white southern veterans were more supportive of black voting rights by the early 1960s.

CONCLUSION

This chapter demonstrates that, for the most part, white attitudes were not broadly liberalized on race and civil rights as a result of World War II. There is some evidence of a decrease in certain (although not all) measures of white racial prejudice, and it is possible that there was a slight liberalization in support for abolishing the poll tax (although the extent to which this was perceived as a racial issue by respondents remains ambiguous). This is counterbalanced, however, by evidence that white opposition to federal antilynching legislation actually seems to have increased by the war's aftermath. While data limitations preclude a clear statement about temporal trends in opposition to military integration, it is very clear that whites were widely opposed to this policy. Although the shifts in prejudice are suggestive and important, this chapter raises doubts about scholarship that has simply assumed the war had a liberalizing impact on white racial attitudes without analyzing the relevant data. This perspective – especially in its more declarative forms, and especially when the focus is on policy issues that were explicitly racial – is not supported by the available survey evidence.

Scholars should generally take care when making claims about wartime attitudinal change without reference to the survey evidence

---

toward voting rights in the early 1960s, which were actually much more supportive than many might assume. See Chapter 3.

[102] Judith N. Shklar, *American Citizenship: The Quest for Inclusion*, (Cambridge: Harvard University Press, 1991), 2, 56.

presented here. Popular interpretations of Myrdal that emphasize the necessity of racial attitude change during the war seem inconsistent with the evidence in this chapter. Myrdal's book is better seen as a primary source representing the contemporaneous expectations of a particular strand of white racial liberalism than as an empirical treatment of white attitudes. Similarly, claims based on secondary references to survey results reported in newspaper and historical accounts could be better substantiated with reference to the more extensive and methodologically attentive analysis of the available survey evidence presented in this chapter.

This analysis of white racial attitudes also has implications for understanding the response of national political actors to civil rights advocates. Popular support for antilynching legislation did not increase during the war, nor was the white public in favor of new wartime civil rights policy goals like the integration of the armed forces. Combined with the growth in executive discretion that tends to happen during times of war, this produced a particularly compelling environment for advocates to appeal to the president for unilateral executive action, a topic that I examine in Chapters 4 and 5.

Before turning to the executive branch, however, there is at least one other way to examine the racial liberalization hypothesis. To complement the aggregate figures and temporal trends described in this chapter, Chapter 3 considers potential differences in the racial attitudes of otherwise similar white veterans and nonveterans. To what extent did white veterans return home with more liberal views on race and civil rights politics than their nonveteran counterparts? The next chapter gathers the available survey evidence to offer the best possible assessment of this question.

3

White Veterans and Racial Attitudes, 1946–1961

Van T. Barfoot, a white lieutenant from Carthage, Mississippi, received the Medal of Honor for his service in Italy during World War II. When Mississippi senators James Eastland and Theodore Bilbo – two of the most infamous white supremacists in national politics of the era – posed for a photo session with the returning veteran, Bilbo asked him whether he had "much trouble with nigras over there." Barfoot, however, did not go along with him. "I found out after I did some fighting in this war that the colored boys fight just as good as the white boys," he told Bilbo. "I've changed my ideas a lot about colored people since I got into this war and so have a lot of other boys from the South."[1]

Barfoot's story wasn't the only anecdote of white veterans whose racial views had been profoundly affected by the war. Amid the racial violence that broke out in Detroit in June 1943, three white sailors happened upon a white mob "beating unmercifully a slender Negro youth." When one of the mob asked why they were getting involved, one of the sailors pointed to his service in World War II. "There was a colored guy in our outfit in the Pacific and he saved the lives of two of my buddies," he said. "Besides, you guys are stirring up here at home something we are fighting to stop!"[2] This suggestive anecdote is drawn from NAACP leader Walter White's 1945 book, *A Rising Wind*. Although perhaps apocryphal – White had a tendency to capture dialogue in a manner

---

[1] James C. Cobb, "World War II and the Mind of the Modern South," in *Remaking Dixie: The Impact of World War II on the American South*, ed. Neil R. McMillen, (Jackson: University Press of Mississippi, 1997), 6.

[2] Walter White, *A Rising Wind*, (Garden City, NY: Doubleday, Doran and Company, Inc., 1945), 124–125.

that seems awkwardly folksy to contemporary ears – such tales nevertheless reached a wide audience and were consistent with other accounts at the time suggesting the war had liberalized the previously racist views of white soldiers fighting for democracy.

When White went to visit European theaters of combat during the war, he met several other white soldiers whose racial views left him optimistic. One white soldier recounted his experiences at the Stage Door Canteen in New York City prior to being sent overseas. The first time the soldier went there, he found black hosts and servicemen and he left in anger. But because the canteen was the standard gathering place for soldiers unfamiliar with the city, he went back several times and had a change of heart. "If we can play together, why can't we fight together?" he asked White. When informed of proposals to establish an integrated unit that white and black soldiers could volunteer to join, he replied, "I'd like to be the first to volunteer. Then I wouldn't feel like a Goddamned hypocrite when people over here ask why, in fighting a war for democracy, the United States sends over one white and one Negro army."[3]

But it wasn't just Walter White who shared such anecdotes. More academic work also connected military service to potential changes in racial attitudes. In 1943's *To Stem This Tide: A Survey of Racial Tension Areas in the United States*, Charles Johnson and his associates shared an anecdote from Evansville, Indiana, where a train conductor ordered a group of white and black soldiers from the same town to separate, but a white soldier refused the order and threatened to "fight the entire train crew."[4] In the war's aftermath, University of North Carolina sociologist Howard Odum, writing in 1948, described "a relatively large number of young college students and returning G.I.'s advocating a more liberal practice with reference to race relations" in the white South.[5]

Was this reflective of a general trend? Scholarship on the attitudinal and behavioral impacts of the war on veterans has focused almost entirely on black veterans.[6] Work on white veterans has been more local and specific. Jason Sokol's history of white southern reactions to civil

---

[3] Ibid., 36–37.

[4] Charles S. Johnson and Associates, *To Stem This Tide: A Survey of Racial Tension Areas in the United States*, (New York: AMS Press, 1943), 38.

[5] Howard W. Odum, "Social Change in the South," *Journal of Politics* 10(2), 1948, 244.

[6] Christopher S. Parker, *Fighting for Democracy: Black Veterans and the Struggle Against White Supremacy in the Postwar South*, (Princeton: Princeton University Press, 2009). For an earlier, more qualitative analysis of how southern black veterans thought about

rights quotes individual white southern men who, as a result of their service in World War II, came to learn "that freedom means more than just freedom for the white man," as one phrased it. Sokol suggests, however, that such attitude changes were small, constituting "only a small fraction of white southern servicemen."[7] Although Sokol's analysis is enlightening in many respects, it is not intended to be generalizable by the standards of political scientists.

Perhaps the best research on white veterans is Jennifer Brooks's analysis of veterans in postwar Georgia. While many southern black men returned from World War II determined to tear down white supremacy, Brooks suggests that the impact of military service on returning white veterans was more heterogeneous. "A small but vocal minority of southern white veterans also defined the war's meaning and their own participation in it as a mandate to implement a political freedom that applied to all Georgians," she writes. These white veterans joined returning black soldiers in their efforts. This push for racial equality, however, "provoked an immediate backlash from other white veterans determined to sustain all the power and prerogatives of white supremacy."[8]

The military was certainly not interested in being used as a sociological laboratory during the war, a point General Dwight Eisenhower made rather bluntly when Walter White talked to him about the issue. Referring to a discussion with an unnamed New York journalist, Eisenhower "almost belligerently" exclaimed to White, "He told me my first duty was to change the social thinking of the soldiers under my command, especially on racial issues. I told him he was a damned fool – that my first duty is to win wars and that any changes in social thinking would be purely incidental. Don't you think I was right?"[9] Such conversations suggest that the link between white military service and civil rights liberalism might not necessarily be so clear.

---

their service, see Neil R. McMillen, "Fighting for What We Didn't Have: How Mississippi's Black Veterans Remember World War II," in *Remaking Dixie: The Impact of World War II on the American South*, ed. Neil R. McMillen, (Jackson: University Press of Mississippi, 1997), 93–110.

[7] Jason Sokol, *There Goes My Everything: White Southerners in the Age of Civil Rights*, (New York: Alfred A. Knopf, 2006), 19, 20, 25.

[8] Jennifer E. Brooks, *Defining the Peace: World War II Veterans, Race, and the Remaking of Southern Political Tradition*, (Chapel Hill: The University of North Carolina Press, 2004), 36. Brooks's analysis covers both enlisted soldiers and officers, as well as those who served in roles like chaplains.

[9] White, *A Rising Wind*, 63.

I begin this chapter with a discussion of how military service might shape attitudes in general and racial attitudes in particular. I then offer a variation of the racial liberalization hypothesis, but this time applied specifically to differences between veterans and nonveterans. I also discuss the available datasets and the opportunities and limitations related to identifying veteran status. The remainder of the chapter then assesses this hypothesis with respect to issues of racial prejudice and policy attitudes, both in the immediate postwar years and in the early 1960s.

I demonstrate that white veterans were generally not less racially prejudiced in the war's immediate aftermath and they were likewise not more willing to support an integrated military. They were, however, more likely to support federal antilynching legislation. Moving ahead to the early 1960s, I demonstrate that white veterans in the South were again not distinguishable on attitudes toward segregation and the sit-in movement. They were, however, more supportive of black voting rights than nonveterans. After presenting these results, I also discuss research conducted within the military at this time, which offers suggestive evidence that service in an integrated World War II–era military might have had more transformative consequences for white racial attitudes than service in the segregated one that actually fought the war.

MILITARY SERVICE AND RACIAL ATTITUDES

Why might military service be expected to have an effect on racial attitudes? Beyond the general linkage between war and rights claims described in Chapter 1, there are also more basic psychological reasons for why wartime is likely to be a transformative experience for soldiers. Most soldiers serve during the "impressionable years" of their late teens and early twenties, when attitudes of all sorts are most likely to crystallize.[10] In this favorable environment for attitudinal change, exposure to any racially liberal cues might be more likely to be effective.

---

[10] Parker, *Fighting for Democracy*, 72–73. See also Howard Schuman and Jacqueline Scott, "Generations and Collective Memories," *American Sociological Review* 54(3), 1989, 359–381. For a more general discussion of the impressionable years hypothesis, see Duane F. Alwin, Ronald L. Cohen, and Theodore M. Newcomb, *Political Attitudes over the Life Span: The Bennington Women After Fifty Years*, (Madison: University of Wisconsin Press, 1991); Duane F. Alwin and Jon A. Krosnick, "Aging, Cohorts, and the Stability of Sociopolitical Orientations over the Life Span," *American Journal of Sociology* 97(1), 1991, 169–195.

Perhaps the most compelling argument for the military's effects on racial attitudes, at least today, is the contact hypothesis: Coming into contact with people from different racial backgrounds might make soldiers more racially tolerant as a result. The institutional features of the military, according to some accounts, make it an especially likely place for the contact hypothesis to find support. John Sibley Butler and Kenneth Wilson note several such features in their study of racial attitudes in the military in the early 1970s. The military's rigid rank structure, for example, means that black and white soldiers of the same rank "possess the same authority, prestige and pay." The "authority structure of the military has set a norm that legitimates favorable racial contact," they further note. "It goes without saying that the rewards of military personnel are highly associated with adhering to the norms of that institution."[11] These are compelling mechanisms in theory. In practice, however, World War II was the last major US war fought with a segregated military, which means that these mechanisms were not present for white soldiers during that War.

What other factors, then, might have played a role? Researchers have emphasized the importance of military service for black men. Christopher Parker, for example, analyzes the "radicalizing experience" of military service for southern black men in particular.[12] He presents a theoretical framework to explain black veterans' attitudes and behavior. Building on the citizen-soldier tradition in republican political thought, Parker examines how black veterans interpreted the meaning of their military experience, then argues that this led to a new belief system he calls "black republicanism."[13]

In many ways, this framework is specific to the experience of black soldiers. For instance, Parker highlights the tension between how black soldiers were treated and the ideals for which they were fighting. White soldiers were simply not treated with the same sort of second-class status. His discussion of the effects of being deployed overseas, however, raises interesting questions about effects on white soldiers. Parker, though, clearly distinguishes between white and black soldiers in this

---

[11] John Sibley Butler and Kenneth L. Wilson, "*The American Soldier* Revisited: Race Relations and the Military," *Social Science Quarterly* 59(3), 1978, 465–466.

[12] Parker, *Fighting for Democracy*, 61. He relates this directly to Foner's discussion of black military service in the Civil War and its effects on political behavior during Reconstruction. See Eric Foner, *Reconstruction: America's Unfinished Revolution*, (New York: Harper and Row, 1988).

[13] Parker, *Fighting Democracy*, 60–87.

discussion. "For white servicemen, travel overseas resulted in increased self-awareness," he writes. "For black servicemen, especially from the South, experiencing life overseas went beyond self-awareness. Deployment during the World War II and the Korean War exposed well over a million black Southerners – who were accustomed to discrimination and oppressive conditions – to a model of race relations in which the indigenous, dominant group often treated them with a measure of respect." This, he argues, gave them additional motivation "to question the legitimacy of white supremacy."[14]

Although they were differentially situated, white soldiers were nonetheless similarly exposed to such variation in race relations. As Parker notes in a general sense, "exposing people to new patterns of social relations and cultural norms tends to expand their worldview by enlarging their perceptions of what is possible." This logic, he argues, leads to an expectation that "black Southerners who were exposed to different, more egalitarian cultures" would "have begun an aggressive interrogation of white supremacy."[15] The extent to which such exposure might also shift white attitudes, however, merits some examination as well.

White soldiers experienced the war differently than did whites on the home front. Like black soldiers, white soldiers were also exposed to "more progressive cultures elsewhere," where "dominant groups often treated [black soldiers] with a measure of respect." We should not expect "an aggressive interrogation of white supremacy," as Parker's framework predicts for black veterans. Insomuch as the experience could have "enlarg[ed] their perceptions of what is possible," however, it might have at least led to new questions. It seems plausible, then, that exposure to new possibilities could have led at least some white veterans to be more open to racial liberalism. If any whites were to be liberalized as a result of the war, veterans would seem to be plausible candidates. While all whites were in some sense "treated" by the war, those who served in the military were certainly affected more directly.

THE RACIAL LIBERALIZATION HYPOTHESIS FOR VETERANS

To assess the potential effects of their military service, this chapter examines a variation on the racial liberalization hypothesis focused on

---

[14] Ibid., 72.
[15] Ibid., 95.

distinctions between white veterans of the war and those who did not serve:

Racial Liberalization Hypothesis for Veterans: World War II liberalized the racial attitudes of white veterans, relative to their nonveteran counterparts.

The racial liberalization hypothesis for veterans shifts the focus from temporal trends in the aggregate white public to differences between otherwise similar veterans and nonveterans. There are several reasons we might expect to find evidence in support of this hypothesis. First, while white Americans in general might be expected to have been influenced by the anti-Nazi cause, whites who served in the military were actually fighting it directly. Second, soldiers were exposed to relatively more egalitarian cultures in places like France, where American racial norms were not fully replicated by locals. This relative egalitarianism should not be overstated – obviously France has a history of colonialism and lingering problems with racism – but insomuch as Parker emphasizes this as a key mechanism emboldening returning black veterans to fight Jim Crow in America, examining the extent to which it might have had effects for white veterans is at least worth exploring.

There is, however, theoretical grounding for a null result. The most common mechanism for a linkage between military service and racial liberalism is the contact hypothesis, and the conditions for that were not present during World War II. It is also not clear that ordinary soldiers understood their role in the war in such ideological ways. Many white soldiers were likely fighting to defend their way of life – white supremacy and all – rather than for something more transformative. Many white veterans simply wanted to return home and resume life exactly as they had left it. "That often meant supporting Jim Crow as staunchly as ever," Sokol writes. "Many believed they had fought to defend, not overturn, racial customs."[16] Parker, similarly, notes that many white soldiers brought their racial views with them rather than being amenable to new social norms.[17] Indeed, many white soldiers from outside the South were exposed to southern Jim Crow for the first time in the military, as the military segregated soldiers by race.[18] The extent to which various contradictory outcomes are entirely plausible suggests the merits of

---

[16] Sokol, *There Goes My Everything*, 20, 23.
[17] Parker, *Fighting for Democracy*.
[18] While in theory this exposure to different regional norms could work in both directions, in practice it was overwhelming northerners coming to the southern states. Eight of the nine army training centers with capacities for 50,000 or more military personnel were located in the South. Morton Sosna, "Introduction," in *Remaking Dixie: The Impact of*

carefully assessing the evidence for this variant of the racial liberalization hypothesis.

To examine these competing possibilities, I analyze public opinion surveys from two distinct time periods: the mid-to-late 1940s, to assess the more immediate impact of the war; and the early 1960s, to assess the longer-term impact. The methodological challenge here is finding surveys that ask about race or civil rights and also identify veteran status. I utilize three surveys from the 1946–1948 period that meet these criteria, as well as an additional survey from 1961. These surveys provide unique opportunities to compare veterans and nonveterans in this time period, but they do have certain limitations. The measures of veteran status are generally dichotomous – respondents are simply identified as having served in the military or not – which precludes any possible analysis distinguishing between different lengths and locations of service, as well as potential differences between enlisted men and officers. Another concern is subgroup sample size, something that is less of a problem in the relatively larger-N 1940s datasets, but more of a concern in the smaller 1961 study. While these drawbacks should be kept in mind – and I refer to them throughout when appropriate – these datasets can nonetheless offer a valuable perspective on white racial attitudes in the aftermath of World War II.

The first section uses surveys introduced in the previous chapter, but with a focus on the difference between veterans and nonveterans. I assess differences between veterans and nonveterans in the 1946 survey that asked four racial prejudice questions, the 1948 survey that asked two versions of a question about integrating the military, and a 1948 survey that asked a question about lynching.[19]

I then move ahead in time and use the Negro Political Participation Study, a survey of black and white southerners – defined as the former Confederate states – conducted in 1961 by principal investigators Donald Matthews and James Prothro at the University of North Carolina.[20]

World War II on the American South, ed. Neil McMillen, (Jackson: University Press of Mississippi, 1997).

[19] These datasets ("USNORC1946-0241: Minorities; United Nations"; "USAIPO1948-0419: Gallup Poll #419"; and "USAIPO1948-0413: Inflation/Business/Presidential Election") were all obtained from the iPoll Databank, http://ropercenter.cornell.edu/ipoll-database/.

[20] This dataset was obtained from the Inter-University Consortium for Political and Social Research (ICPSR) at the University of Michigan. ICPSR Website, www.icpsr.umich.edu/icpsrweb/ICPSR/. See also Donald R. Matthews and James

This survey uses the more modern ANES sample design. Thus, while it is limited by the lack of a nonsouthern comparison group, it does not face the limitations of the quota-controlled samples used in the previous surveys. This is the survey used by Parker, who focused on the black sample. I utilize the white sample to address the questions stated earlier. I discuss the question wordings in the relevant sections.

Methodologically, my goal here is to estimate the relationship between veteran status and racial attitudes, controlling for other factors.[21] I start with descriptive cross-tabulations of all white respondents, then break the numbers down by gender and veteran status. While this is a useful way to start, these numbers might obscure other demographic differences. World War II veterans, for instance, were obviously younger on average than nonveterans. To more rigorously assess the relationship between veteran status and racial attitudes, I then estimate regression models on the male subset of the white population that is of the age range that could have plausibly served in the war.[22] These models also control for region, educational attainment, and age.[23]

Because I am primarily interested in a comparison between veterans and nonveterans, this chapter does not include original analysis of data from *The American Soldier*, which emphasizes variation within the military rather than comparisons between soldiers and civilians. Beyond this substantive focus, I also want to highlight how other, underutilized surveys from this era might offer additional vantage points from which to assess questions about the war's consequences for white attitudes. I do

---

W. Prothro, *Negroes and the New Southern Politics*, (New York: Harcourt, Brace & World, Inc., 1966).

[21] This chapter examines relatively immediate effects of the war (with the exception of an examination of white veterans in 1961). Longer-term effects – and effects of the sort that cannot be identified with survey data – are still possible. Another open question is whether any observed effects were immediate but then decayed over time or whether effects were more permanent. Unfortunately, the questions I am able to analyze for the late 1940s were not asked in the 1960s. I argue, however, that looking at the available survey evidence is still a useful analytical perspective that can provide an important empirical baseline.

[22] For the models using the 1946 dataset, I analyzed only those individuals age 50 and below. For the 1948 datasets, I used age 52 as the cutoff. For the 1961 dataset, I looked only at those between 34 and 65 to best assess World War II veterans. In the regression models, no opinion responses are dropped. I graph the regression results, following advice from Jonathan P. Kastellec and Eduardo L. Leoni, "Using Graphs Instead of Tables in Political Science," *Perspectives on Politics* 5(4), 2007, 755–771.

[23] Concerns about possible posttreatment bias, particularly in the 1961 dataset, are addressed in the appendix.

TABLE 3.1: *Antiblack prejudice, 1946 (veterans vs. nonveterans)*

Question Wording	White Male Vets	White Male Nonvets
"Do you think Negroes should have **as good a chance** as white people to get any kind of job, or do you think white people should have the first chance at any kind of job?"	56%	45%
"In general, do you think Negroes **are as intelligent** as white people – that is, can they learn just as well if they are given the same education?"	58%	50%
"As far as you know, is Negro blood **the same** as white blood, or is it different in some way?"	51%	39%
"If you were sick in a hospital, would it be **all right with you** if you had a Negro nurse, or wouldn't you like it?"	46%	46%

Note: Percentages refer to the percent of whites answering with the option in bold.

return to this study toward the end of the chapter, however, as part of a larger discussion on whether an integrated military might have led to different attitudinal consequences during World War II.

VETERANS' RACIAL ATTITUDES IN THE IMMEDIATE POSTWAR ERA

The 1946 NORC survey introduced in the previous chapter contained several questions about racial prejudice. Fortunately for the purposes of this chapter, it also identified veteran status. I begin by presenting cross-tabulations to offer some sense of whether any potential differences exist between veterans and nonveterans. To better discern whether any seeming differences between veterans and nonveterans hold up once other demographic characteristics are accounted for, I follow this by discussing regression results.

Table 3.1 presents aggregate percentages, while Figures 3.1 and 3.2 present the regression results. I discuss each survey question in turn, starting with whether African Americans should have the same chance as whites at a job. Overall, 47 percent of whites said African Americans

Veterans' Racial Attitudes in the Immediate Postwar Era 77

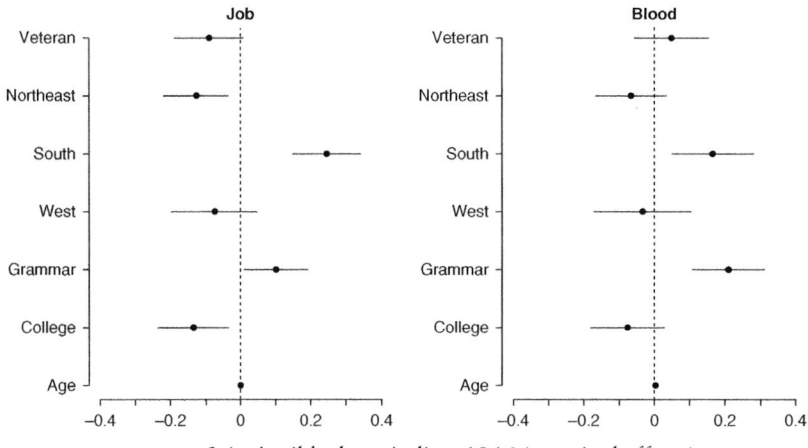

FIGURE 3.1: Antiblack prejudice, 1946 (marginal effects)

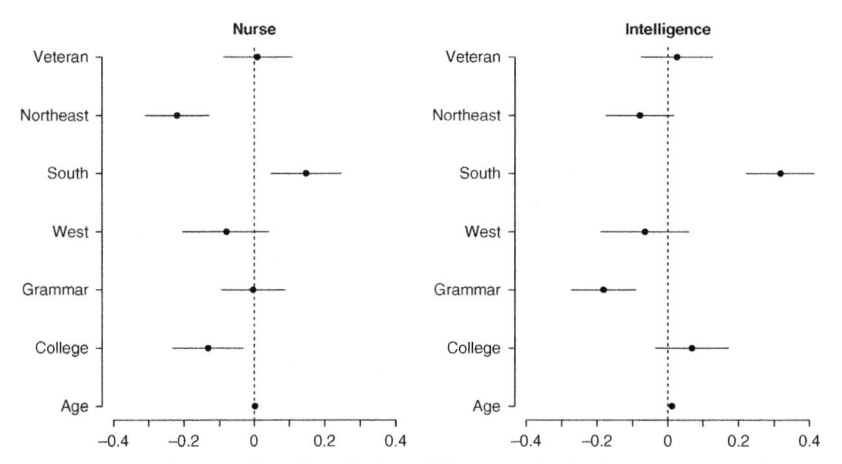

FIGURE 3.2: Antiblack prejudice, 1946 (marginal effects), continued

should have the same chance, with 50 percent disagreeing. There was no real difference with respect to gender. There does appear, at least at first glance, to be an interesting distinction between male veterans and nonveterans. Among veterans, 56 percent said African Americans should have the same chance as whites, while only 45 percent of nonveterans agreed with this sentiment. To what extent, though, is this difference simply a function of other characteristics, particularly age? Figure 3.1 presents the marginal effects calculated from a logistic regression where opinion among white men in the appropriate age range is modeled as a function of veteran status, region, educational attainment, and age.

The results indicate that veterans were 9 percentage points less likely to say that white people should get the first chance at a job, but this marginal effect is only significant at the .07 level.[24] This is suggestive of greater racial liberalism among white veterans, but the evidence is weaker in terms of statistical significance than one might like.

Another potential difference emerges in the question about blood. In this case, however, the regression results are clear that any estimated difference is not statistically significant. Overall, 40 percent of whites said black blood was biologically the same as white blood, with 33 percent saying it was different and 28 percent saying they do not know. There are again no major gender differences: Among white men, 41 percent said it was the same, compared to 38 percent of white women. Looking at veterans and nonveterans, however, does reveal a potential difference: While both groups were equally likely to say black blood was different (33 percent), there appears to be a discernible difference in the same and don't know responses. Among veterans, 51 percent said black blood was the same and only 17 percent said they did not know. In contrast, 39 percent of nonveterans said it was the same, with a much higher 28 percent stating that they did not know. While this is an intriguing distinction, it does not hold up in a multivariate regression framework (Figure 3.1).[25]

In other cases, there is clearly no difference between veterans and nonveterans. Consider the question about having a black nurse. Overall, 47 percent of whites said that they would be comfortable having a black nurse, compared to 51 percent who said that they would not be comfortable with this. Among white men, a similar proportion, 45 percent, said it would be acceptable, compared to 52 percent who said it would not be acceptable. The numbers for veterans and nonveterans are strikingly similar: 46 percent of both veterans and nonveterans said that it would be acceptable, while 53 percent of veterans and 52 percent of nonveterans said it would not be acceptable. Not surprisingly, the marginal effect calculated from the logistic regression affirms that there is no distinction between veterans and nonveterans on this question (Figure 3.2).[26]

---

[24] This might be reasonable since $N = 714$, but if the conventional 0.05 significance level is maintained, the effect does not meet the criteria for statistical significance.

[25] The estimated marginal effect of military service is a 5 percentage point increase in thinking that black blood is different, but the p-value is 0.37, far above conventional thresholds of statistical significance.

[26] The estimated marginal effect is a 1 percentage point increase in being uncomfortable having a black nurse, with a p-value of 0.85.

Veterans' Racial Attitudes in the Immediate Postwar Era 79

The question about black intelligence is not quite as clear cut, but overall the difference that emerges is hard to distinguish from sampling error. Overall, 55 percent of whites said black people were as innately intelligent as white people, compared to 38 percent saying they were not and 7 percent saying that they did not know. Among white men, 52 percent said they were as intelligent, with 42 percent saying they were not and 6 percent saying they did not know. In the cross-tabulation, there appears to be a difference between veterans and nonveterans. While 58 percent of veterans said black people are as intelligent, only 50 percent of nonveterans did so. The regression results demonstrate, however, that this difference disappears when age, region, and educational attainment are accounted for, suggesting the slight bivariate difference is not the outcome of military service in itself (Figure 3.2).[27]

Perhaps white veterans were more likely to express racially liberal attitudes on issues involving the military itself. One of the most prominent civil rights issues of the 1940s was the effort to integrate the armed forces, and the linkage between civil rights and military service might be especially clear for those with military experience. Here I examine two survey questions from 1948, which are the same question asked in slightly different ways. Some respondents were asked whether they would "favor or oppose having Negro and white troops throughout the U.S. Armed Services live and work together – or should they be separated as they are now?" Other respondents were told, "It has been suggested that white and colored men serve together throughout the U.S. Armed Services – that is, live and work in the same units." They were then asked whether they "think this is a good idea or a poor idea?"

The results are presented in Table 3.2 and Figure 3.3. Overall, 68 percent of whites said that white and black troops should remain separated, with 23 percent saying they should live and work together (another 10 percent that they did not know). There is a slight gender divide, with white men being somewhat more likely to support racial segregation than white women (70 percent vs. 66 percent). Among white men, however, there is no major difference in the percentage of veterans and nonveterans who take this position (71 percent and 69 percent, respectively). The results are similar for the other version of the question.[28] Like the

---

[27] The estimated marginal effect is a 3 percentage point increase in thinking that black people are not as intelligent, but the *p*-value is 0.62.
[28] 25 percent of whites overall supported integration when this question wording was used. This can be broken down into 22 percent support among white men and 28 percent

TABLE 3.2: *Military segregation, 1948 (veterans vs. nonveterans)*

Question Wording	White Male Vets	White Male Nonvets
"Would you **favor** or oppose having Negro and white troops throughout the U.S. Armed Services live and work together – or should they be separated as they are now?"	21%	21%
"It has been suggested that white and colored men serve together throughout the U.S. Armed Services – that is, live and work in the same units. Do you think this is a **good idea** or a poor idea?"	23%	21%

Note: Percentages refer to the percent of whites answering with the option in bold.

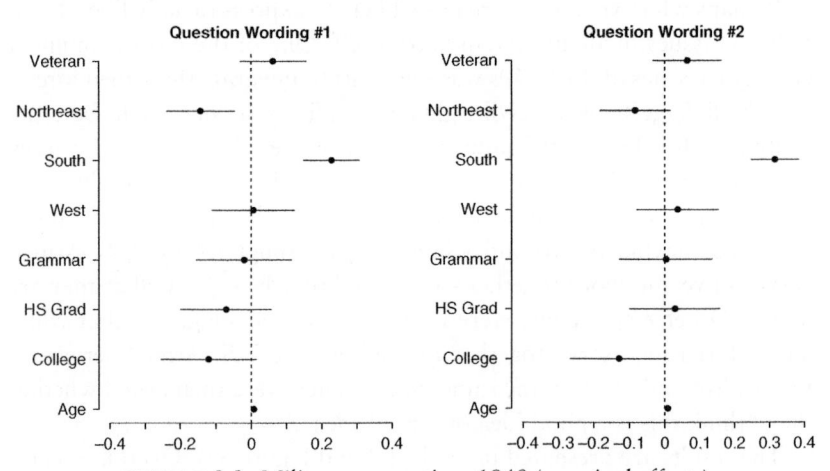

FIGURE 3.3: Military segregation, 1948 (marginal effects)

cross-tabulations, the regression results, presented in Figure 3.3, clearly show no relationship between veteran status and support for military integration.[29] Given the salience of the military integration policy debate in the postwar period – and the ideological tension between a war for democracy waged by a segregated military – this null result is quite striking.

support among white women. Among men, 23 percent of veterans and 21 percent of nonveterans offered support.

[29] The estimated marginal effect is a 6 percentage point increase in opposition to military integration, but significant at only the 0.20 level (the results for the second question wording are nearly identical).

TABLE 3.3: *Lynching, 1948 (veterans vs. nonveterans)*

Question Wording	White Male Vets	White Male Nonvets
"At present, state governments deal with most crimes committed in their own states. In the case of a lynching, do you think the **United States (Federal) Government should have the right to step in and deal with the crime** – or do you think this should be left entirely to the state government?"	53%	38%

Note: Percentages refer to the percent of whites answering with the option in bold.

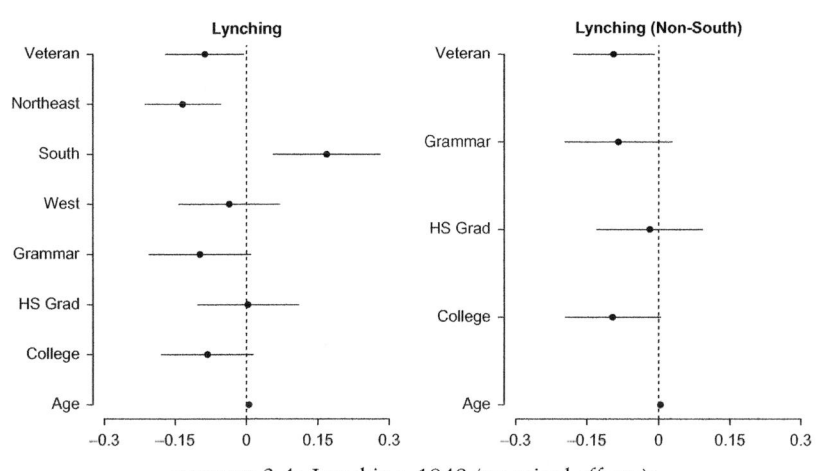

FIGURE 3.4: Lynching, 1948 (marginal effects)

If white veterans were not more likely to support integration of the armed forces, perhaps they were more willing to take a stand against racial violence. Here, I examine a February 1948 question asking respondents, "At present, state governments deal with most crimes committed in their own states. In the case of a lynching, do you think the United States (Federal) Government should have the right to step in and deal with the crime – or do you think this should be left entirely to the state government?"

The results are presented in Table 3.3 and Figure 3.4. Overall, 40 percent of whites supported federal antilynching legislation, while 42 percent opposed it and 18 percent said they did not know. Looking specifically at white men, 41 percent supported it, while 46 percent opposed it and 13 percent said they did not know (interestingly, white women were much more likely to say that they did not know, with 24 percent giving this response). Comparing white men who were veterans and those who were not reveals that 53 percent of veterans supported antilynching legislation, compared to only 38 percent of nonveterans – a 15 percentage point gap. To control for other factors that might account for this difference, Figure 3.4 presents the marginal effects calculated after a logistic regression that controls for age, region, and education. Controlling for these other factors, otherwise similar veterans were 9 percentage points less likely to take the states' rights stance than the federal intervention stance.

When I estimate separate models by region, however, this turns out to be an entirely nonsouthern effect. Among southern whites, there is no relationship between veteran status and attitudes towards antilynching legislation.[30] Among nonsouthern whites, by contrast, veterans were 9 percentage points less likely to take a states' rights stance than nonveterans (see Figure 3.4).[31] Overall, the case of lynching provides the strongest positive evidence supporting the hypothesis that white veterans were liberalized on race, although this liberalization was evident only outside the southern states.

THE CIVIL RIGHTS ERA: EARLY 1960S

While the immediate consequences of military service on racial attitudes are interesting, the potential relationship between military service and racial attitudes later in life also merits examination, especially in the era when civil rights politics were more nationally prominent. This analysis also allows me to relate this project more directly to Parker's work on the attitudinal and behavioral impact of black veterans' military service. Relying on the southern white sample of the 1961 Negro Political Participation Survey, I examine the following questions: whether the respondent favors "integration, strict segregation, or something in between"; their agreement with the statement, "[c]olored people ought to be allowed to vote"; their assessment of the sit-in movement ("that is, some of the

---

[30] The estimated marginal effect is a 2 percentage point increase in opposition, but significant at only the 0.88 level.
[31] If the estimates are not rounded, the marginal effect for nonsouthern veterans is a 9.4 percentage point decrease, compared to an 8.8 percentage point decrease among veterans overall.

young colored people going into stores, and sitting down at lunch counters, and refusing to leave until they are served"); and their agreement with the statement, "Demonstrations to protest integration of schools are a good idea, even if a few people have to get hurt." I also examine a question asking whether they have "ever known a colored person well enough that you would talk to him as a friend" in the following section.

This study actually identified veteran status in a slightly more fine-grained way, distinguishing between veterans who served abroad and those who never left the United States during their service. Unfortunately, the potential analytical value to be gained from this distinction is negated by the small sample size. While surveys from the quota sampling era tended to have unusually large sample sizes (often between two and three thousand per survey), the Negro Political Participation Study interviewed just 694 white adult respondents, along with 610 black adult respondents. Within the sample of 694 white adults, the dataset contains 108 white male veterans in the appropriate age range, with another 92 while male respondents in the same age range available as a comparison group for the regression models. Of these 108 veterans, 81 served outside the United States, 15 served domestically but outside the southern states, 9 served domestically in the southern states, two served in their state of residence, and one said that they did not know where they served. Because of the small sample size, I operationalize veteran status in the same dichotomous manner as in the earlier surveys.[32]

Even when all veterans are collapsed into a single dichotomous measure, however, the relatively small size of the sample might raise concerns. While this issue is certainly worth keeping in mind, it is not a reason to disregard the dataset entirely. Even though the sample is smaller for this study than the other studies used in earlier in this book, the sampling procedure employed is actually much closer to contemporary standards. Since the study was well designed, the small sample size is likely to mean that there is a bias away from statistical significance rather than toward

---

[32] In contrast to the 1940s questions where the survey specifically asked about service in World War II, this survey asked about military service generally. To provide the best proxy for World War II–era service, my veteran variable codes as "1" only veterans in the age range that could have served in World War II, while all others – including veterans outside this range (i.e., people who are listed as veterans but are too old or young to have plausibly served during World War II) – are coded as "0."

it.[33] The black adult sample is actually somewhat smaller than the white adult sample, but other scholars have effectively used it to address similar questions about black military service.[34] Overall, with these limitations acknowledged, this dataset provides a unique perspective on the relationship between military service and white racial attitudes at an important historical moment.

Table 3.4 and Figures 3.5–3.6 present the results. The strongest support for the racial liberalization hypothesis for veterans is found in the question assessing support for black voting rights. Overall, 73 percent agreed "quite a bit" that African Americans should be allowed to vote, 15 percent agreed "a little," 4 percent disagreed "a little," and 7 percent disagreed "quite a bit." There were no discernible differences in the attitudes of men and women. There does, however, appear to be a difference between men who were veterans and those who were not. Among veterans, 84 percent agreed "quite a bit" and another 10 percent agreed "a little," with only 1 percent disagreeing "a little" and 4 percent disagreeing "quite a bit." By contrast, among nonveterans, 68 percent agreed "quite a bit" and 16 percent agreed "a little," with 6 percent disagreeing "a little" and 11 percent disagreeing "quite a bit." Overall, veterans were more likely to agree (combining the "quite a bit" and "a little" answers shows that 94 percent of veterans agreed, compared to 84 percent of nonveterans), but in particular were much more likely to strongly agree. By contrast, nonveterans were much more likely to disagree, and in particular to disagree strongly. To examine whether this difference holds when controlling for age and education, I estimate an OLS regression model. The results are presented in Figure 3.5. Consistent with the difference in the cross-tabulation, the coefficient on the veteran variable is statistically significant in the racially liberal direction.[35]

---

[33] In other words, it is possible that nonsignificant statistical relationships observed in this dataset might hypothetically be statistically significant in a larger sample size, but unfortunately there is no way to know this definitively.

[34] Parker, *Fighting for Rights*; Christopher S. Parker, "When Politics Becomes Protest: Black Veterans and Political Activism in the Postwar South," *Journal of Politics* 71(1), 2009, 113–131.

[35] The OLS coefficient is -0.48 (the outcome variable ranges from 1 to 4, coded so that conservative responses are higher) and is statistically significant at the 0.001 level ($N = 198$). The OLS results are consistent with the results from an ordered probit model, although the latter does a better job of capturing the uneven differences between categories. The results are also robust to excluding controls for education (which might generate post-treatment bias due to the GI Bill). To avoid unwieldy statistical details, these alternative specifications are included in the appendix.

TABLE 3.4: *Voting rights, segregation, and sit-ins, 1961 (veterans vs. nonveterans)*

Question Wording	White Male Vets	White Male Nonvets
"Now, I'd like to read some of the kinds of things people tell me when I interview them and ask you whether you **agree** or disagree with them... Colored people out to be allowed to vote."	94%*	84%*
"What about you? Are you in favor of **integration**, strict segregation, or something in between?"	10%	7%
"What is your feeling about this?" Asked to those who answered yes to, "Have you ever heard of the sit-in movement – that is, some of the colored people going into stores, and sitting down at lunch counters, and refusing to leave until they are served?" [Numbers are for those who **approve**.]	11%*	8%*
"Now, I'd like to read some of the kinds of things people tell me when I interview them and ask you whether you agree or disagree with them... Demonstrations to protest integration of schools are a good idea, even if a few people have to get hurt." [Numbers are for those who **disagree**.]	84%*	79%*

Note: Percentages refer to the percent of whites answering with the option in bold.
* denotes that strong and weak support are added together.

There is no difference, however, between veterans and nonveterans on assessments of the sit-in protests or general attitudes toward segregation. While black voting received strong support among whites overall, these issues were much more unpopular, and military background seemed not to have any effect.[36] Overall, among whites who had heard of the sit-ins movement, 62 percent disapproved, with an additional 18 percent "strongly" disapproving, while 6 percent said they approved and just

[36] It is possible that veterans were generally more opposed to lawbreaking, which might mask greater support for civil rights advocacy per se. Unfortunately, there is not a question in this study that asks about lawbreaking more generally with which to compare.

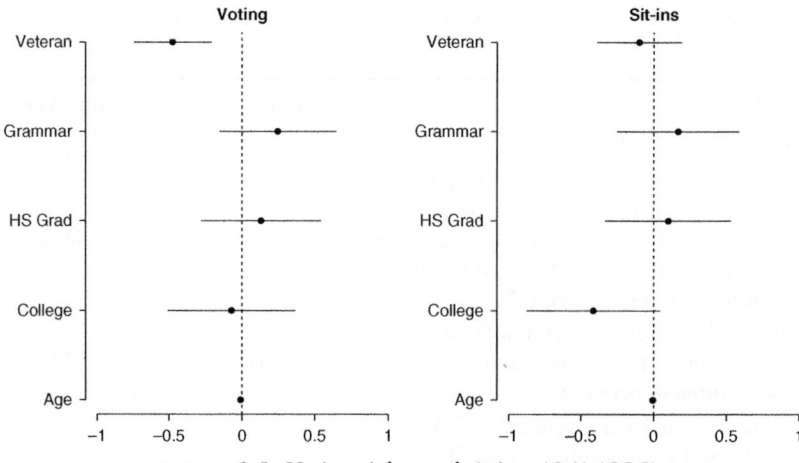

FIGURE 3.5: Voting rights and sit-ins, 1961 (OLS)

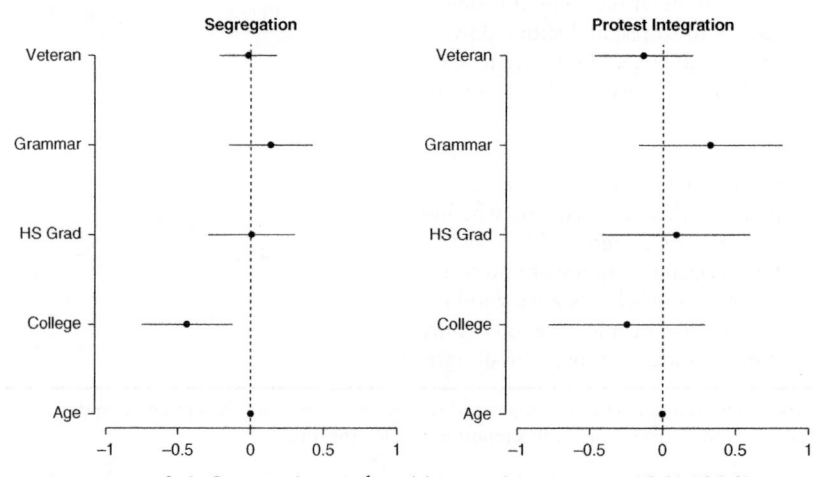

FIGURE 3.6: Segregation and anti-integration protests, 1961 (OLS)

2 percent said they "strongly approved." An additional 11 percent said they were neutral. White men were more likely to "strongly" disapprove than women, with 22 percent offering this response and another 57 percent saying they disapproved. The numbers for veterans and nonveterans are barely distinguishable: there is no relationship between military service and views on the sit-ins movement, a claim that is consistent with the regression results displayed in Figure 3.5.[37]

---

[37] The OLS coefficient is only significant at the 0.51 level in this model. If the controls for education are excluded, however, the coefficient increases in size and the *p*-value drops

Whites were overwhelmingly supportive of segregation, with very few supporting full integration. Overall, 64 percent of whites said they supported segregation, with just 6 percent saying they supported integration and 28 percent saying they supported something "in between." The numbers for men and women are striking similar, with 63 percent of white men saying they support segregation, 8 percent supporting integration, and 28 percent saying something in between. Veterans were slightly less supportive of segregation than nonveterans in their responses, but the small differences are indistinguishable from sampling error. Ten percent of veterans supported integration, compared to 7 percent of nonveterans, with 60 percent of veterans supporting segregation and 65 percent of nonveterans doing so (29 percent of veterans and 28 percent of nonveterans said they supported the in between option). The regression results shown in Figure 3.6, however, demonstrate that there is no statistically significant relationship between veteran status and opinions on segregation.[38]

The lack of a clear relationship between veteran status and these issues is a challenge to the racial liberalization hypothesis. Segregation was at the core of the southern racial status quo, and military service seems to have had no moderating effect on how southern white men felt about the issue. Similarly, the sit-in movement was a critical aspect of the 1960s civil rights movement, and military service likewise seems to have had no impact on white assessments of it.

The question about violent anti-integration protests is less clear-cut, but ultimately the evidence for the racial liberalization hypothesis is not as strong as it was for the black voting rights question. While southern whites largely supported segregation, most expressed disapproval of anti-integration protests that might involve violence. Overall, 68 percent of whites said they disagreed "quite a bit" with anti-integration protests if it meant "a few people have to get hurt," with another 11 percent disagreeing "a little bit." A smaller group of whites supported such protests, with 7 percent supporting them "a little bit" and 11 percent supporting them "quite a bit." Another 4 percent said they did not know. There were no major differences by gender, with 67 percent of white men strongly disagreeing with violent anti-integration protests, 13 percent disagreeing

---

to 0.14. While this is still below conventional thresholds of statistical significance, it is more suggestive than the main model, particularly given the small N. See the appendix for more details.

[38] The OLS coefficient is only significant at the 0.86 level. When controls for education are excluded, though, the coefficient does increase in size and the p-value drops to 0.18. See the appendix.

a little, 6 percent agreeing, and 11 percent agreeing strongly. Veterans and nonveterans were basically identical in the middle two categories, but veterans were less likely to take the strongly agree stance (8 percent, compared to 13 percent for nonveterans) and more likely to take the strongly disagree stance (71 percent, compared to 65 percent for nonveterans). As Figure 3.6 shows, however, this result does not hold up in a regression framework. When age and education are controlled for, there is no statistically significant relationship between veteran status and attitudes toward violent anti-integration protests.[39] While less clear-cut than the segregation and sit-ins questions, ultimately the racial liberalization hypothesis does not clearly find support in this question either, leaving the voting rights question to stand alone as clear evidence for greater racial liberalism among veterans for the 1960s civil rights era issues.

THE CONTACT HYPOTHESIS AND WORLD WAR II

Today, the military is one of America's most racially integrated institutions, and some researchers have found evidence that the contact hypothesis holds for the armed forces.[40] As described in the next chapter, however, the military remained segregated during World War II. Despite this less favorable institutional context for the growth of white racial liberalism, this chapter presents a couple of intriguing pieces of evidence that military service had a moderating effect on the racial attitudes of at at least some white men during this period. White veterans outside the South were more supportive of federal intervention in state lynching cases than their nonveteran counterparts, and white veterans in the South offered stronger support for black voting rights than nonveterans.

Although the military remained segregated, some white veterans did find themselves having more positive contact with African Americans in the war's aftermath. Consider the 1961 survey of white southerners

---

[39] The coefficient is significant at the 0.44 level. In a model where educational control variables are excluded, though, the coefficient size increases from −0.13 to −0.24 and is significant at the 0.15 level (still below conventional thresholds, but more suggestive). See the appendix for more details.

[40] Scott E. Carrell, Mark Hoekstra, and James E. West, "The Impact of Intergroup Contact on Racial Attitudes and Revealed Preferences," NBER Working Paper 20940, National Bureau of Economic Research, Cambridge, MA, 2015. For a contradictory assessment, however, see Tatishe M. Nteta and Melinda R. Tarsi, "Self-Selection Versus Socialization Revisited: Military Service, Racial Resentment, and Generational Membership," *Armed Forces & Society* 42(2), 2016, 362–385. See also George H. Lawrence and Thomas D. Kane, "Military Service and Racial Attitudes of White Veterans," *Armed Forces & Society* 22(2), 1995, 235–255.

again. Respondents were asked whether they had "ever known a colored person well enough that you would talk to him as a friend." Overall, 68 percent of white men said they knew a black person well enough to call them a friend, while 32 percent said they did not. The number for World War II–era veterans, though, is higher: 74 percent of veterans said they knew a black person well enough to call them a friend, compared to 65 percent of nonveterans overall and 55 percent of nonveterans in the same age range.[41] While the "black friend" trope is a cliche one, it lends some support to the idea that white veterans' relative moderation, at least on some issues, was potentially fueled, in part, by contact.

This raises an interesting counterfactual: Had the United States military fought a war against Nazi Germany with a fully integrated force, would the liberalizing effects of the military service have been stronger and more consistent?[42] While it is impossible to be sure, the limited experiments in integrated units that took place near the war's end provide some evidence that can be brought to bear on this question.

During May and June of 1945, the Research Branch Information and Education Division in the European Theater of Operations fielded a survey of white company grade officers and platoon sergeants to assess their feelings toward black rifle platoons that had joined their companies in March and April of that year, fighting alongside white troops until V-E Day. Overall, 250 whites were surveyed, including all available company grade officers and what the report determined to be a representative sample of platoon sergeants. By a two-to-one margin, both white officers and noncommissioned officers said they were initially not favorably disposed toward the idea. More than three-fourths, however, said that, after having served with the black troops, their opinions became more favorable. Both groups agreed that white and black soldiers had generally gotten along well.[43]

---

[41] This relationship holds up in a regression framework. Controlling for age and educational attainment, these veterans were actually 18 percentage points more likely to report having a black friend than white men in the same age range. These logistic regression results are presented in the appendix.

[42] Compared to later conflicts, the combination of contact with the ideological logic of the anti-Nazi crusade could have been a much more powerful combination than the interracial contact involved in, for example, the Korean War, Vietnam War, etc.

[43] "Opinions About Negro Infantry Platoons in White Companies of 7 Divisions," July 3, 1945, Record Group 220: Records of the President's Committee on Equality of Treatment and Opportunity in the Armed Services, Army, Negro Platoons in White Companies, available online: www.trumanlibrary.org/whistlestop/study_collections/desegregation/large/documents/index.php?documentid=10-11&pagenumber=1.

That said, there were limitations to this newfound tolerance. When asked whether black soldiers were to be used as infantry in the future, a majority stated that while they were willing to have a platoon of black soldiers in the same company as white soldiers, they preferred the platoon itself to be separate (62 percent of white officers expressed this position, along with 89 percent of white noncommissioned officers). Only 7 percent of white officers – and 1 percent of white noncommissioned officers – advocated black soldiers serving in integrated platoons.[44]

The researchers also conducted a survey of 1,710 white enlisted men in European Theater of Operations field forces. In response to the question of how the respondent would feel if their outfit was set up as a company including both white and black platoons, responses differed with respect to contact. In units that had no black platoons in white companies (1,450 of the 1,710 respondents), 62 percent said they would "dislike it very much." By contrast, of those in companies that had a black platoon (80 of the 1,450 respondents), only 7 percent said so.[45] Asked more generally whether "it is a good idea or a poor idea to have the same company in a combat outfit include Negro platoons and white platoons," only 18 percent of those in units without a black platoon said this was a "very good" or "fairly good" idea. For those in a company with a black platoon, however, 64 percent of respondents said so.[46]

These studies by the Research Branch would come to serve as the sources for *The American Soldier*, the landmark study of social psychology that found that contact led white soldiers to be more supportive of integration and to have better relationships with black soldiers, relative to other soldiers.[47] The findings also made their way into the Truman civil rights committee's report, *To Secure These Rights*, which declared

---

[44] Ibid.

[45] Ibid. There were also two middle groups: 24 percent of respondents in the same division but not the same regiment as black troops said they would dislike it, as well as 20 percent of respondents in the same regiment but not the same company as black troops.

[46] Ibid. Fifty percent of those in the same division but not the same regiment as black troops approved, as did 66 percent of those in the same regiments but not the same company as black troops.

[47] Samuel A. Stouffer, Edward A. Suchman, Leland C. DeVinney, Shirley A. Star, and Robin M. Williams, Jr., *Studies in Social Psychology in World War II: Volume I: The American Soldier: Adjustment During Army Life*, Princeton: Princeton University Press, 1949); Samuel A. Stouffer, Arthur A. Lumsdaine, Marion Harper Lumsdaine, Robin M. Williams, Jr., M. Brewster Smith, Irving L. Janis, Shirley A. Star, and Leonard S. Cottrell, Jr., *Studies in Social Psychology in World War II: Volume II: The American Soldier: Combat and Its Aftermath*, (Princeton: Princeton University Press, 1949). For an in-depth analysis of the books, see Joseph W. Ryan, "What Were They Thinking?

that "the closer white infantrymen had been to the actual experience of working with Negroes in combat units the more willing they were to accept integrated Negro platoons in white companies as a good idea for the future."[48]

To what extent might these small-scale experiments have been replicated on a larger scale, leading to a transformation of the racial attitudes of white soldiers in the war's aftermath? There are certainly reasons to be skeptical. The contact hypothesis is appealing to many. "But identity is highly contextual," Ronald Krebs writes, "and one should not be surprised to see soldiers adopting regional, class, gendered, religious, or ethnic perspectives when they are off base or out of uniform or when they have returned to civilian life."[49] Soldiers, Krebs argues, are not "passive receivers," as "cultural systems always contain enough contradictory material so that individuals can challenge hegemonic projects."[50]

Indeed, despite the ideological logic of racial liberalism many civil rights advocates linked to the war, it is not obvious that soldiers themselves – particularly white ones – understood their mission in these terms. Even under an official policy of integration, individual white soldiers might have served alongside black soldiers without any actual change of hearts and minds. Writing in 1966, for example, the sociologist Charles Moskos described how "the segregationist-inclined white soldier regards racial integration as something to be accepted pragmatically, if not enthusiastically, as are so many situations in military life."[51] Indeed, the Stouffer et al. *American Soldier* study contained similar nuances that often get overlooked by those looking for a quick citation. "It should be remembered, however, that not all the white support of using Negroes as infantrymen necessarily reflected 'democratic' or 'pro-Negro'

Samuel A. Stouffer and *The American Solider*," (PhD dissertation, University of Kansas, 2010).

[48] President's Committee on Civil Rights, *To Secure These Rights: The Report of the President's Committee on Civil Rights*, (Washington, DC: US Government Printing Office, 1947), www.trumanlibrary.org/civilrights/srights4.htm, 84. The committee also cited an article in *Public Opinion Quarterly*, which found that, among white merchant seamen, "it would appear that many of our respondents could not afford the luxury of an anti-Negro prejudice while at sea." Ibid., 85. Ira N. Brophy, "The Luxury of Anti-Negro Prejudice," *Public Opinion Quarterly* 9(4), 1945–46, 466.

[49] Krebs, *Fighting for Rights*, 9.

[50] Ibid., 8. Krebs directs this critique primarily at socialization arguments but notes that it applies to the contact hypothesis "to an extent."

[51] Charles C. Moskos, "Racial Integration in the Armed Forces," *American Journal of Sociology* 72(2), 1966, 142.

attitudes," the authors of *The American Soldier* wrote. "It could be simply a reflection of the desire of combat men to have their own burden lightened by letting others do part of the fighting; it might even conceal the most extreme attitudes of racial superiority leading to the reasoning that inferior Negro lives should be sacrificed before white lives. Moreover, the Negroes were still in separate platoons, which, to some Southern respondents, preserved at least the principle of segregation."[52]

World War II provided a unique opportunity for the contact hypothesis to be at its most effective, with the fight against Nazism offering a compelling ideological push toward tolerance, at least in theory. In practice, however, the relevant institutional mechanisms required for the contact hypothesis to function were largely not present. Consider the mechanisms, like a rank structure that mandates equality of authority and a clearly understood military norm of equality that had material payoffs for soldiers that abided by it, noted as important for the contact hypothesis in later decades by Butler and Wilson.[53] While the small experiments in integration during World War II are intriguing, they generally only constituted contact in its weakest form. While white and black soldiers literally came into contact with one another, such experiments did not include providing black soldiers with access to high-ranking officer positions, and they certainly did not involve a massive top-down implementation of racial equality. White soldiers could have easily seen such integration as a temporary exception from the norm rather than a new norm that would require new behavior over the longer term.

Counterfactually, if the armed serves were integrated in a genuine way during World War II (with all the accompanying components important to the contact hypothesis described by Butler and Wilson), would this have led to a more substantial growth in white racial liberalism? While there are reasons to be skeptical (like those noted by Krebs), it is quite possible that the combination of top-down integration enforcement and the war's unusually egalitarian ideological logic would have at least provided an unusually likely setting for attitudinal change.[54] Ultimately,

---

[52] *The American Soldier*, Vol. I, 590. Quoted in Ryan, "What Were They Thinking?," 66.
[53] Butler and Wilson, "*The American Soldier* Revisited," 465–466.
[54] The war's effects on contact between black men and white men were complex. On the home front, black soldiers stationed in southern training centers came into contact with both white soldiers and nonmilitary whites. Black men and white men also were more likely to work together in the defense industry than they had been before the war. This increased contact certainly did not lead easily to toleration and integration, as race riots and other incidents of racial violence on the home front make clear. Kryder, *Divided*

there is no way to truly know, as President Roosevelt refused to integrate the armed forces during World War II. Advocates of military integration had to wait until Truman's executive order in the postwar period, by which time the especially favorable ideological context of a war against Nazism had passed.

CONCLUSION

This chapter provides evidence that white veterans' military service corresponded with more moderate racial attitudes on some issues, but not others. White veterans were less likely to oppose federal intervention in state lynching cases in 1948, although this seems to have been concentrated among nonsoutherners. Southern white veterans, however, did offer stronger support for black voting rights in 1961 than did their nonveteran counterparts in the region. Notably, though, this moderation did not extend to broader claims about racial integration. The southern white veterans analyzed in the 1960s were just as supportive of Jim Crow segregation as southern whites who did not serve, and they were not any more sympathetic to the sit-in movement. Perhaps most striking of all, white veterans in general were not more supportive of integrating the armed forces in the immediate postwar period than those who did not serve. On the one hand, then, while far from a universal trend toward racial liberalism, there is at least some limited evidence that on attitudes toward particular civil and political rights, white veterans were distinctive from those who did not serve in the war. On the other hand, though, it is harder to find evidence that military service was associated with less racial prejudice, and questions related to integration seem to have been especially difficult to change.

Having now spent two chapters examining white racial attitudes, the next two chapters turn to the executive branch's response to civil rights advocacy. The contours of white racial attitudes in this era provide important contextual information for understanding why the politics of civil rights more broadly proceeded as it did. There are, for example, striking parallels between the finding that veterans were more likely to oppose the extremes of white supremacist violence and the most blatant

Arsenal. Historians of housing politics have likewise demonstrated intense antiblack sentiments among white urban residents who came into contact with growing black populations. See, for example, Arnold Hirsch, *Making the Second Ghetto: Race and Housing in Chicago, 1940–1960*, (Chicago: University of Chicago Press, 1998).

form of democratic exclusion (yet offer similar levels of support as nonveterans for a maintenance of the racial status quo in other ways) and the story of President Truman's evolving civil rights positions, which had important implications for the Truman administration's actions on civil rights.

More broadly, the extent to which the long-standing congressional civil rights agenda item of antilynching legislation likely grew less popular over the course of the war meant that Congress remained an unfavorable venue for civil rights policy advances. The newer issues of integrating the military and stopping discrimination in the defense industry were likewise unpopular among the white public. An important difference, however, is that these issues could be tied directly to the war effort, and the growth in executive power during wartime meant that unilateral action by the president offered an alternative venue for policy victories. The next two chapters describe the response to this advocacy, beginning with the Roosevelt administration.

4

The Roosevelt Administration and Civil Rights During World War II

A week after the attack on Pearl Harbor, Ralph Knox, a black man living in Philadelphia, decided to join the Army. His grandfather had served in the Civil War, and Knox felt it was his "duty to do something to uphold those rights and privileges for which he made possible for me." When he arrived at the custom house to volunteer, however, he was told no "colored units" were available for enlistment. "I am going to do everything within my power to keep steadfast inspite of this obstacle," he wrote Congressman John E. Sheridan. "[N]evertheless, I am terribly hurt."[1]

Representative Sheridan forwarded his letter to President Roosevelt. "I could take the Floor of the House and go off in a lengthy tirade," he wrote, "but I feel this would not be beneficial to the national unity which we now have and desire to hold." Sheridan instead hoped that the matter might be dealt with internally, describing his "inherent belief in your fairness and that immediate steps will be instituted to correct this grave error."[2] Marvin McIntyre, one of Roosevelt's advisors, took note of the letter's potential importance. "I hate to bother you with this but it looks important," he told Roosevelt. "Either the Secretary of War or someone should give it attention in my opinion."[3]

---

[1] Letter, Ralph Knox to John Sheridan, December 15, 1941, Folder: Colored Matters (Negroes), Jan–Feb 1942, Box 4, Official File 93 (hereafter OF 93), Franklin D. Roosevelt Library, Hyde Park, NY (hereafter FDRL).

[2] Letter, John Sheridan to Franklin Roosevelt, December 17, 1941, Folder: Colored Matters (Negroes), Jan–Feb 1942, Box 4, OF 93, FDRL.

[3] Memorandum, Marvin McIntyre to Franklin Roosevelt, December 19, 1941, Folder: Colored Matters (Negroes), Jan–Feb 1942, Box 4, OF 93, FDRL.

The president decided to respond to the letter in his own name. Mark Ethridge, one of Roosevelt's advisors, was tasked with drafting a reply.[4] In his draft, Ethridge called for the heads of the armed services to meet with the president, who would "advise them that it will be necessary for them to revise the policies of their departments at once to accept as volunteers or as selected service men all Americans on the basis of their qualifications and fitness and without regard to their race, creed, or color." The letter then turned to the ideology of the war. "It is transparently clear that we shall need to employ to their fullest all our resources, material and moral, in our struggle to maintain democracy in the world," he wrote. "We can do so only if we marshal all of our forces in a democratic fashion and eliminate internal inconsistencies which bring into question the reality of the objectives for with your country is fighting."[5]

This blunt acknowledgment of the discrepancy between the ideals of the war effort and the reality of Jim Crow was striking. It echoed the calls of civil rights organizations and black newspapers, which regularly drew attention to the seeming contradiction between the expressed aims of the war effort abroad and the maintenance of the racial status quo on the home front. This statement was never formally made, however. Ethridge was clearly aware of the political delicacy of the matter. "I have drafted a proposed letter which you may not care to send," he told the president. "As you will see, it calls for some discussion of the matter. The situation has been intensified by the Pearl Harbor incident and it is such that I feel the Army and Navy will have to face it realistically sooner or later."[6] When McIntyre read the letter, he told Grace Tully, the president's secretary, that he doubted Roosevelt would want to sign it. "[I]t has some dynamite in it," he wrote.[7]

McIntyre's assumption was correct. When he saw Ethridge's draft, Roosevelt told McIntyre to "answer the letter yourself and tone it

---

[4] Memorandum, Franklin Roosevelt to Mark Ethridge, December 22, 1941, Folder: Colored Matters (Negroes), Jan–Feb 1942, Box 4, OF 93, FDRL.

[5] Letter Draft, Mark Ethridge, Undated, Folder: Colored Matters (Negroes), Jan–Feb 1942, Box 4, OF 93, FDRL. In the letter draft, Ethridge also described Knox's situation as presenting "a problem which has vexed us in peace time and which must now be faced squarely and directly because of the issues involved in the present war." Ibid.

[6] Letter, Mark Ethridge to Franklin Roosevelt, January 5, 1942, Folder: Colored Matters (Negroes), Jan–Feb 1942, Box 4, OF 93, FDRL.

[7] Memorandum, Marvin McIntyre to Grace Tully, January 12, 1942, Folder: Colored Matters (Negroes), Jan–Feb 1942, Box 4, OF 93, FDRL.

down."[8] On January 19, 1942, Representative Sheridan finally received a reply. It came from McIntyre rather than Roosevelt, however, and the calls for "eliminating internal inconsistencies" were entirely absent. The tone was instead formal, perhaps even dismissive:

> Mr. Knox should be informed that the number of voluntary enlistments for both white and colored units which can be accepted for the Army at any moment depends upon the vacancies present or anticipated in existing troop units. The troop basis, in turn, depends upon appropriations, equipment, and other similar considerations.
> On December 11, the War Department authorized a new increase in enlistments for colored men in each corps area as the previous allotments were known to be nearly exhausted. Apparently word of this increase had not reached the recruiting office where Mr. Knox applied; hence his enlistment was turned down in the application of routine administrative procedure for reasons wholly apart from considerations of race.
> Mr. Knox can, of course, volunteer at any time for induction under the Selective Service Act.[9]

Knox's plea, and the administration's internally divided response regarding how to handle it, is reflective in many ways of broader trends in how the Roosevelt administration dealt with race and civil rights during World War II. In this chapter, I assess the Roosevelt administration's response to wartime civil rights advocacy, focusing both on rhetoric and policy. The chapter begins by demonstrating that the administration was familiar with the Double-V campaign and describing their efforts to ignore, or at least downplay, such issues when possible. I then turn to the policy issues that were at the top of the wartime civil rights agenda. After briefly discussing the long-standing issues of lynching and the poll tax, the remainder of the chapter focuses on the two primary items the administration was pressed on: the struggle against military discrimination, which became a central issue as black soldiers were asked to fight Nazi racism in segregated units; and defense industry employment discrimination, which saw the first and perhaps only real civil rights accomplishment of the Roosevelt presidency.

Taken together, the material in this chapter sheds new light on debates about the administration's relative inaction on civil rights by highlighting

---

[8] Letter, Franklin Roosevelt to Marvin McIntyre, January 13, 1942, Folder: Colored Matters (Negroes), Jan–Feb 1942, Box 4, OF 93, FDRL.

[9] Letter, Marvin McIntyre to John Sheridan, January 19, 1942, Folder: Colored Matters (Negroes), Jan–Feb 1942, Box 4, OF 93, FDRL.

the central but heterogeneous role of World War II.[10] Absent wartime activism, it is unlikely that Roosevelt ever would have signed an executive order combatting any kind of racial discrimination in employment. Yet while the war served as a compelling force on this issue, it was an insufficient juncture to pressure the president to integrate the armed forces in the midst of combat. While activists framed the exigency of wartime as requiring a more rational utilization of the capabilities of black soldiers, War Department officials interpreted the war's exigent nature as instead requiring a maintenance of the segregated status quo. Despite the creative activism of civil rights advocates, Roosevelt sided with the War Department on this issue, meaning that America's fight against Nazi Germany would be fought with a military segregated along racial lines.

THE ADMINISTRATION'S PERSPECTIVE ON WARTIME ADVOCACY

The debate over wartime civil rights issues related to a broader debate that was happening inside the White House. During a December 28, 1943, press conference, President Roosevelt declared that, effectively, "Dr. New Deal" had been replaced by "Dr. Win-the-War."[11] This turn of phrase came to symbolize the White House's transition from a focus on New Deal domestic policies to one almost entirely dedicated to the military aspects of World War II. It was in this context that civil rights advocates tried to convince the president and other members of the executive branch that their demands merited a policy response. In this section, I describe the efforts by various executive branch actors to make sense of, and develop a response to, such wartime demands.

Despite the administration's focus on the war effort, there is clear evidence that important executive branch actors were familiar with

---

[10] On the Roosevelt administration's general inaction on civil rights, particularly as it related to the broader effort at maintaining the support of southern Democrats, see Robert C. Lieberman, *Shifting the Color Line: Race and the American Welfare State*, (Cambridge: Harvard University Press, 1998); Ira Katznelson, *Fear Itself: The New Deal and the Origins of Our Time*, (New York: Liveright Publishing Corporation, 2013). For a revisionist account, see Kevin J. McMahon, *Reconsidering Roosevelt on Race: How the Presidency Paved the Road to Brown*, (Chicago: University of Chicago Press, 2004).

[11] Franklin D. Roosevelt, "Excerpts from the Press Conference," December 28, 1943, Online by Gerhard Peters and John T. Woolley, The American Presidency Project, www.presidency.ucsb.edu/ws/?pid=16358.

the rhetoric of the Double-V campaign. For example, in an October 1, 1942, letter from Lawrence Cramer, executive secretary of the Fair Employment Practices Committee (FEPC), to Marvin McIntyre, one of Roosevelt's secretaries, the campaign was discussed quite bluntly. "The argument is frequently advanced," Cramer wrote, "that we are fighting Hitler and all of his doctrines, including the doctrine of race superiority, and that there should be a clear and forceful statement by the President pointing out that the doctrine of race superiority is what our enemies are fighting for, not what we are fighting for."[12] Cramer continued:

Frequently letter-writers seize upon a statement by the President, or by a high administrative officer of the government directed against the German or Vichy-French government for inhumanities against Jews, religious organizations or minority groups, and argues that if these matters are of concern to our government, inhumanities or differentiation in legal or economic rights of citizens of or residents in this country should be given similar notice by the President or by high administrative officers. Where there is a demand for action by the Federal government in an area where it does not have jurisdiction, it is possible to point out that the matter is beyond the jurisdiction of the Federal government. Where, however, the demand is merely for a statement by the President similar to those made in the case of persecuted church officials in Norway, Poles and Jews in Germany or France, and others, it is more difficult, for me, to answer.[13]

Prominent members of the Cabinet were likewise familiar with it. Later that year, on December 15, Attorney General Francis Biddle sent Grace Tully, another one of the president's secretaries, a note. "I thought the President might like to see the enclosed November issue of *Survey Graphic* edited by Professor Alain Locke and devoted to the Negro problem, particularly Negroes in war," Biddle wrote. "It has had wide circulation and has been very favorably commented on."[14] There is no clear indication that the president ever actually followed up on Biddle's suggestion, however. It seems that Biddle remained at least somewhat interested in such matters, though. On November 8, 1944, he sent a letter to Roosevelt congratulating him on winning the election. "I do not think that the great issues of the war can be separated from

---

[12] Letter, Lawrence Cramer to Marvin McIntyre, October 1, 1942, Folder: Colored Matters (Negroes) Sept–Dec 1942, Box 5, OF 93, FDRL.

[13] Ibid.

[14] Letter, Francis Biddle to Grace Tully, December 15, 1942, Folder: Colored Matters (Negroes) Sept–Dec 1942, Box 5, OF 93, FDRL.

the domestic issues," he wrote. "International cooperation necessarily involves a tolerant and liberal outlook."[15]

The White House often received mail from a variety of individuals and organizations that engaged in a form of "rights talk" linked directly to the war effort.[16] Sometime in early 1944, for example, the Negro Newspaper Publishers Association submitted a "Statement of Negro War Aims" to the White House. "Negro Americans on every battlefront are giving their lives to defend the soil, the homes and the democratic ideals of their native land," the statement declared. "They, and we, are fighting for the freedom of America and of all oppressed and exploited peoples." While emphasizing the importance of winning the war, the statement declared that the authors believed "[t]hat second-class citizenship now imposed in many ways upon Negroes in America violated the principles of the Declaration of Independence and the Constitution of the United States, prevents full utilization of the material and moral resources of our country at war and destroys all possibility of a just and enduring peace." The authors maintained "[t]hat it is our duty and obligation to fight for every right guaranteed by the Constitution to all people, for to refrain from doing so would impair our Democracy at home and abroad by weakening the principles on which it is founded," and "[t]hat the Federal Government should begin now to use its authority and powers of persuasion to end abridgment of the Negro's citizenship, so as to bring about a more truly democratic America. Such action would support our claim that we fight for a world order in which economic equality, political self-determination and social justice will prevail."[17]

The general goal of executive branch actors, however, was to deflect attention away from such claims. On February 22, presidential administrative assistant Jonathan Daniels sent a memorandum to presidential correspondence secretary William Hassett about the organization's statement. "I suggest that we duck it," Daniels wrote.[18]

---

[15] Letter, Francis Biddle to Franklin Roosevelt, November 8, 1944, Folder: Roosevelt, Franklin D., Box 2, Francis Biddle Papers (hereafter Biddle Papers), FDRL.

[16] The type of "rights talk" in such correspondence has parallels to the letters received by the Civil Rights Section of the Justice Department starting in 1939. For an extensive analysis of how ordinary Americans used the language of rights in letters to this agency, see George I. Lovell, *This Is Not Civil Rights: Discovering Rights Talk in 1939 America*, (Chicago: University of Chicago Press, 2012).

[17] Negro Newspaper Publishers Association, "Statement of Negro War Aims," undated, Folder: Colored Matters (Negroes), Jan–March 1944, Box 6, OF 93, FDRL. The statement closed with a list of policies to work toward.

[18] Memorandum, Jonathan Daniels to William Hassett, February 22, 1944, Folder: Colored Matters (Negroes), Jan–March 1944, Box 6, OF 93, FDRL.

Some administration officials were leery of growing white southern fears that civil rights organizations were using the wartime context as an accelerant for their demands. In trying to hold together its unwieldy alliance between northern liberals and southern whites, the administration did not want to be seen as an active civil rights ally by racial conservatives. For example, in a November 25, 1942, memorandum to the president about the FEPC investigation of the Capital Transit Company, Daniels wrote that the move was likely to "create Southern fears that the government may be moving to end Jim Crow laws in transportation in the South under the guise of the war effort."[19]

On the other hand, some within the executive branch were fearful that discrimination against African Americans could be utilized by Japanese propagandists. In his description of a March 6, 1942, Cabinet meeting, Biddle noted that he had been told that stories regarding "the housing situation in Detroit" had been "short-waved to India, South America and Japan" and that "negroes are tearing up their draft cards and the blow to morale is serious."[20] In July of that year, Victor Rotnem, head of the Justice Department's Civil Rights Section, sent a memorandum to Assistant Attorney General Wendell Burge that addressed, among other topics, "Negro cases," in which he referred to "the importance of Negro morale to the war effort and the apparent effectiveness of Nazi propaganda, especially the Japanese."[21] The Office of War Information (OWI) was leery of the existence of what it called "pan-colored feeling" among African Americans toward Japanese people. A 1942 OWI study concluded that 18 percent of African Americans thought they would be

---

[19] Memorandum, Jonathan Daniels to Franklin Roosevelt, November 25, 1942, Folder: Colored Matters (Negroes) Sept–Dec 1942, Box 5, OF 93, FDRL. "It may also lift Negro hopes only to drop them again," Daniels added.

[20] Meeting Notes, March 6, 1942, Folder: Cabinet Meetings, Jan–June 1942, Box 1, Biddle Papers, FDRL. For an analysis of Japanese radio broadcasts aimed at African Americans, see Sato Masaharu and Barak Kushner, "'Negro Propaganda Operations': Japan's Short-Wave Radio Broadcasts for World War II Black Americans," *Historical Journal of Film, Radio and Television* 19(1), 1999, 5–26.

[21] Memorandum, Victor Rotnem to Wendell Burge, July 23, 1942, Folder: Civil Rights/Fair Employment, Box 1, Biddle Papers, FDRL. The quote can be found on p. 8. Writing in the *Washington University Law Review*, Rotnem led with an account of the 1942 lynching of Cleo Wright in Sikeston, Missouri, noting that "[w]ithin forty-eight hours thereafter, the German and Japanese short wave radio broadcasters featured discussions of the 'Sikeston Affair' in all its sordid details." Victor W. Rotnem, "The Federal Civil Right 'Not to Be Lynched,'" *Washington University Law Review* 28(2), 1943, 57.

treated better under Japanese rule, with another 31 percent thinking that they would be treated the same.[22]

Civil rights advocates sometimes tried to use these concerns to their advantage, although generally with only limited success. When the Dies Committee accused several prominent black leaders of being Communists, Walter White wrote to Dies directly to challenge him, using the fear of Japanese propaganda as a rhetorical tool. White sent Roosevelt a copy of the letter, along with a note referring to Dies' "morale-destroying attack."[23] The accusations, White wrote to Dies, "will be exceedingly useful to Tokyo in its broadcasts to the one billion colored peoples of the Orient in efforts to convince them that they should cast in their lot with Japan" instead of the Allied forces. "You have supplied excellent ammunition to the enemies of America," White continued. "Hitler and Hirohito should express their thanks to you."[24] White's rhetoric was striking – and it offered a preview of a logic that would become more prevalent during the Cold War – but there is no evidence that the letter had any impact inside the White House.

Despite reluctance on the administration's part to engage their claims, black newspapers joined advocacy organizations to press the administration to acknowledge the link between the war abroad and their struggle at home. In particular, Michael Carter, a reporter at the Baltimore *Afro-American*, made a concerted effort to get prominent public officials to address the relationship between American participation in the war and the demands of civil rights activists.[25] Indeed, the list of questions he sent to such figures is nearly identical to the ones a contemporary researcher might come up with were they given access to a time machine and a survey firm. The back-and-forth between Carter and prominent executive branch actors clearly illustrates some of the tensions between rights advocates and White House elites at this time.

---

[22] Clayton R. Koppes and Gregory D. Black, "Blacks, Loyalty, and Motion-Picture Propaganda in World War II," *Journal of American History* 73(2), 1986, 385–386.

[23] Letter, Walter White to Franklin Roosevelt, September 25, 1942, Folder: Colored Matters (Negroes) Sept–Dec 1942, Box 5, OF 93, FDRL.

[24] Letter, Walter White to Martin Dies, September 25, 1942, Folder: Colored Matters (Negroes) Sept–Dec 1942, Box 5, OF 93, FDRL.

[25] "Michael Carter" was actually the "working name" of Milton Smith, as he acknowledged in a 1942 letter to FDR. Since his articles were published under the name Michael Carter, though, I use this name in the main text. Letter, Milton Smith to Franklin Roosevelt, August 31, 1942, Folder: Colored Matters (Negroes) July–Aug 1942, Box 4, OF 93, FDRL. See also Sara Blair, *Harlem Crossroads: Black Writers and the Photograph in the Twentieth Century*, (Princeton: Princeton University Press, 2007), 19.

Carter's requests were often denied. He tried twice to secure an interview with President Roosevelt on the topic, first on August 31, 1942, and then later in the aftermath of the Detroit race riot on June 25, 1943. "The basic ideas behind these interviews is to interpret, through a channel which Negroes respect and use, the war and our relationship to it," he wrote in the 1942 attempt. "The interviews combat the dangerous Axis serving and perhaps Axis inspired propaganda that is trickling into urban Negro communities. Armed with your answers to the enclosed questions the Negro would be encouraged to even greater efforts towards total victory."[26] Roosevelt's secretaries were not amenable to the request, however.[27]

In Carter's 1943 attempt at securing an interview with the president, he acknowledged that his previous request was declined. But, Carter declared, "[n]ow, something else, something terrible has happened. Those riots have sapped Negro morale, changed Negro attitude towards the war, America, democracy and race relations. If it were possible for you, as it is for me, to over hear conversations in pool parlors, beer gardens, beauty parlors, YMCA's barracks etc. you should really understand the nature of the body blow to Negro morale." He used this setup to frame his request. "I beg you to grant me an interview – a statement – a talk with a White House representative, anything to antidote the poison, to assure the Negro that this is still his war and that his most murderous enemies are in Berlin," Carter wrote. "Such an interview would be equal

---

[26] Letter, Milton Smith to Franklin Roosevelt, August 31, 1942, Folder: Colored Matters (Negroes) July–Aug 1942, Box 4, OF 93, FDRL. Carter also mentioned how he was directly helped by the Federal Writers' Project, perhaps in an attempt to appeal to FDR's interests more generally.

[27] Letter, Stephen Early to Milton Smith, August 31, 1942, Folder: Colored Matters (Negroes) July–Aug 1942, Box 4, OF 93, FDRL. Notably, Carter did secure interviews with Wendell Willkie (the 1940 Republican presidential candidate) and Thomas Dewey (who would go on to be the 1944 and 1948 Republican presidential candidate) around this time period. Both gave positive assessments of wartime activism. "Yes siree," he quoted Willkie as saying, "I do not think that the colored man should stop his honest struggles for democracy because of the war. I see absolutely no inconsistency in the two aims." Dewey was similarly positive. "A large portion of our population is being thwarted in its patriotism and deprived of its right to take full part in the national effort," he said. "This is not only ugly and hateful; it is downright stupid. It is not simply a blunder; it is a crime." Michael Carter, "America Will Lose the Peace Unless It Gives Equal Duties and Opportunity to Everyone," *Afro-American*, August 15, 1942, ProQuest Historical Newspapers; Michael Carter, "Race Hate Choking All of Nation – Dewey," *Afro-American*, October 24, 1942, ProQuest Historical Newspapers.

to gunpowder. It would rebuild confidence in the Negro."[28] His second request was also denied.[29]

While the president was not willing to grant an interview to Carter, three important executive branch actors did correspond with him: Harold Ickes, Eleanor Roosevelt, and Henry Wallace. To the extent that these three figures represented the more racially liberal parts of the administration, their comments are illustrative of what sympathetic white elites were willing to say, as well as where they tended to draw the rhetorical line.[30]

Ickes wrote to Carter to express "regret that my schedule is so heavy that I am unable to find time for an interview on the subject of the Negro and the war." He was, however, willing to respond in writing to a list of questions Carter had included in his request. Overall, Ickes expressed support for civil rights advocacy, but insisted on a clear distinction between military victory in the war and civil rights policy victories at home. In response to a question about whether "the Negro [should] continue his drive for ethnic freedom during the course of the war," Ickes wrote, "In my personal opinion, yes – provided that it does not seriously interfere with the prosecution of the war, which must come first."[31]

---

[28] Letter, Michael Carter to Franklin Roosevelt, June 25, 1943, Folder: Colored Matters (Negroes), May–June 1943, Box 5, OF 93, FDRL.

[29] Letter, Stephen Early to Michael Carter, June 29, 1943, Folder: Colored Matters (Negroes), May–June 1943, Box 5, OF 93, FDRL. Carter also unsuccessfully requested an interview with one of Roosevelt's secretaries, Marvin McIntyre. "I would like your advice as to what I ought to do about this," McIntyre wrote William Hassett. "Naturally, I want to turn it down but I don't want to hurt any feelings." McIntyre politely declined Carter's request a few days later. "Were it not for the fact that I have very consistently refrained from press interviews and from any writing, I would be glad to cooperate with you," he wrote. "As you know, my work as Secretary is entirely divorced from the public relations, and I have always felt that I should refrain from public expression of my personal views." Memorandum, Marvin McIntyre to William Hassett, January 20, 1943, Folder: Colored Matters (Negroes), Jan–April 1943, Box 5, OF 93, FDRL, Letter, Marvin McIntyre to Michael Carter, January 22, 1943, Folder: Colored Matters (Negroes), Jan–April 1943, Box 5, OF 93, FDRL, Letter, Michael Carter to Marvin McIntyre, January 14, 1943, Folder: Colored Matters (Negroes), Jan–April 1943, Box 5, OF 93, FDRL.

[30] For discussion of the contours of Ickes's racial liberalism in particular, see John B. Kirby, *Black Americans in the Roosevelt Era: Liberalism and Race*, (Knoxville: University of Tennessee Press, 1980), 17–35.

[31] Letter, Harold Ickes to Michael Carter, April 13, 1943, Folder: Negroes, 1933–1945, Box 213, Harold L. Ickes Papers (hereafter Ickes Papers), Library of Congress, Manuscript Division, Washington, DC (hereafter LOC); Letter, Michael Carter to Harold Ickes, March 30, 1943, Folder: Negroes, 1933–1945, Box 213, Ickes Papers, LOC.

Similarly, when asked if "the war [can] be considered won if at its conclusion the status of the Negro, in American life, remains unchanged," Ickes responded, "This is a question of definition. We must not confuse the winning of the war, which is a military problem, with the winning of democratic rights. We can win the war on the battlefield and still have to go on fighting to protect or preserve certain rights."[32] In his *Afro-American* write-up of the interview, Carter noted that Ickes "hedges a little" on military segregation. "In war time questions concerning army policy should be decided purely on the basis of what would produce least friction and most military success," Ickes said. "This is for the War Department and the general staff to decide." That was "buck passing," Carter wrote, "but if it came to a vote I suspect I know where he would stand."[33]

Carter also secured a response from Eleanor Roosevelt. He led the article with her response to the question, "Should the colored man take advantage of the present crisis to further his own ends?" The First Lady responded, "No one who realizes why this war is being fought and no one who knows what the loss of freedom means, should take advantage of this crisis in history to further his own ends unless in furthering them he does so with the interest of the whole country in mind... Surely nothing will be gained by colored people's efforts to advance themselves at the expense of the total war effort, unless we all work together for

---

[32] Ibid. Notably, one question asked by Carter was, "The last war was punctuated by a series of race riots. To date there have been none, or at least, but few. To what do you attribute the happy change? Need Negroes fear a repetition of riots against them?" Ickes responded, "I believe that the absence of race riots in this war is largely the result of President Roosevelt's consistent policy of attacking discrimination against Negroes, particularly in plants that do war work." Unfortunately for Ickes' optimism, it would be only two months until racial violence erupted in Detroit.

[33] Michael Carter, "I Have Done Everything to Abolish Discrimination," *Afro-American*, June 5, 1943, ProQuest Historical Newspapers. A few days before Carter's request, on March 27, Ickes received a letter from John H. Johnson, managing editor of the *Negro Digest*, asking him to write an article addressing the question, "Have you ever thought about what you would do if you were a Negro?" Ickes responded on April 15: "I regret very much that lack of time makes it impossible for me to contribute an article on the subject, 'If I Were a Negro,' to your magazine. I have always felt that discrimination on the basis of race, color, or religion, is a disgrace to any country where it exists. The treatment of the Negro in this country is nothing for any American to be proud of, but I am happy to say that the situation is definitely improving. The road to equality of opportunity is still long and hard, and 'If I Were a Negro' I would not stop until I had reached the goal." Letter, Harold Ickes to John H. Johnson, April 15, 1943, Folder: Negroes, 1933–1945, Box 213, Ickes Papers, LOC; Letter, John H. Johnson to Harold Ickes, March 27, 1943, Folder: Negroes, 1933–1945, Box 213, Ickes Papers, LOC.

the one end; peace and a chance to build a better world." She did, to be clear, criticize racially discriminatory policies, but like Ickes she was not willing to advocate using the war as a means of overcoming them.[34]

Carter also interviewed Vice President Henry Wallace, who made a number of generally racially liberal comments. Wallace, however, was not entirely optimistic about the future. "The interview ended on a depressing tone," Carter wrote in his article. "I told the Vice President that there was a democratic awareness in America. White people *I* thought, were becoming more conscious of the fact that we were denied normal American privileges and that we deserved better treatment." Wallace, though, "had no such optimism," replying, "I only hope you are right. I wish there were a greater spirit of fair play and a greater knowledge of the real spirit of this war. The need for fraternity and unity is still great."[35]

For the most part, though, the executive branch was focused almost entirely on the international arena. The Department of War came to capture more and more of Roosevelt's attention, and – as will be seen in the sections to come – it was staunchly opposed to calls for the military to help alleviate racial inequities. Even Secretary of Labor Frances Perkins, a major figure in planning domestic social policies in the 1930s, agreed. Regarding the president's shift from emphasizing the New Deal to "win-the-war," she later said, "Well, that was a proper thing to say. What he meant by it was let us temporarily suspend these various humanitarian movements that we have been breathing into the law of this land, and

---

[34] Michael Carter, "U.S. Must Give Vote and Equal Pay to Everyone – Mrs. FDR," *Afro-American*, July 14, 1942, ProQuest Historical Newspapers.

[35] Michael Carter, "No Freedom Here for Colored People, says V-President Wallace: 'We Haven't Solved Problem Anywhere'," *Afro-American*, October 23, 1943, ProQuest Historical Newspapers. Carter also interviewed other executive branch officials, including War Manpower Commission Chairman Paul McNutt. See Michael Carter, "U.S. Not Using Enough Colored War Workers, Warns Paul V. McNutt," *Afro-American*, December 12, 1942, ProQuest Historical Newspapers. Truman Gibson, then civilian aide to the Secretary of War, also agreed to an interview where he told Carter that "[w]e must not stop hitting at jim crow," but praised the Army for its efforts. "I think the army is as much opposed to injustice as anyone else," he said. "I know what they are doing against brutality." Michael Carter, "An Interview With: Truman K. Gibson Civilian Aide to Secretary of War," *Afro-American*, July 17, 1943, ProQuest Historical Newspapers. As will be described in the next chapter, however, Gibson was less restrained in criticizing the military in internal documents than he was in this public statement.

bend all our energies on winning the War. When the War's over, we'll see what we can do then."[36]

In this context, sympathetic figures inside the White House were reluctant to press the issue, particularly if that involved taking a public stand. On February 10, 1944, Marshall Field, Edwin Embree, and Charles Johnson wrote a letter to Ickes inviting him to attend a meeting of the Southern Regional Council in Chicago. "The war has forced to the front the question of race and color," the letter began. "This is not a new problem, but its mounting acuteness, as a factor in world civilization, demands that fresh attention be given to what is happening and is likely to happen in America."[37] On February 17, Ickes responded in a letter addressed to Embree. "What you and your co-signers say in your letter of February 10, is, unfortunately, accurate, and I would love to attend the proposed conference," Ickes wrote. "Unfortunately, I cannot do so." Ickes then proceeded to describe his vacation plans with his wife. "All things considered, and despite my very real interest in the discussion that you are planning, I do not feel that, in justice to myself or in fairness to Mrs. Ickes, I can again disappoint her."[38]

While most executive branch officials were not interested in pursuing domestic issues generally, and civil rights issues especially, during the war, civil rights advocates nonetheless perceived the war as offering a unique window of opportunity. The next three sections examine the executive

---

[36] Reminiscences of Frances Perkins (1961), Interview 8, Session 1, p. 527, in the Oral History Research Office Collection of the Columbia University Libraries. Perkins apparently viewed the wartime FEPC as a "nuisance" and a presidential order that "[d]idn't have any standing." Ibid., 909.

[37] Letter, Marshall Field, Edwin Embree, and Charles Johnson to Harold Ickes, February 10, 1944, Folder: Negroes, 1933–1945, Box 213, Ickes Papers, LOC.

[38] Letter, Harold Ickes to Edwin Embree, February 17, 1944, Folder: Negroes, 1933–1945, Box 213, Ickes Papers, LOC. Ickes maintained his deference to the president even after leaving the Truman White House. When the Civil Rights Congress asked him to sign a petition urging Truman to investigate a police raid in Columbia, Tennessee, in August 1946, Ickes refused. "I have very strong feelings on the subject matter with which your letter deals," he replied. "I have spoken vigorously in the past about lynchings and Negro persecutions, and I shall again in the future. However, I do not feel like joining in the proposed petition to President Truman." Letter, Harold Ickes to Vincent Sheean and George Marshall, September 19, 1946, Folder: Negroes, 1946–1951, Box 75, Ickes Papers, LOC. In May 1947, he declined a request from the NAACP to advertise their membership drive in his column. Although his letter declining the request offered a more generic reason, privately he worried about southern opposition to the NAACP, noting that he had "a number of subscribers among the southern newspapers." Memorandum, Harold Ickes to Dr. Clark, Undated, Folder: Negroes, 1946–1951, Box 75, Ickes Papers, LOC.

branch's response to these efforts. I start with a brief overview of how wartime rhetoric started being associated with the long-standing issues of lynching and the poll tax. I then offer a more extensive analysis of the executive branch's response to the new wartime issues of segregation in the military and job discrimination in the defense industry.

LYNCHING, THE POLL TAX, AND WARTIME RHETORIC

The effort to end segregation in the armed forces and discrimination in the defense industry eventually came to take precedence over long-standing efforts to end lynching and the poll tax. While they declined in prominence, however, advocacy on these issues nonetheless contained interesting hints of the wartime rhetoric to come. In 1936, for example, Senator Edward Costigan cosponsored an antilynching bill and told his fellow senators bluntly that the bill gave the country "a choice between Hitler and Mussolini on the one side, and Washington, Jefferson, Lincoln, Henry Grady, Woodrow Wilson, and Franklin Delano Roosevelt on the other."[39] Like all such bills, however, it never became law. Roosevelt viewed antilynching legislation as a serious threat to the New Deal coalition between northern and southern constituents and representatives. In 1934, Roosevelt had told Walter White that he could not publicly support antilynching legislation because he had "to get legislation passed by Congress to save America," referring to the early New Deal's economic measures. "If I come out for the anti-lynching bill," he told White, southern congressmen would "block every bill I ask Congress to pass to keep America from collapsing. I just can't take that risk."[40]

While they were never successful, this did not stop civil rights advocates from pressing the president, and this pressure gradually started to link antilynching efforts to the rise of totalitarianism in Europe. On February 5, 1938, Carl Murphy of the *Afro-American* newspapers wrote to presidential secretary Marvin McIntyre. "Our people feel keenly the fact that the President has made no public statement on the anti-lynching bill since it has been in Congress," he wrote. "They feel that such a public word will bring encouragement to advocates of the measure and dismay to those who are opposed to it." He acknowledged the coalitional issues

---

[39] Klinkner and Smith, *The Unsteady March*, 138–139.
[40] Katznelson, *Fear Itself*, 160.

related to southern Democrats, but compared the rhetoric of such senators to that heard in the totalitarian regimes of Europe. "It is not doing us as a party any good to have the Congressional Record and the public press filled, day after day, with anti-Negro propaganda matching in bigotry and prejudice anything published in Germany, Russia or Italy against Jews, Catholics and aliens," he wrote.[41]

Lynching did not completely exit the agenda during the war. On December 11, 1942, for example, Biddle stayed after a Cabinet meeting to talk with Roosevelt about the issue. "I suggested to the President that he direct me, to which he agreed, to call a group of the outstanding people interested in the Negro situation to work out with them a more competent handling of the whole problem," Biddle wrote in his meeting notes. "I reported to the President our investigation of and authorization of a grand jury proceeding in the recent Mississippi lynching case of Howard Walsh, a negro who was lynched as a result of the jailer leaving unlocked the door of his cell so that the mob entered and dragged him out. The President was pleased with the way we handled it."[42] The issue, though, certainly declined in prominence as the war pushed other issues onto the agenda like military segregation and defense industry discrimination, and the congressional antilynching campaign started to falter. An antilynching law, perhaps the most prominent item on the early twentieth-century NAACP's policy agenda, would never be passed.

The poll tax debate, too, contained hints of the wartime rhetoric to come. As Steven Lawson writes, the "outbreak of World War II armed the antipoll-tax forces with powerful ideological weapons."[43] As Kimberley Johnson notes, however, southern white elites were able to find a rhetorical balance between the democratizing thrust of the war effort by offering a racially exclusionary critique of the poll tax that would extend the franchise to poorer whites, but not black southerners. "By writing out or eliminating race from the issue, they could square the American democratic revival with the Jim Crow order," Johnson writes. "Abolishing the poll tax became a way of reclaiming and reasserting the South's adherence to democratic norms (albeit for whites only)."[44]

---

[41] Letter, Carl Murphy to Marvin McIntyre, February 5, 1938, Folder: Lynching 1938–1944, Box 7, OF 93, FDRL.
[42] Meeting Notes, Francis Biddle, December 11, 1942, Folder: Cabinet meetings, July–December 1942, Box 1, Biddle Papers, FDRL.
[43] Steven F. Lawson, *Black Ballots: Voting Rights in the South, 1944–1969*, (New York: Columbia University Press, 1976), 65.
[44] Johnson, *Reforming Jim Crow*, 99.

While issues related to lynching and access to the ballot remained important to advocates, two newer issues became the primary ones pressed by civil rights advocates: discrimination in the defense industry and segregation in the armed forces. In the following sections, I examine these two new issues in greater detail. Civil rights advocates were able to successfully convince Roosevelt to issue an executive order addressing discrimination in the defense industry, but not one addressing segregation in the armed forces. In the aftermath of this, civil rights advocates had a model of job discrimination enforcement, but were never able to achieve a national policy beyond the temporary measures for the defense industry. They also continued pushing for military integration, an effort that would find success in the Truman administration.

SEGREGATION IN THE ARMED FORCES

I start with the fight against the segregated military. In this case, there was a divide between civil rights advocates and military leaders, and Roosevelt sided with the military. This meant that success in the struggle against military segregation would have to wait until the Truman presidency. The strategy of civil rights advocates, however, was developed earlier in the decade, both during the mobilization phase and the actual fighting of World War II.

Troop policy debates emerged well before US entry into World War II. This was partially the result of the experience of black soldiers serving in World War I, which activists like W. E. B. Du Bois thought – incorrectly, it turned out – would lead to major civil rights advances. As American participation in World War II became increasingly likely, civil rights advocates took a more proactive approach in lobbying the administration. For example, on March 9, 1939, Roy Wilkins wrote the president, enclosing an article in *The Crisis* titled "Old Jim Crow in Uniform," as well as a copy of a letter that had been sent to Secretary of War Harry Woodring. The editorial was about military discrimination during World War I. On March 13, McIntyre acknowledged receipt of the editorial and said that he would show it to Roosevelt, but there is no indication that the White House took it particularly seriously.[45]

---

[45] Letter, Roy Wilkins to Franklin Roosevelt, March 9, 1939, Folder: Lynching 1938–1944, OF 93, Box 7, FDRL; Letter, Marvin McIntyre to Roy Wilkins, March 13, 1939, Folder: Lynching 1938–1944, Box 7, OF 93, FDRL

At the beginning of the 1940s, African Americans had only a "very marginal presence" in the military, representing no more than 2 percent of personnel in any service branch.[46] Most served in the Army, where black soldiers were only allowed to participate in segregated Army Reserve and National Guard units, along with just four all-black Regular Army regiments.[47] While the Navy actually had a history of racial integration in the nineteenth century, on the eve of World War II, the majority of black sailors were segregated into steward positions.[48] The Marine Corps, a part of the Navy, excluded African Americans entirely.

As US participation in World War II was becoming an increasingly likely prospect, pressure from advocacy organizations and the reality of mobilization led to a formalization of US military racial policy. The most prominent part of this policy was the emergence of a 10 percent ceiling quota for black enlistment, a number that reflected the group's population share. Referred to as the "balanced force" concept, in practice enlistment figures tended to be lower – slightly so for the Army and significantly so for other branches.[49] In addition to this limit on black enlistment, the military also insisted on a second condition: strict racial segregation for those African Americans that served.

Black soldiers were disproportionately placed in noncombat, service-oriented positions. In the Army, where most black soldiers served, they were clustered in nontechnical positions in the infantry, Corps of Engineers, and Quartermaster Corps. Such segregation meant that many of the least prestigious positions in the Army were actually staffed by black men well above the 10 percent quota, while more elite units were far below that figure.[50] Segregation in the Navy was especially limiting. Not

---

[46] Sherie Mershon and Steven Schlossman, *Foxholes & Color Lines: Desegregating the U.S. Armed Forces*, (Baltimore: Johns Hopkins University Press, 1998), 1.

[47] These were the Twenty-Fourth and Twenty-Fifth Infantry Regiments and the Ninth and Tenth Cavalry Regiments, units that could be traced back to the Reconstruction era. Ibid., 2–3.

[48] Ibid., 9. The Navy had actually banned new black enlistment from the end of World War I through 1933, and when enlistment opened again, it pertained only to the stewards branch.

[49] Ibid., 27–28.

[50] Between 1940 and 1942, three-fifths of black Army soldiers were placed in nontechnical infantry positions, the Corps of Engineers, or the Quartermaster Corps. By the end of 1942, 19.7 percent of black enlisted personnel, compared to 40 percent of white enlisted personnel, were in combat units. Conversely, 48.6 percent of black enlisted personnel, compared to 21.6 percent of white enlisted personnel, were employed in support service and overhead work. Ibid., 54. There were two all-black combat divisions: the Ninety-third Infantry Division and Ninety-second Infantry Division. Ibid., 5.

only did nearly 72 percent of black sailors serve as stewards, but approximately half actually worked on shore inside the continental United States during the war.[51]

Civil rights advocates pressed for greater opportunities for black soldiers and sailors, as well as an end to segregation. Perhaps the most prominent event related to race and troop policy prior to Pearl Harbor came on September 27, 1940, when civil rights leaders met the president and military leaders in the White House. Civil rights advocates had pressed White House secretaries for the meeting, but succeeded only when they submitted the request through the more sympathetic First Lady. The eventual meeting consisted of A. Philip Randolph, Walter White, Secretary of the Navy Frank Knox, Assistant Secretary of War Robert Patterson, and the president.

The War Department had no interest in listening to the civil rights leaders' demands. In his diary, Secretary of War Henry Stimson wrote that he sent Patterson "because I really had so much else to do." Patterson apparently told him it was "an amusing affair – the President's gymnastics as to politics. I saw the same thing happen 23 years ago when Woodrow Wilson yielded to the same sort of demand and appointed colored officers to several of the Divisions that went over to France, and the poor fellows made perfect fools of themselves." His overall assessment of black capacities was blunt. "Leadership is not embedded in the Negro race yet," he wrote, "and to try to make commissioned officers to lead the men into battle is only to work disaster to both."[52]

Randolph and White pressed the administration for meaningful policies to address civil rights. The president was jovial, if noncommittal and, at times, slightly demeaning (in response to Randolph's inquiry about the rank of black members of the Navy, Roosevelt said, "There's no reason why we shouldn't have a colored band on some of these ships, because they're darn good at it").[53] Most accounts, however, suggest that Randolph and White left thinking some progress had been made. This turned out not to be the case.

On October 8, Patterson sent a memorandum to President Roosevelt about black participation in national defense. He included a statement

---

[51] Ibid., 65. The stewards percentage comes from a February 1943 assessment.
[52] Doris Kearns Goodwin, *No Ordinary Time: Franklin and Eleanor Roosevelt: The Home Front in World War II*, (New York: Simon & Schuster Paperbacks, 1994), 169.
[53] William Doyle, *Inside the Oval Office: The White House Tapes from FDR to Clinton*, (New York: Kodansha International, 1999), 15.

of War Department policies, which had been informally approved by the Secretary of War and Chief of Staff. While stating that technical training of some black troops would be accelerated, the statement was insistent that segregation be maintained. "The policy of the War Department is not to intermingle colored and white enlisted personnel in the same regimental organizations," the statement read. "This policy has proven satisfactory over a long period of years and to make changes would produce situations destructive to morale and detrimental to the preparations for national defense." Using language that would later be echoed in debates about LGBT military service, the War Department concluded by insisting that "no experiments be tried with the organizational set-up of these units at this critical time."[54]

Stephen Early returned the memorandum on October 9 with the president's penciled-in approval, and a statement of the policy was released to the press on that same day.[55] The press release infuriated civil rights activists, who felt it implied they condoned the military's policy of segregation. The NAACP sent out its own press release with the headline, "White House charged with trickery in announcing Jim Crow policy of Army." White wrote a letter to Ickes, attaching the release and stating, "I want you to see the enclosed story on an issue of very great importance not only to the Negro but to many white people who are fair-minded and who believe in practicing democracy as well as talking about it."[56]

On October 21, David Niles wrote to Early regarding a proposed statement responding to the controversy ("I think this statement is restrained, makes no commitment, and may do the trick," Niles wrote).[57] On October 25, the president sent letters to White, Randolph, and Arnold Hill. "I regret that there has been so much misinterpretation of the Statement of War Department Policy issued from the White House on October ninth," the letter began. "I regret that your own position, as well as the attitude of both the White House and the War Department,

---

[54] Nancy J. Weiss, *Farewell to the Party of Lincoln: Black Politics in the Age of FDR*, (Princeton: Princeton University Press, 1983), 277.
[55] See document dated October 8, 1940, that contains a description of correspondence between Robert Patterson and Stephen Early. Folder: Segregation, 1933–45, Box 7, OF 93, FDRL.
[56] Letter, Walter White to Harold Ickes, October 16, 1940, Folder: Colored Matters (Negroes) Oct–Dec 1940, Box 3, OF 93, FDRL.
[57] Letter, David Niles to Stephen Early, October 21, 1940, Folder: Colored Matters (Negroes) Oct–Dec 1940, Box 3, OF 93, FDRL.

has been misunderstood." He went on to promise better use of black troops. He also wrote that William Hastie – a prominent black legal figure – had been appointed as Civilian Aide to the Secretary of War.[58] The letter was received favorably by its recipients, but none of this led to meaningful shifts in the military's manpower policy.[59]

Civil rights leaders attempted to pressure the White House for further results. On March 13, 1941, for example, White wrote President Roosevelt to suggest a conference on racial exclusion in national defense, but his request was declined.[60] The new year did see one victory in terms of executive branch personnel. In February 1941, Truman Gibson – a black lawyer from Chicago – was brought into the executive branch as an assistant to Hastie. His initial experiences left him slightly skeptical of his role, however. On February 10, Gibson wrote his wife. "Today, the Youth Congress has been picketing the War Department, with the pickets marching around chanting, 'Down with Jim Crow'. I had to go out and saw these fifty or so kids, mostly Negroes." The protesters apparently caused quite a bit of resentment among army officers who were nearby, with a member of the General Staff leaving a message for Gibson to "hold himself in readiness – for what I don't know. Maybe he wanted me to rush out and stop them with my bare hands."[61]

After the December 1941 attack on Pearl Harbor and the following US declaration of war, the participation of African American troops in actual international combat formalized the structure of the debate. Civil rights leaders like Walter White were able to visit military bases and hear about discriminatory treatment firsthand. On the other hand, the War Department became even more frustrated with activist pressures as they focused exclusively on the military aspects of the conflict, convinced that segregating black troops was the most efficient strategy for winning the war. I discuss each in turn.

---

[58] Letter, Franklin Roosevelt to Walter White, October 25, 1940, Folder: Colored Matters (Negroes) Oct–Dec 1940, Box 3, OF 93; FDRL. The other letters are worded identically.

[59] Letter, Arnold Hill to Franklin Roosevelt, October 31, 1940, Folder: Colored Matters (Negroes) Oct–Dec 1940, Box 3, OF 93; FDRL; Letter, A. Philip Randolph to Franklin Roosevelt, November 1, 1940, Folder: Colored Matters (Negroes) Oct–Dec 1940, Box 3, OF 93; FDRL.

[60] Letter, Walter White to Franklin Roosevelt, March 13, 1941, Folder: Colored Matters (Negroes), Jan–May 1941, Box 3, OF 93, FDRL; Letter, Edwin Watson to Walter White, April 8, 1941, Folder: Colored Matters (Negroes), Jan–May 1941, Box 3, OF 93, FDRL.

[61] Letter, Truman Gibson to Isabelle Gibson, February 10, 1941, Folder: Family papers, correspondence, Jan–Mar 1941, Box 1, Truman K. Gibson Papers (hereafter Gibson Papers); LOC.

White maintained the NAACP's pressure campaign in part by visiting military bases and reporting to President Roosevelt on prospects for integration. For example, on October 28, 1942, White wrote the president to contrast the integrated training of officer candidates at Fort Sill in Oklahoma with the segregated training of Women's Army Auxiliary Corps (WAAC) recruits in Iowa. "I came away from the former more heartened regarding the possibilities of actual practice of democracy in the United States Army than I have ever been before," he wrote, describing "young Negroes who are quartered with, eat with, and study with white fellow candidates, Southern and Northern." Based on his conversations there, White attributed the prevailing "liberal unprejudiced attitude" to the leadership efforts of a prior Fort Sill commandant. White contrasted his positive take on Fort Sill with criticism of the training of recruits in Des Moines. "But, unfortunately, in a Northern City, at Des Moines, in the training of WAACs, there is just the reverse of the situation in the South," he continued. "The segregation at Des Moines is, in my opinion, both unnecessary and distinctly hurtful of morale." It is, White declared, contrary to "the ideals for which the war is being fought."[62]

White kept this up in the following years as well, reporting from his visits to Europe and beyond. On April 22, 1944, for example, he sent a memorandum to the War Department about his visits to the North African and Middle Eastern Theatres. "My first and strongest impression is the difference in racial attitudes in active theatres of war as contrasted with those in theatres of preparation for action," White wrote. "As men approach actual combat and the dangers of death, the tendency becomes more manifest to ignore or drop off pettinesses such as racial prejudice." He gave the example of the Anzio beachhead, where he said "men eat, sleep, and associate together with apparent complete ignoring of race or color of their neighbors." The reason for this tolerance, White wrote, was simple. "When German shells and bombs are raining about them, they do not worry as much about the race or creed of the man next to them."[63]

---

[62] Letter, Walter White to Franklin Roosevelt, October 28, 1942, Folder: Colored Matters (Negroes) Sept–Dec 1942, Box 5, OF 93, FDRL. The description of Fort Sill is found in a copy of a lengthy letter White originally sent to Henry Stimson and Oveta Hobby, director of the Women's Army Auxiliary Corp (WAAC). Letter, Walter White to Henry Stimson and Oveta Hobby, October 28, 1942, Folder: Colored Matters (Negroes) Sept–Dec 1942, Box 5, OF 93, FDRL.
[63] Memorandum, Walter White to War Department, April 22, 1944, Folder: Colored Matters (Negroes), Apr–May 1944, Box 6, OF 93, FDRL.

White argued that these effects seemed to hold over into nonbattle environments. "Memories of danger shared appear to leave a greater tolerance," he wrote. White criticized the tendency to place black soldiers in service duties rather than combat ones, arguing the latter would be more beneficial to improving perceptions of their true capacities.[64] In November of that year, White tried to convince the president and secretary of war to give "special recognition of Army personnel who have taken a decent attitude on the matter of race and color," but this letter does not appear to have received a response.[65]

Military officials were generally not persuaded by such advocacy. On December 29, 1943, John Sengstacke, President of the Negro Newspaper Publishers Association, wrote the president requesting a conference about "the status of the Negro in the United States Navy." This exchange is most revealing for the response it generated from military officials. Sengstacke's concluding paragraph chided various figures in the Navy Department for responses that "indicate a wide gap between the thinking of the top men in the Navy and the Negro people. We also believe they indicate a failure on the part of Navy officials to appreciate the importance of the issue." He closed by appealing to the war effort. "No one knows better than you, Mr. President, the pernicious effect this situation has on national unity," he wrote. "No one knows better than you how it weakens our cause before the entire world."[66]

Administration officials sent the letter around for comments. The response from the Chief of Naval Personnel is especially revealing. He blamed the black press for problems with black morale and focused his attention on the potential white response. "The individual negro finds it difficult to sublimate his race consciousness and become an integral part of the established Navy program," he wrote. "The Navy will continue to effect integration only to the extent that the attitude of both negroes and whites indicates that integration is practicable. To do otherwise would ignore the fact that racial prejudices on the part of both negroes and whites do exist on a national scale." He also indicated that he did not expect a change in the immediate future. "Until the national attitude has been so conditioned that these prejudices no longer

---

[64] Ibid.
[65] Letter, Walter White to Franklin Roosevelt, November 22, 1944, Folder: Colored Matters (Negroes), Oct–Dec 1944, Box 5, OF 93, FDRL.
[66] Letter, John Sengstacke to Franklin Roosevelt, December 29, 1943, Folder: Colored Matters (Negroes), Jan–March 1944, Box 6, OF 93, FDRL.

exist on a national scale – and it is believed that the attitude of the negro press in deliberately developing race consciousness and undue sensitivity to discrimination on the part of the negro in the Navy is retarding national progress in this direction – the Navy cannot undertake in time of war a program which will be detrimental to its war effort and serve only to further the interests of a racial minority," he concluded.[67]

Such negative military sentiments toward civil rights activists were fairly common. The day after Sengstacke wrote his letter, Jeanette Welch Brown, Executive Secretary of the National Council of Negro Women, requested that Mary McLeod Bethune be sent to war fronts to see black soldiers. President Roosevelt asked the First Lady for advice. "A young woman would have to go with her and a man would have to go on a tour such as was planned by Walter White, but I think it would be very good," she replied. The president then asked Jonathan Daniels, who responded by attaching a draft letter declining the request. "The Army does not want her to go," Daniels stated quite concisely.[68]

Eleanor Roosevelt's involvement in this internal debate is indicative of the more general role she played inside the White House on such issues, often as a foil to Stimson and others in the War Department. In 1940, she had accepted an invitation from A. Philip Randolph to speak at the Convention of Sleeping Car Porters, which, according to Goodwin, "set into motion a chain of events that would carry her into the center of a convulsive battle for racial equality in the armed forces."[69] With Stimson at the forefront of defending what civil rights activists took to calling the

---

[67] Memorandum, Chief of Naval Personnel to Secretary of Navy, January 5, 1944, Folder: Colored Matters (Negroes), Jan–March 1944, Box 6, OF 93, FDRL. Inside the White House, one advisor wrote to another that the president should not get too involved, as "the professional agitator would never be satisfied." Memorandum, Wilson Brown to Edwin Watson, January 10, 1944, Folder: Colored Matters (Negroes), Jan–March 1944, Box 6, OF 93, FDRL.

[68] Letter, Jeannette Welch Brown to Franklin Roosevelt, December 30, 1943, Folder: Colored Matters (Negroes), Jan–March 1944, Box 6, OF 93, FDRL; Memorandum, Franklin Roosevelt to Eleanor Roosevelt, January 3, 1944, Folder: Colored Matters (Negroes), Jan–March 1944, Box 6, OF 93, FDRL; Memorandum, Eleanor Roosevelt to Franklin Roosevelt, January 7, 1944, Folder: Colored Matters (Negroes), Jan–March 1944, Box 6, OF 93, FDRL; Memorandum, Franklin Roosevelt to Jonathan Daniels, January 10, 1944, Folder: Colored Matters (Negroes), Jan–March 1944, Box 6, OF 93, FDRL; Memorandum, Jonathan Daniels to Franklin Roosevelt, January 15, 1944, Box 6, OF 93, FDRL.

[69] Goodwin, *No Ordinary Time*, 161.

"Negro is too dumb to fight" policy, he and the First Lady frequently butted heads over the issue.[70]

Unfortunately for civil rights advocates, the president tended to side with the War Department in such cases. In October 1942, for example, the First Lady left for a trip to England inspecting military camps. Prior to leaving, she had written Stimson after hearing from various sources about racial tension due to white southern soldiers being "very indignant" at relations between black American soldiers and white English women. "I think we will have to do a little educating among our Southern white men and officers," she wrote. In his diary, Stimson wrote that he went to see the president prior to the First Lady's trip, asking him to warn his wife not to make any public statements about "the differential treatment which Negroes receive in the United Kingdom from what they receive in the U.S." Despite the concerns raised in her letter, Eleanor Roosevelt said nothing about race relations during the trip.[71]

In early 1944, an Advisory Committee on Negro Troop Policies was established, with its first meeting taking place on February 29.[72] On April 26 of that year, the committee met with Walter White, who pressed the military to alleviate racial inequities in its midst. The military representatives saw things differently. "There is too much pressure on the Army to change conditions in the United States," an exasperated General Porter stated at one point.[73]

While the ideological logic of the war was a useful rhetorical toolbox for civil rights advocates, it did not compel the president or military leaders to see the war in the same light. Beyond their ideological claims, civil rights advocates also argued that integration would lead to a more efficient military. The quota system, they argued, hindered

---

[70] Ibid., 566.
[71] Ibid., 383.
[72] The meeting was held in McCloy's office and began with a discussion of black troops, before turning to the Red Cross's segregated blood donor policies. "The Red Cross gets the blood, and the Army uses it. This is the policy of the Red Cross," Gibson said. "The Surgeon General made the request to segregate the blood." The blood segregation "offends the colored people," acknowledged one general in attendance. The committee, however, decided to take no action on the issue. "Minutes of Meeting of Advisory Committee on Negro Troop Policies," February 29, 1944, Folder: Subject File, War Department, Correspondence & Related Materials, 1944–65, nd., Box 3, Gibson Papers, LOC. See p. 5 of the meeting notes for these quotes.
[73] "Minutes of Meeting of Advisory Committee on Negro Troop Policies," April 26, 1944, Folder: Subject File, War Department, Correspondence & Related Materials, 1944–65, nd., Box 3, Gibson Papers, LOC. See p. 3 of the meeting notes for Porter's quote.

enlistment rates, and segregation in training and assignments prohibited the military from making full use of the capabilities of black soldiers. The War Department, however, disagreed, seeing white resistance to integration as the primary lens through which to understand the military segregation debate: because there were more white soldiers than black soldiers – and because white southerners were disproportionately represented among the whites – the War Department emphasized white morale at the expense of black morale. Ultimately, this perspective won out during the Roosevelt years, with Roosevelt siding with the War Department over the objections of civil rights advocates. In 1945, with the Allied forces drawing closer to the defeat of the Nazi regime, the United States military remained segregated by race.[74]

JOB DISCRIMINATION IN THE DEFENSE INDUSTRY

A second issue on the wartime civil rights agenda was discrimination in the defense industry.[75] Concerns about discriminatory employment practices had of course been raised in the past, but the defense industry provided a more concrete target, one that could be rhetorically tied to the broader aims of the war effort. And because advocates focused on the defense industry only, it was an easier sell than a broader antijob discrimination agenda targeting all private business. Unlike the military integration debate, this time the Roosevelt administration was willing to side with civil rights advocates against the War Department, albeit more for strategic than for ideological reasons.

The massive material undertaking necessitated by US mobilization for the war effort required workers to meet the demands resulting from an increase in federal defense spending. For many African Americans, however, such opportunities were limited by racial discriminatory hiring policies. Even when they were hired, they were often treated in a discriminatory manner, with a disproportionate tendency to be hired into service

---

[74] Some black soldiers were even given "undesirable" discharges after they made challenges to segregation. Margot Canaday, *The Straight State Sexuality and Citizenship in Twentieth-Century America*, (Princeton: Princeton University Press, 2011), 148.

[75] For a contemporaneous discussion of reasons employers gave against hiring African Americans, as well as other racial and ethnic minority groups, see Francis J. Haas and G. James Fleming, "Personnel Practices and Wartime Changes," *The Annals of the American Academy of Political and Social Science* 244, 1946, 48–56.

and unskilled positions instead of skilled occupations.[76] "While we are in complete sympathy with the Negro, it is against company policy to employ them as aircraft workers or mechanics," declared the president of the North American Aviation Company, noting that there will be "some jobs as janitors" available to black workers.[77]

Just like the military's growing manpower needs created an opportunity to pressure that institution for integration, so too did the needs generated by a booming defense industry result in an advocacy campaign to help African Americans benefit equitably from it. In early 1941, A. Philip Randolph organized the March on Washington Movement. The more active stance was in no small part a result of the dissatisfaction with the September 1940 meeting at the White House and its ensuing controversies. While White and the NAACP based their strategy around elite contacts and private outreach, Randolph grew increasingly cynical and looked to new methods to force the government to move on civil rights. Randolph observed the massive size of the wartime defense industry and saw an opportunity to use this to the advantage of civil rights advocacy. Moving beyond the NAACP's elite contacts approach, Randolph advocated direct political protest. The public announcement of the organization's motives came on January 15, and in the ensuing months Randolph worked to build support for a massive march to protest racial discrimination. His approach was not entirely appreciated by national organizations like the NAACP and the National Urban League, who did relatively little to promote it.[78] Individual leaders like White and the National Urban League's Lester Granger, however, did affiliate themselves with the march, and White in particular would be important in convincing the president that Randolph's march was a serious threat.

By February, black newspapers were covering the proposed march.[79] In May, Randolph's *Black Worker* published a "Call to Negro America to March on Washington for Jobs and Equal Participation in National

---

[76] Herbert Garfinkel, *When Negroes March: The March on Washington Movement in the Organizational Politics for FEPC*, (New York: Atheneum, 1973), 17.
[77] Ibid.
[78] Ibid., 40.
[79] For an early example of coverage, see "A. Philip Randolph," *Chicago Defender*, February 8, 1941, ProQuest Historical Newspapers. The *Chicago Defender* was skeptical Randolph would be able to pull the march off, but wrote that they "fervently hope this one will happen before the battle of England is over, and in the manner prayed for by Mr. Randolph." See also Garfinkel, *When Negroes March*, 55.

Defense on July 1, 1941."[80] The language of Randolph's call was much more militant than anything found in the NAACP's rhetoric. "In this period of power politics," he wrote, "nothing counts but pressure, more pressure, and still more pressure, through the tactic and strategy of broad, organized, aggressive mass action behind the vital and important issues of the Negro." A march on Washington would "shake up white America" and "shake up official Washington," "give encouragement to our white friends to fight all the harder by our side," "gain new respect for the Negro people," and "create a new sense of self-respect among Negroes."[81]

Randolph also preempted a number of anticipated critiques, in particular those related to national unity. "We believe in national unity which recognizes equal opportunity of black and white citizens to jobs in national defense and the armed forces, and in all other institutions and endeavors in America," he wrote. "We condemn all dictatorships, Fascist, Nazi and Communist. We are loyal, patriotic Americans all." For Randolph, however, this did not mean abstaining from protest. "But if American democracy will not defend its defenders; if American democracy will not protect its protectors; if American democracy will not give jobs to its toilers because of race or color; if American democracy will not insure equality of opportunity, freedom and justice to its citizens, black and white, it is a hollow mockery and belies the principles for which it is supposed to stand," he wrote.[82]

The White House soon took note. By June, Roosevelt was expressing displeasure at the proposed march. In a June 7 memorandum, Roosevelt asked Marvin McIntyre to inform Dr. F. O. Williston, a local black leader in Washington, DC, that "the President is much upset to hear (yesterday) that several negro organizations are planning to March on Washington on July first, their goal being 100,000 negroes and I can imagine nothing that will stir up race hatred and slow up progress more than a march of that kind and the best contribution Williston can make is to stop that march." A June 16 memorandum to the president said that Williston "has been to see [Roosevelt secretary Marvin McIntyre] several times

---

[80] Ibid., 56. In the call, the number proposed was ten thousand. The call referred both to defense jobs and the military, although the FEPC order would focus only on the defense industry.
[81] A. Philip Randolph, "Black Workers Call for a March on Washington," HERB: Resources for Teachers, accessed January 6, 2017, https://herb.ashp.cuny.edu/items/show/113.
[82] Ibid.

and he told [McIntyre] that your action is having a marvelous effect and that he has talked with several Negro leaders, who were in favor of the 'march', but he feels now that there is a good chance that nothing will happen."[83] This, however, turned out to be naive.

On June 5, Randolph wrote to Eleanor Roosevelt, describing the proposed march and asking if she would provide supportive remarks in her newspaper column.[84] "I have talked over your letter with the President," she responded on June 10, "and I feel very strongly that your group is making a very grave mistake at the present time to allow this march to take place."[85] She also sent a note to Under Secretary of War Robert Patterson. "The President suggested that I send this over to you in the hopes that everything possible is being done to prevent this march on Washington," she wrote.[86] Three days later, New York Mayor Fiorello La Guardia organized a meeting with Randolph and White in his City Hall office. Eleanor Roosevelt and the National Youth Administration's Aubrey Williams were in attendance. This outreach did not dissuade Randolph, however.[87]

On June 18, the president held a White House conference with Randolph, White, Stimson, Knox, and several others. Stimson was not pleased by the meeting. He wrote in his diary that it was "one of those rather harassing interruptions with the main business with which the Secretary of War ought to be engaged – namely, in preparing the Army for defense."[88] In the meeting, Randolph promised to bring one hundred thousand people to march on Washington if the president did not issue an executive order abolishing defense industry discrimination.

---

[83] Memorandum, Franklin Roosevelt to Marvin McIntyre, June 7, 1941, Folder: Colored Matters (Negroes) June–July 1941, Box 4, OF 93, FDRL; Memorandum, "G." to Franklin Roosevelt, June 16, 1941, Folder: Colored Matters (Negroes) June–July 1941, Box 4, OF 93, FDRL.

[84] Letter, A. Philip Randolph to Eleanor Roosevelt, June 5, 1941; www.fdrlibrary.marist.edu/_resources/images/ersel/ersel077.pdf.

[85] Letter, Eleanor Roosevelt to A. Philip Randolph, June 10, 1941; www.fdrlibrary.marist.edu/_resources/images/ersel/ersel077.pdf. See also Kenneth Robert Janken, *White: The Biographic of Walter White, Mr. NAACP*, (New York: The New Press, 2003), 255–257.

[86] Note, Eleanor Roosevelt to Robert Patterson, Undated; www.fdrlibrary.marist.edu/_resources/images/ersel/ersel077.pdf. In response, Patterson sent her a three-page memorandum describing efforts to improve the racial policies of the War Department. Memorandum, Robert Patterson to Eleanor Roosevelt, June 13, 1941; www.fdrlibrary.marist.edu/_resources/images/ersel/ersel077.pdf.

[87] Garfinkel, *When Negroes March*, 60.

[88] Goodwin, *No Ordinary Time*, 252.

When Roosevelt looked to White, thinking that Randolph was bluffing (and he probably was), White nonetheless backed up Randolph's number. The president eventually agreed, and the drafting of the order began.[89]

The War Department objected. On June 24, Patterson and Under Secretary of the Navy James Forrestal sent a memorandum to the president regarding the coming executive order. "While we are in sympathy with the policy, we are not in favor of this step," they wrote. They gave five reasons for the department's objection: first, the order "would be a dead letter" in the South; second, since some labor unions discriminated against black workers, contractors working under a closed shop with such unions had no choice in the matter; third, contractors might fear litigation and not make bids on war contracts; fourth, it would be difficult to administer, as the "[t]he only effective remedy for breach would be cancellation of the contract," which he argued would be "most unwise" in the case of "munitions urgently needed" for the war effort; and fifth, "prejudices might be aroused, rather than allayed, by such a measure," and the "substantial progress toward eliminating prejudice might suffer a setback." If such an order were administered, however, they suggested that the language be toned down. "[W]e suggest that the clause be to the effect that the contractor will observe, so far as practical and consistent with the expeditious performance of the work, the policy of the Government that there be no discrimination because of race, creed, or color," he said. "Any board set up to hear grievances should not have the power to direct cancellation of any defense contract."[90]

This time the War Department lost out, at least initially. The executive order was released the next day, and debates ensued about what the order would mean in practice.[91] Civil rights leaders were initially quite celebratory. This attitude later turned slightly more cynical, as many activists felt

---

[89] Bynum indicates it was La Guardia who convinced the others that he was "rather confident" Randolph wouldn't cancel the march unless they could "work out something definite and specific...to deal effectively with this problem." Cornelius L. Bynum, *A. Philip Randolph and the Struggle for Civil Rights*, (Urbana: University of Illinois Press, 2010), 173.

[90] Memorandum, Robert Patterson to Franklin Roosevelt, June 24, 1941, Folder: Colored Matters (Negroes) June–July 1941, Box 4, OF 93; FDRL.

[91] Franklin D. Roosevelt: "Executive Order 8802 – Reaffirming Policy of Full Participation in the Defense Program by All Persons, Regardless of Race, Creed, Color, or National Origin, and Directing Certain Action in Furtherance of Said Policy," June 25, 1941. Online by Gerhard Peters and John T. Woolley, The American Presidency Project. www.presidency.ucsb.edu/ws/?pid=16134.

the committee would not live up to its potential.[92] On August 20, Mark Ethridge wrote to Stephen Early. "As you know, the Negroes wanted the executive order as a sort of second Emancipation Proclamation. They wanted the setup entirely outside of OPM with La Guardia as chairman and, I suppose, somebody like Winston Churchill would have satisfied them as executive secretary," he stated. "I think the agitators had got themselves into such a position with a threatened march that they wanted to make the abandonment of the march appear to come as the result of a great victory."[93]

Implementation and enforcement of the order proved to be a challenge. The committee on fair employment practices was initially set up in the Office of Production Management (OPM). The war, which had provided the necessary context to achieve the victory, soon came to be used as a cudgel against enforcement of the very order. Congressional pressure – combined with his full attention turning to the war effort – led Roosevelt to transfer the FEPC to the War Manpower Commission and place it under the control of Paul McNutt, which Randolph believed weakened its powers considerably.[94] In 1942, McNutt suspended hearings into railroad discrimination, which had been opposed by a powerful coalition of white southerners and northern industrialists, a move heavily criticized by FEPC advocates.[95] In February 1943, McNutt convened a

---

[92] In this way, there is some similarity to the Department of Justice's Civil Rights Section (CRS). Lovell describes a wide array of letters from ordinary Americans asking the CRS for help, usually to be told that the organization did not have the capacity to offer such assistance as they had requested. Lovell, *This Is Not Civil Rights*.

[93] Letter, Mark Ethridge to Stephen Early, August 20, 1941, Folder: Colored Matters (Negroes) Aug–Dec 1941, Box 4, OF 93, FDRL. Indeed, Randolph had referred to the FEPC as a "new Emancipation Proclamation." Bynum, *A. Philip Randolph and the Struggle for Civil Rights*, 179. Mary Beth Bethune wrote to Eleanor Roosevelt that she was "happy that we were able to ward off the March on Washington," and praised the order as the most "memorable day" since Lincoln signed the Emancipation Proclamation. Kirby, *Black Americans in the Roosevelt Era*, 119.

[94] Bynum, *A. Philip Randolph and the Struggle for Civil Rights*, 177–178. For a discussion of congressional maneuvering, see Will Maslow, "FEPC: A Case Study in Parliamentary Maneuver," *University of Chicago Law Review* 13(4), 1946, 407–444.

[95] Bynum, *A. Philip Randolph and the Struggle for Civil Rights*, 178. In May 1943, Roosevelt issued Executive Order 9346, creating a new FEPC with explicit authorization to conduct "investigations and hearings." Franklin D. Roosevelt: "Executive Order 9346 Establishing a Committee on Fair Employment Practice," May 27, 1943. Online by Gerhard Peters and John T. Woolley, The American Presidency Project. www.presidency.ucsb.edu/ws/?pid=16404. For an examination of the amended FEPC's railway investigations, see Alexa B. Henderson, "FEPC and the Southern Railway Case: An Investigation into the Discriminatory Practices of Railroads During World War II," *Journal of Negro History* 61(2), 1976, 173–187.

meeting to discuss their concerns. If the FEPC did not take a more active stance against discrimination, Walter White told him, "all that we are fighting for in this war is going to be lost."[96]

The war, here, brought up a new issue – discrimination in the defense industry – and in so doing it prompted perhaps the only real civil rights achievement of the Roosevelt presidency. Yet this accomplishment was limited in at least two ways. The specific order was weakened by mixed sentiments in the executive branch, which naturally led to discretion in implementation. More broadly, by focusing so intensely on the defense industry – a rhetorically convenient site in the context of the war – employment discrimination protections were applied narrowly rather than broadly. While there is no polling data on Roosevelt's FEPC executive order, the postwar evidence on state fair employment legislation suggests that white attitudes were not supportive.[97] It is perhaps no surprise, then, that this limited victory came via unilateral executive action, was applied only to a subset of workers tied directly to the war effort, and was never made permanent through the legislative process.

Although the wartime FEPC would not be as powerful as advocates had hoped, it would nonetheless provide a model for civil rights advocacy going forward.[98] In September 1943, Randolph formed the National Council for a Permanent FEPC. They were, in their own statement, "keenly aware of the limited powers and transiency of this wartime agency" and "felt it was necessary to give it a permanent legislative base."[99] Anthony Chen argues that this (ultimately unsuccessful) effort to save the wartime FEPC "served as a catalyst for grass-roots mobilization" and "spurred a wider range of liberal interest groups to collaborate more closely with each other – in the name of civil rights – than ever before in the twentieth century." While a permanent FEPC was never passed in Congress, the experience with the wartime FEPC

---

[96] Bynum, *A. Philip Randolph and the Struggle for Civil Rights*, 182.
[97] See Chapter 2. See also Anthony S. Chen, *The Fifth Freedom: Jobs, Politics, and Civil Rights in the United States, 1941–1972*, (Princeton: Princeton University Press, 2009).
[98] The historian Kevin Schultz describes the wartime FEPC as "[b]orn out of guilt, undernourished as a child, and dead at the age of five." However, he argues that "the FEPC cause lived on long after the war" and "helped create and sustain a coalition of civil rights liberals." Kevin M. Schultz, "The FEPC and the Legacy of the Labor-Based Civil Rights Movement of the 1940s," *Labor History* 49(1), 2008, 71. For an empirical analysis of the wartime FEPC's effectiveness, see William J. Collins, "Race, Roosevelt, and Wartime Production: Fair Employment in World War II Labor Markets," *American Economic Review* 91(1), 2001, 272–286.
[99] Bynum, *A. Philip Randolph and the Struggle for Civil Rights*, 183.

led to "a specific regulatory ideal and concrete legislative program" for the immediate postwar period.[100]

CONCLUSION

Although most executive branch officials would have preferred to ignore the issue entirely, especially during wartime, civil rights leaders were able to force their demands onto the policy agenda during World War II. The actual policy outcomes, however, were mixed. Despite their efforts, Roosevelt sided with the War Department in favor of maintaining racial segregation in the armed forces, even in a war waged in part against Nazi Germany. Civil rights leaders had more success with job discrimination in the defense industry after the threat of a March on Washington successfully pressured the president to sign an executive order on this issue.

There is little reason to think that President Roosevelt would have issued an executive order to combat job discrimination of any sort in the absence of this wartime activism, which in turn reflected strategic decisions by civil rights leaders to use both the war's logic and labor requirements to their advantage. The war, in this sense, was a compelling force, much to the chagrin of many executive branch officials. Yet the war had constraining effects for civil rights activism as well. In the midst of the war, Roosevelt sided with the War Department over civil rights advocates on the issue of segregation in the armed forces, deferring to their judgment that integration would hinder rather than help the war effort. Their understanding of what the exigencies of war required won out over the arguments of civil rights advocates that integration would lead to a more effective force. Even though the war's ideological logic was helpful for activists, then, in the case of military segregation this was not sufficient for change to occur.

The World War II–era civil rights movement's strategies also offered a preview of the Cold War's tendency to constrain the rhetoric and aims of the movement in the decades that followed. On the one hand, the Double-V campaign allowed them to link their agenda to the goals of the war, which was undoubtedly helpful in some areas. Activists, however, felt compelled to tone down more radical claims. Some even felt the need to preempt criticism from moderates. For example, on June 8, 1942, A. Philip Randolph wrote Mary McLeod Bethune. "May I also

[100] Chen, *The Fifth Freedom*, 33.

say that the meetings which we are holding are not in any way intended to hinder the war. I want to see the war won by the United Nations and the wiping out of Hitler, Hirohito, and Mussolini," he told her. "But I think it is proper for Negroes to insist upon their democratic rights of being permitted to play their part in the Army, Navy, Air and Marine Corps, defense industries, and the government as equals with the White people in this country. This will help rather than weaken America in the prosecution of the war."[101] If a particular civil rights strategy could credibly be claimed to be hindering the execution of the war, it would have immediately been less persuasive to political elites. Advocates, then, had to frame their demands both ideologically and practically, showing the consistency of their arguments with the success of the war effort.

The Truman administration would present new challenges and surprising opportunities for civil rights advocates. While some were initially skeptical of the Missourian, Truman would eventually sign two important executive orders dealing with civil rights, one establishing a committee to study the issue, and then, after congressional inaction on its policy proposals, a second that would begin the gradual process of integrating the armed forces. As the next chapter describes, however, this was not a move that the military establishment welcomed with open arms.

---

[101] Letter, A. Philip Randolph to Mary McLeod Bethune, June 8, 1942, Folder: March on Washington Movement, Correspondence, A-B 1942, Box 26, A. Philip Randolph Papers, LOC.

5

The Truman Administration, Military Service, and Postwar Civil Rights

In the midst of debates about President Truman's proposed civil rights package, Mary Jane Truman – the president's sister – told a North Carolina reporter, "Harry is no more for nigger equality than any of us." Around the same time, Truman replied to a letter from a concerned southern Democrat. Acknowledging that he understood the concerns of the white South, he nonetheless proceeded to defend his civil rights stance. He pointed to the role of military service as a particularly powerful justification. "But my very stomach turned over when I learned that Negro soldiers, just back from overseas, were being dumped out of army trucks in Mississippi and beaten," he wrote. "Whatever my inclinations as a native of Missouri might have been, as President I know this is bad." Then, in a moralistic tone common in his rhetoric, Truman concluded, "I shall fight to end evils like this."[1]

Like many white Missourians of his time, Truman possessed more than his fair share of racial prejudice. Although the state itself was technically midwestern, his hometown of Independence was, according to his most prominent biographer, "pervadingly southern – Antebellum Old South, unreconstructed."[2] Later, during his presidency, when his daughter Margaret jokingly asked her grandmother if she wanted to sleep in Lincoln's bed, the president's mother declared with disgust that given the option she would prefer to sleep on the floor.[3] In early courtship letters to Elizabeth Wallace – the eventual First Lady Bess Truman – Truman

---

[1] David McCullough, *Truman*, (New York: Simon & Schuster, 1992), 588.
[2] Ibid., 53.
[3] Ibid., 385.

casually used a wide range of racial slurs.[4] Such habits of speech would not disappear entirely even by the time he became president.[5] In the later years of Truman's life, he was even critical of the civil rights movement of the 1950s and 1960s, especially tactics like sit-ins and marches, which he considered lawlessness.[6]

Yet, during the Truman administration, civil rights leaders found more support for their policy goals than they had seen under any previous Democratic administration. When Truman was preparing to leave office in January 1953, Roy Wilkins – who would succeed Walter White to become executive secretary of the NAACP just two years later – wrote him a letter. "I want to thank you and to convey to you my admiration for your efforts in the civil rights field, for your pronouncements and definitions of policy on racial and religious discrimination and segregation," he wrote. "Mr. President, no Chief Executive in our history has spoken so plainly on this matter as yourself, or acted so forthrightly."[7] While the letter's tone was perhaps partly deference to the executive office, it is hard to imagine Wilkins writing the same letter to Roosevelt.

What explains the Truman administration's more supportive response to civil rights advocacy? Perhaps the most common explanation is electoral pressure as a result of black migration out of the southern states. While 77 percent of African Americans lived in the South in 1940, this number had declined to 68 percent by the end of World War II.[8] African

---

[4] In one letter, he declared, "One man was as good as another, so long as he's honest and decent and not a nigger or a Chinaman." Later, in reference to his uncle, Truman wrote, "He sure does hate Chinks and Japs. So do I. It is race prejudice I guess. But I am strongly of the opinion that negroes ought to be in Africa, yellow men in Asia, and white men in Europe and America." Ibid., 83–88.

[5] He still used racial slurs privately, "as if that were the way one naturally referred to blacks." Ibid., 588. When Adam Clayton Powell protested First Lady Bess Truman's decision to accept an invitation to tea with the Daughters of the American Revolution, he was referred to as "that damn nigger preacher" in a Cabinet meeting. Ibid., 576.

[6] This, too, provides an interesting connection between Truman's thought and trends among white veterans described in Chapter 3.

[7] Letter, Roy Wilkins to Harry Truman, January 12, 1953, Folder: OF 596: July 1950–53, Box 1666, White House Central Files, Official File, Harry S. Truman Papers (hereafter Truman Papers), Harry S. Truman Library, Independence, Missouri (hereafter HSTL).

[8] Morton Sosna, "Introduction," in *Remaking Dixie: The Impact of World War II on the American South*, ed. Neil R. McMillen, (Jackson: University Press of Mississippi, 1997), xv. This trend was especially notable among black veterans. More than half of black World War II veterans who served during their twenties lived in a different region

Americans who left the South disproportionately went to states with strong city machine politics. Tom Pendergast, the boss of Kansas City who introduced Harry Truman into Democratic political office, "was perhaps the first of the Democratic bosses to win over the new urban blacks," according to John Frederick Martin, "and he did so in a state where the Klan was a power in politics."[9] This northern migration led to the development of a theory that black voters represented the "balance of power" in several closely contested swing states.[10] Indeed, some within Truman's inner circles saw the black vote as critical for his 1948 reelection hopes. In a confidential report, James Rowe wrote approvingly of the notion that "the northern Negro vote today holds the balance of power in Presidential elections for the simple arithmetical reason that Negroes not only vote in a block but are geographically concentrated in the pivotal, large and closely contested electoral states such as New York, Illinois, Pennsylvania, Ohio, and Michigan."[11]

Another explanation, which complements the previous one, is the growing linkage between economic and racial liberalism in the ideologies of northern state Democratic parties by the postwar era.[12] Pro–civil rights unionism played a key role in this, particularly the interracial vision of union leadership provided by the Congress of Industrial Organizations (CIO). Other white-led interest groups also came to support civil rights, including Americans for Democratic Action, an organization that played a key role in pressuring party delegates to adopt a more liberal civil rights plank at the 1948 Democratic National Convention, in turn prompting a number of Deep South delegates to walk out in protest.[13] The result of all this was the emergence of a nonsouthern, racially liberal

---

than they were born into by 1950, compared to a third of otherwise similar nonveterans. John Modell, Marc Goulden, and Sigurdur Magnusson, "World War II in the Lives of Black Americans: Some Findings and an Interpretation," *Journal of American History* 76(3), 1989, 839.

[9] John Frederick Martin, *Civil Rights and the Crisis of Liberalism: The Democratic Party 1945–1976*, (Boulder: Westview Press, 1979), 50.

[10] Henry Lee Moon, *Balance of Power: The Negro Vote*, (Garden City, NY: Doubleday, 1948).

[11] McCullough, *Truman*, 590.

[12] On the linking of economic and racial liberalism, see Eric Schickler, *Racial Realignment: The Transformation of American Liberalism, 1932–1965*, (Princeton: Princeton University Press, 2016).

[13] Steven M. Gillon, *Politics and Vision: The ADA and American Liberalism, 1947–1985*, (New York: Oxford University Press, 1987); Kari A. Frederickson., *The Dixiecrat Revolt and the End of the Solid South, 1932–1968*, (Chapel Hill: University of North Carolina Press, 2001).

Democratic coalition that could credibly challenge the power of the party's white southern bloc, thereby creating genuine pressure for a more pro–civil rights stance among party leaders.

While not downplaying these important factors, this chapter emphasizes the contextual role played by World War II and its aftermath. Given the rise of a more racially liberal Democratic Party outside the South, it is not, at least in retrospect, surprising that something happened on civil rights at all. These factors in themselves, however, cannot explain the often rather military-centric nature of Truman-era civil rights reforms. Arguably the most important civil rights accomplishment of the Truman era was the executive order that led to the gradual integration of the armed forces. Along with this, there was also a proposal by the president's civil rights committee to prohibit discrimination in public accommodations, but only against military veterans. Although this was never implemented, it does further illustrate the particular concern the Truman administration had with protecting black soldiers and veterans rather than African Americans more generally.

These policy outcomes were the result of a variety of struggles inside the executive branch bureaucracy, particularly between actors sympathetic to civil rights and military officials leery of, and in some cases adamantly opposed to, changes to the policy of segregation. Sympathetic presidential assistants, as well as members of two prominent committees established by the president to study civil rights issues, played a key role in providing a pathway for civil rights leaders to finally achieve their goal of moving the military towards racial integration. Such figures were ultimately able to successfully challenge military officials committed to the status quo, contrary to what had happened in the Roosevelt administration. Absent Truman's support, however, these committees would have had little influence, and indeed might not have even existed in the first place. To a much greater extent than in the Roosevelt chapter, then, Truman's own multifaceted understanding of civil rights politics plays an important role here.

While Truman's racial attitudes were certainly formed in part by his Missouri upbringing, his military service in World War I seems to have mediated those views somewhat. Truman's wartime experience was, by his own account, the defining experience of his life. Alonzo Hamby writes that "[t]here should be little wonder that throughout his life Truman valued his military comrades above most other acquaintances;

they were, after all, reminders of his most satisfying experience."[14] This personal experience seems to have shaped his response to accounts of violence against black veterans of World War II. Note, for instance, the vivid language, quoted at the beginning of this chapter, Truman used to describe his reaction to "Negro soldiers, just back from overseas," being beaten in Mississippi. Truman was not sympathetic to more extensive liberal arguments about universal rights, but republican claims about rights earned via military service had a greater emotional resonance for him.[15]

The particular concern about mistreatment of black veterans overlapped in important ways with Truman's approach to making value judgments. Roosevelt, according to David McCullough, "loved the subtleties of human relations" and was "sensitive to nuances in a way Harry Truman never was." Because of his rural background and limited education (he is the most recent president not to have graduated from college), McCullough argues Truman "was inclined to see things in far simpler terms, as right or wrong, wise or foolish."[16] This black-or-white, right-or-wrong sensibility provides a useful analytical lens. It allowed Truman to see violence against black veterans and vow to fight "evils like this," yet it also left him influenced by traditions, including the tradition of "social segregation" in society more broadly.[17]

---

[14] Hamby describes Truman's military experience as "enormously beneficial for his sagging self-esteem." Alonzo L. Hamby, "An American Democrat: A Reevaluation of the Personality of Harry S. Truman," *Political Science Quarterly* 106(1), 1991, 40–41.

[15] This also provides a useful vantage point for statements like the one by Roy Wilkins, who, reflecting on the differences between Truman and Roosevelt later in life, said, "I feel that Truman was a friend of civil rights and he wanted to do the fair thing." Reminiscences of Roy Wilkins (1960), in the Oral History Research Office Collection of the Columbia University Libraries. In the context of the times, "fairness" did not necessarily mean full liberal equality, but rather a more limited recognition of certain rights derived from service. If military service endowed black soldiers with the right to serve with white men and not to be beaten or lynched when they returned home, it did not necessarily follow, for Truman, that they also deserved the full range of citizenship rights in a liberal polity. In this way, Truman's commitments were primarily focused on the rights of *civil* citizenship described by Marshall. See Chapter 1.

[16] McCullough continues: "He dealt little in abstractions. His answers to questions, even complicated questions, were nearly always direct and assured, plainly said, and followed often by a conclusive 'And that's all there is to it,' an old Missouri expression, when in truth there may have been a great more 'to it'." McCullough, *Truman*, 325.

[17] For a discussion of "political" versus "social" rights in this time period, see this contemporaneous discussion in *Public Opinion Quarterly*, which noted, "In general, more respondents favored granting additional rights in the political than in the social realm."

In this chapter, I begin by describing how civil rights leaders succeeded in bringing news of violence against returning black veterans into the Truman White House, in turn prompting the president to establish a committee to study civil rights. The committee eventually released an influential report on the topic, which included a list of policy proposals. I then describe how, after it became apparent that Congress was not going to act, Truman eventually issued an executive order that would start the process of integrating the armed forces. Along with providing background information on discussions of military racial policy in the war's immediate aftermath, I analyze the hearings of the committee tasked with figuring out a way to implement the order in the face of opposition within the military. I conclude the chapter by reflecting on the ways in which World War II is critical for making sense of the civil rights record of both the Roosevelt and Truman administrations, albeit in different ways.

BLACK VETERANS, WHITE VIOLENCE, AND THE PCCR

In September 1946, Philleo Nash, a presidential assistant known to be supportive of civil rights, received a newspaper clipping. The story began:

> The flat, unemotional voice of Isaac Woodward, Jr., does not change when he says, "Then the cop gouged out both my eyes with the end of his billy stick." Sitting in his parents' apartment at 1100 Franklin Ave., Bronx, the 27-year-old Negro veteran was telling how South Carolina, his home state, welcomed him back from the war.

Claude Dahmer, Jr. and Elliott McGinnies, "Shifting Sentiments Toward Civil Rights in a Southern University," *Public Opinion Quarterly* 13(2), 1949, 241. While Truman's civil right legacy is linked, perhaps above all else, with the desegregation of the armed services, Truman was not an antisegregationist. "I wish to make it clear that I am not appealing for social equality of the Negro," Truman had told the National Colored Democratic Association in 1940. "The Negro himself knows better than that, and the highest types of Negro leaders say quite frankly that they prefer the society of their own people. Negroes want justice, not social relations." Truman, however, was not of a similar mind with the most committed of white supremacists in the US Senate like Theodore Bilbo. In his election announcement earlier that year, Truman declared, "I believe in the brotherhood of man; not merely the brotherhood of white men; but the brotherhood of all men before the law." William C. Berman, *The Politics of Civil Rights in the Truman Administration*, (Columbus: Ohio State University Press, 1970), 12.

As if not expecting you to take his word for it, Woodward takes off his dark glasses to show you his sightless eyes. He says they were made that way by an Aiken, S.C., cop last Feb. 13, five hours after Woodward had been handed his honorable discharge papers, and while he was still in Army uniform.[18]

The case of Sergeant Isaac Woodard – often misspelled as "Woodward" by journalists at the time – is perhaps the most striking example of the role violence against black veterans played in shaping the Truman administration's civil rights agenda.[19] Although the case did not reach the attention of individuals in the executive branch until September, the story began much earlier in the year. On February 12, 1946, Woodard was traveling on a Greyhound bus from Georgia's Camp Gordon to see his family in North Carolina. When the bus stopped just outside Augusta, Woodard went to use a restroom. At some point, the driver called local police and described Woodard as drunk and disorderly. Police officers – including the Chief of Police – beat him with nightsticks, arrested him, and left him in jail overnight.[20] In the attack, Woodard "suffered bleeding of both eyeballs, and breaking of the cornea in the right eye."[21] He was never able to see again.

The Woodard case eventually captured the attention of national civil rights organizations as well as black newspapers. The *Chicago Defender* was clear in its condemnation. "Though the Negro veterans of World War II fought to save this country from Hiterlism and its racial implications," the article read, "he has a greater battle yet to fight to win for himself the status of an American citizen, said Isaac Woodard Jr., veteran of overseas service whose eyes were gouged out in February by race-hating South Carolina cops."[22]

---

[18] *PM* Clipping, Folder: Lynching – Woodard [Woodward], Isaac, Box 45; Philleo Nash Papers (hereafter Nash Papers), HSTL.

[19] For statements suggesting this violence played a role in Truman's behavior, see Martin, *Civil Rights and the Crisis of Liberalism*, 78; Klinkner and Smith, *The Unsteady March*, 202–203, 207. "It began with the returning black veterans of World War II," presidential assistant Philleo Nash later declared. See Memorandum, Philleo Nash to Clark Clifford, undated, Folder: Civil Rights [2001 accretion], Box 113, George M. Elsey Papers, HSTL.

[20] This is the rough outline, but as Klinkner and Smith note, "[a]ccounts of the Woodard beating vary." Klinkner and Smith, *The Unsteady March*, 385f1.

[21] "POLICE CHIEF FREED IN NEGRO BEATING: Federal Court Jury Acquits South Carolina Officer After Blind Veteran Accuses Him," *New York Times* (New York), November 6, 1948, Proquest Historical Newspapers.

[22] *Chicago Defender* clipping, Folder: Lynching – Woodard, [Woodward] Isaac, Box 45, Nash Papers, HSTL.

The NAACP organized a national tour featuring Woodard. As Kari Frederickson notes, unlike many previous examples where relatives of victims of racial violence had been featured, the NAACP could now "present northern audiences with a walking, breathing victim of southern racial injustice. Because Woodard was a veteran, because he was maimed, because his attacker was an officer of the law, and because he survived, he became an emblem of what was terribly wrong with the South."[23] It wasn't until the fall, however, that the Woodard case received federal attention. In September 1946, a meeting was held at the White House with the National Emergency Committee Against Mob Violence (a coalition composed of representatives from the NAACP, Urban League, Federal Council of Churches, and the American Federation of Labor).[24] When presented with stories of such violence, Truman supposedly said, "My God! I had no idea that it was as terrible as that! We have to do something."[25]

Walter White later described the meeting as indicative of an important difference between Roosevelt and Truman. "Roosevelt issued his famous Executive Order 8802 establishing a Fair Employment Practice Committee only when he was convinced that a threatened March on Washington was not a bluff," White argued. Truman, he argued, was different. "When a small delegation representing labor, church and civic groups presented to him on September 19th, 1946, the facts regarding the wave of lynchings and other antiminority practices which were then sweeping the country, Truman's face became pale with horror. His voice trembled with deep emotion as he assured us the steps must be taken immediately to stop this wave of terrorism before it got out of hand."[26] While the meeting details are filtered through White's writing style (particularly his tendency to capture dialogue in a folksy manner), it nonetheless seems to be the case that Truman was emotionally affected by the meeting.

---

[23] Frederickson, *Dixiecrat Revolt*, 56.
[24] Edith S. Riehm, "Forging the Civil Rights Frontier: How Truman's Committee Set the Liberal Agenda for Reform 1947–1965" (PhD dissertation, Georgia State University, 2002), 56.
[25] McCullough, *Truman*, 50–51. The quote, though, originates from Walter White's autobiography, so it is filtered through White's perspective. Walter White, *A Man Called White: The Autobiography of Walter White*, (New York: The Viking Press, 1948).
[26] Walter White, "The President Means It," February 12, 1948, Folder: [1948] 1949–1952, Box 26, David K. Niles Papers; (hereafter Niles Papers), HSTL.

McCullough argues that such stories of violence against black veterans "made an everlasting impression on Truman, moving him in a way no statistics ever would have."[27] Matthew Connelly, the president's press secretary, would later describe Truman as having "a special feeling for soldiers."[28] On September 20, Truman sent a memorandum to David Niles, one his advisors, attaching a copy of a letter he sent to Attorney General Tom Clark. "I am very much in earnest on this thing and I'd like very much to have you push it with everything you have," Truman wrote to Niles. "I had as callers yesterday some members of the National Association for the Advancement of Colored People and they told me about an incident which happened in South Carolina where a negro Sergeant, who had been discharged from the Army just three hours, was taken off the bus and not only seriously beaten but his eyes deliberately put out, and that the Mayor of the town had bragged about committing this outrage," Truman wrote in the letter to Clark. "I have been very much alarmed at the increased racial feeling all over the country," he continued, and proposed appointing a commission to study the topic and present policy solutions to the next Congress.[29]

With the Attorney General's support, Truman signed an executive order establishing the President's Committee on Civil Rights (PCCR) on December 5, 1946.[30] The 15-member committee included representatives from business, labor, universities, and religious organizations,

---

[27] McCullough, *Truman*, 589. Truman seems to have been affected by other incidents of postwar violence as well. In an interview with Robert Goe, one of Truman's assistants in composing his memoirs, Truman referred to "that sheriff in Georgia, who lined up these four Negroes and shot them. Nothing was ever done about it... and that's what set me back on my heels, and I was raised unreconstructed." Interview with President Truman, Folder: Domestic Policy – Civil Rights, Box 643, Harry S. Truman Post-Presidential Papers, HSTL. He also seems to have been concerned about anti-Japanese American violence as well. In December 1945, Eleanor Roosevelt forwarded Truman a letter she had received regarding this subject. "This disgraceful conduct almost makes you believe that a lot of our Americans have a streak of Nazi in them," he wrote back. Alonzo L. Hamby, *Beyond the New Deal: Harry S. Truman and American Liberalism*, (New York: Columbia University Press, 1973), 65.

[28] Frederickson, *Dixiecrat Revolt*, 56.

[29] Memorandum, Harry Truman to David Niles, September 20, 1946, Folder: 1945–June, 1947 [2 of 2], Box 26, Niles Papers, HSTL; Letter, Harry Truman to Tom Clark, September 20, 1946, Folder: 1945–June, 1947 [2 of 2], Box 26, Niles Papers, HSTL.

[30] Harry S. Truman: "Executive Order 9808 – Establishing the President's Committee on Civil Rights," December 5, 1946. Online by Gerhard Peters and John T. Woolley, The American Presidency Project. www.presidency.ucsb.edu/ws/?pid=60711.

among others.³¹ It was broken up into three subcommittees: one to address legislation, one to "consider the broader aspects of the problem," and one to "consider any other related aspects of the civil rights problem."³²

After nine months of meetings from January to September 1947, the PCCR sent Truman its final report on October, 27, 1947.³³ In its "program of action," the report argued there were moral, economic, and international reasons for acting. "The United States is not so strong," the report declared, "the final triumph of the democratic ideal is not so inevitable that we can ignore what the world thinks of us or our record."³⁴ The report then used language that would come to be familiar during the Cold War. "The international reason for acting to secure our civil rights now is not to win the approval of our totalitarian critics," the report declared. "We would not expect it if our record were spotless; to them our civil rights record is only a convenient weapon with which to attack us. Certainly we would like to deprive them of that weapon. But we are more concerned with the good opinion of the peoples of the world."³⁵

---

³¹ The full committee was Sadie T. Alexander (a black lawyer, who was also the first African American woman to receive a PhD in the United States), James B. Carey (Secretary-Treasurer of the CIO), John S. Dickey (President of Dartmouth College), Morris L. Ernst (an anti-communist leader of the American Civil Liberties Union), Rabbi Roland B. Gittelsohn (the first Jewish chaplain in the Marine Corps), Frank P. Graham (president of the University of North Carolina and later senator from North Carolina), Reverend Francis J. Haas (bishop of the Roman Catholic Diocese of Grand Rapids, Michigan, who had previously served on Roosevelt's Committee on Fair Employment Practice), Charles Luckman (businessman), Francis P. Matthews (Director of the Department of Finance in the US Chamber of Commerce [and later Secretary of the Navy]), Franklin D. Roosevelt, Jr. (the former president's son), Reverend Henry Knox Sherrill (an Episcopal clergyman in Massachusetts), Boris Shishkin (an economist with the American Federation of Labor), Dorothy Tilly (a southern activist who favored a more gradual pace for reform), Channing H. Tobias (a black civil rights activist affiliated with the YMCA until 1946, when he became director of the Phelps-Stokes Fund), and Charles E. Wilson (CEO of General Electric) who served as Chairman. Robert K. Carr (a government professor at Dartmouth College) was Executive Secretary.

³² Riehm, "Forging the Civil Rights Frontier," 61.

³³ Notably, the report was actually written by the PCCR staff rather than the members themselves. The staff were generally supportive of federal protection for civil rights, which was reflected in the language of the text. Ibid., 62.

³⁴ President's Committee on Civil Rights, *To Secure These Rights: The Report of the President's Committee on Civil Rights*, (Washington, DC: US Government Printing Office, 1947), www.trumanlibrary.org/civilrights/srights4.htm, 148.

³⁵ President's Committee on Civil Rights, *To Secure These Rights*, 148.

The PCCR's legislative agenda was wide-ranging. Among other policy proposals, the report recommended changes in federal and state law enforcement to "strengthen the machinery for the protection of civil rights," a congressional antilynching bill to "strengthen the right to safety and security of the person," an end to poll taxes and federal protection for voting in national elections to "strengthen the right to citizenship and its privileges," and an end to "separate but equal" and a federal FEPC to "strengthen the right to equality of opportunity."[36]

Importantly for my focus here, the PCCR also made two policy recommendations related to black military service within the category of strengthening "the right to citizenship and its privileges." The report was direct in its condemnation of military segregation, calling for "[t]he enactment by Congress of legislation, followed by appropriate administrative action, to end immediately all discrimination and segregation based on race, color, creed, or national origin, in the organization and activities of all branches of the Armed Services." Their reasoning was twofold. First, "[t]he injustice of calling men to fight for freedom while subjecting them to humiliating discrimination within the fighting forces is at once apparent." This argument was more ideological. Second, "by preventing entire groups from making their maximum contribution to the national defense, we weaken our defense to that extent and impose heavier burdens on the remainder of the population." This argument, by contrast, was more practical. On similar grounds, they referred to the postwar structure of the US military. "The Committee believes that the recent unification of the armed forces provides a timely opportunity for the revision of present policy and practice. A strong enunciation of future policy should be made condemning discrimination and segregation within the armed services."[37] A combination of arguments based on ideology and efficiency, then, set the groundwork for a broader debate about integrating the armed forces.

The report, however, did not stop at military segregation. The PCCR also advocated for "[t]he enactment by Congress of legislation providing that no member of the armed forces shall be subject to discrimination of any kind by any public authority or place of public accommodation, recreation, transportation, or other service or business." This seems more specifically directed to incidents like the Woodard case – and, notably,

[36] Ibid., 151–173.
[37] Ibid., 162–163.

was a proposal only for men who had served in the war, not African Americans generally. Their reasoning was as follows: "The government of a nation has an obligation to protect the dignity of the uniform of its armed services. The esteem of the government itself is impaired when affronts to its armed forces are tolerated. The government also has a responsibility for the well-being of those who surrender some of the privileges of citizenship to serve in the defense establishments."[38] The proposal itself likely would have been difficult to implement. It is difficult to imagine a variant of Jim Crow where black veterans were treated with equality with respect to public accommodations, while otherwise similar nonveterans were not. Nonetheless, the proposal is interesting in its own right as a reflection of the thinking of white liberals close to Truman. Their arguments fall in line with a long association between military service and republican claims on citizenship rights, an association that was very powerful for Truman and his allies.[39]

Whether Truman expected such a forthright statement from the report is unclear.[40] Later in life, though, Truman stood by the report, and pointed to postwar racial violence as a motivating factor in establishing the committee. "I took this action because of the repeated anti-minority incidents immediately after the war in which homes were invaded, property destroyed, and a number of innocent lives were taken," he stated.[41] While political pressures played a substantial role in forcing some action rather than no action, such calculations in themselves say little about the particular form the Truman administration's actions took. Considered in combination with Truman and his allies' understanding of the relationship between military service and rights claims, however, the

---

[38] Ibid., 163.

[39] It is possible, though, that rather than recognizing veterans as meriting special rights, it was instead a response to greater threats posed by white supremacists against black veterans.

[40] Klinkner and Smith are more positive towards Truman. "Truman seems to have hoped that the committee's work would help make public opinion more receptive to his civil right proposals," they write. "Thus he urged its members to come up with a strong report." Klinkner and Smith, *The Unsteady March*, 211. Klinkner and Smith draw here on William E. Juhnke, "President Truman's Committee on Civil Rights: The Interaction of Politics, Protest, and Presidential Advisory Commission," *Presidential Studies Quarterly* 19, 1989. William Berman is more negative. "In all probability *To Secure These Rights* went far beyond anything Truman and his advisors had in mind when they initially commission an investigation of the problems created by the racial violence of 1945 and 1946," he argues. See Berman, *The Politics of Civil Rights in the Truman Administration*, 70–71.

[41] Ibid., 57.

form of the Truman administration's civil rights actions is made more explicable.

Congressional liberals generally reacted favorably. Senator Irving Ives, a liberal Republican from New York, declared the report would be "very helpful when the legislation comes up" in Congress. Illinois Democrat Scott Lucas said the country had to recognize the moral issues raised in the report "sooner or later and the sooner the better." Many prominent newspapers in northern cities expressed their approval, with the *Washington Post*, for example, running several positive editorials and opinion pieces. The *New York Times* also praised the report, but with more cynicism than the *Post* had offered in its write-ups, noting the likelihood a Senate filibuster would inhibit meaningful congressional action.[42]

Black newspapers were also generally approving in their coverage of the report, with the *Chicago Defender* calling it a "new blueprint for freedom." The *Pittsburgh Courier* emphasized the significance of "the first time that an official body, commissioned by the President of the United States, has made such well-considered and far-reaching suggestions for the implementation of American democracy."[43] Both Walter White and A. Philip Randolph praised the report, although Randolph had previously expressed public concern it wouldn't go far enough prior to its release.[44]

The reaction in the white South was one of outrage, particularly in the Deep South. Mississippi provides perhaps the strongest example. Acting Governor Oscar Wolfe was particularly incensed by the antisegregation arguments. "[H]istory shows that where any nation has not practiced segregation of races, but allowed miscegenation and amalgamation of races, the custom has always resulted in the destruction of the nation that permitted this crime against nature," he told reporters.[45] The Mississippi House of Representatives issued a House Concurrent Resolution "Memorializing the Congress of the United States of the Grave Apprehension and Vigorous opposition of the people of this state to

---

[42] William E. Juhnke, "Creating a New Charter of Freedom: The Organization and Operation of the President's Committee on Civil Rights, 1946–48," (PhD dissertation, University of Kansas, 1974), 195. Not all nonsouthern urban newspapers were positive. The *Los Angeles Times*, for example, called the report's recommendations "drastic" and "antagonistic." Ibid., 198.

[43] Juhnke, "Creating a New Charter of Freedom," 196.

[44] Ibid., 195.

[45] Riehm, "Forging the Civil Rights Frontier," 179.

the recommendations of President Truman's Committee on Civil Rights, and urging opposition to Any Congressional enactment of Said Recommendations."[46] John Stennis – who would win his first Senate term later that year after Bilbo's death – was more measured, but nonetheless opposed. "Our customs and traditions may be assailed," he said, "but we can stand firm in our rights to make our decisions about such matters."[47] Although Mississippi is perhaps the strongest case, white opposition extended throughout the entire region, with newspapers from Birmingham to Charlotte publishing critical op-eds.[48]

In the end, despite the fears of southern white elites and the hopes of civil rights advocates, the PCCR did not ultimately lead to major changes in public policy. On February 2, 1948, Truman sent the Congress his civil rights recommendations (a condensed, ten-part version of the PCCR report's suggestions). Southern congressmen reacted with "intense hostility" and "vitriolic defiance," with Georgia Senator William Russell telling a reporter that the proposals were "nothing more or less than an FBI Gestapo to break down race segregation in the South" and Virginia Senator Harry Byrd calling the proposals "a mass invasion of states' rights never before even suggested ... by any previous president in the nation's history."[49] Not surprisingly, considering this southern opposition and the institutional features of the Senate that privileged these members, Congress ultimately failed to enact the recommended legislation.

THE FAHY COMMITTEE AND "EQUALITY OF TREATMENT AND OPPORTUNITY"

Despite the PCCR's clear call for an end to segregation in the armed forces, discrimination in the military would never be addressed by Congress. As was described in Chapter 2, white public opinion was overwhelmingly opposed to military integration. Depending on the question wording, between 64 and 68 percent of whites opposed an integrated military when asked about it in 1948, an unlikely attitudinal context for congressional action.[50] As with fair employment, it would take

---

[46] Ibid. The reference to "the people of this state" was presumably implied to mean white people only.
[47] Ibid.
[48] Juhnke, "Creating a New Charter of Freedom," 197.
[49] Ibid., 210.
[50] See Chapter 2.

unilateral executive action for any change to occur. Truman's February 1948 civil rights message to Congress indicated as much. "During the recent war and in the years since its close we have made much progress toward equality of opportunity in our armed services without regard to race, color, religion or national origin," Truman told Congress. "I have instructed the Secretary of Defense to take steps to have the remaining instances of discrimination in the armed services eliminated as rapidly as possible. The personnel policies and practices of all the services in this regard will be made consistent."[51] Like with antidiscrimination provisions for defense contractors, segregation in the military presented a unique sector where action could take place via executive order.

Although presidents have significant authority over the military, the military establishment was not a particularly receptive audience. The War Department resisted military integration successfully during the Roosevelt presidency, and this resistance lingered into the Truman years as well. Before turning to a discussion of the committee hearings that emerged from Truman's 1948 executive order, I first provide some background on efforts between 1945 and 1948 to press the military for a more equitable utilization of black troops. An August 1945 memorandum describing the military's perception of black troops and an April 1948 meeting of the National Defense Conference on Negro Affairs provide some insights into the military's position.

On August 8, 1945, Truman Gibson, the black lawyer who had been named chief civilian advisor in the War Department by Roosevelt, wrote a memorandum that summarized the arguments being made against military integration at that time. "Since the expansion that began in 1940, the Army has been constantly faced with pressure for a change of its Negro policies," Gibson wrote. "Prior to 1940 there had been several studies into the performance of Negro troops that served as basis for the several statements and policies governing the employment of Negro personnel in the Army." The "following basic premises appear": (1) "Negroes should be segregated into separate units" because of (a) some statutes from the late 1860s that have (b) "proven satisfactory over a long period of years" and (c) "because any other policy would have social repercussions and the Army cannot 'get ahead of' the country on

---

[51] Harry S. Truman: "Special Message to the Congress on Civil Rights," February 2, 1948, online by Gerhard Peters and John T. Woolley, The American Presidency Project, www.presidency.ucsb.edu/ws/?pid=13006.

this question"; (2) "Negro soldiers are not adaptable to modern combat conditions because of certain racial characteristics" (as one commanding officer put it, "As fighting troops the Negro must be rated as second class material; this is due primarily to his inferior intelligence and lack of mental and moral qualifications"); and (3) "Negro officers have failed because of their lack of character and the inherent distrust of Negroes for Negro leadership."[52]

"The general conclusion that has resulted from these studies," Gibson wrote, "has been that the Army should use Negro troops only in segregated units; that as few Negro organizations as possible should be established and that these should be noncombatant." Gibson, however, argued that new studies were needed that did not rely on old assumptions. In particular, he advocated that an inquiry be made into "the present policy of segregation. This is the basic problem before the War Department. As indicated above all of the preceding studies have proceeded on the assumption the segregation is necessary. Experiences during this war in Army hospitals and Officer Candidate Schools and with the integrated Negro platoons in Europe certainly raise questions about the continuance of this policy which should be inquired into." Gibson finally chided the Army for its rhetoric. "It has been often stated that the Army is considerably ahead of the majority of most parts of the country in its handling of Negroes," he wrote. "Unfortunately, this statement is often used as an excuse for not changing policies. Future policy should be predicated on an assumption that civilian attitudes will not remain static."[53]

In response to Gibson's overview, Davidson Sommers, an Air Corps officer assigned to the War Department, sent a memorandum to Assistant Secretary of War John McCloy on August 28. Although Gibson's memorandum "does not call for any action on your part, it raises the question of how the Army is to handle its planning with regard to use of Negroes in the post-war period," he wrote. "It is pretty well recognized that in this field the Army has not found the right answer in terms of the most efficient use of available manpower."[54]

---

[52] Memorandum, Truman Gibson to John McCloy, August 8, 1945, Folder: McCloy Committee, Box 14, RG 220: Records of the President's Committee on Equality of Treatment and Opportunity in the Armed Services (hereafter Fahy Committee Records), HSTL.

[53] Ibid.

[54] Memorandum, Davidson Sommers to John McCloy, August 28, 1945, Folder: McCloy Committee, Box 14, Fahy Committee Records, HSTL.

Progress in the military segregation debate, though, would ultimately require outside pressure, with A. Philip Randolph again playing an important role. Despite Randolph's labor background, he "prioritized the desegregation of the armed forces over the FEPC."[55] How could the FEPC "criticize job discrimination in private industry if the federal government itself were simultaneously discriminating against Negro youth in military installations all over the world," he asked. African Americans, he said, were "more emotionally aroused" about segregation in the army "than by any other single issue," because all families were affected "through intense humiliation of their husbands, sons, brothers, and sisters in the armed forces."[56]

Along with Grant Reynolds, a former Army chaplain and unsuccessful congressional candidate, Randolph organized a Committee Against Jim Crow in Military Service and Training in November 1947. On March 30, 1948, Randolph testified before the Senate Armed Services Committee, telling those in attendance that "Negroes are in no mood to shoulder a gun for democracy abroad so long as they are denied democracy at home." He told them he would "advise Negroes to refuse to fight as slaves for a democracy they cannot possess and cannot enjoy."[57] His comments were not well received. Some reports indicate that Reynolds and Truman Gibson "almost came to blows" at the hearing.[58]

As Randolph and the Committee Against Jim Crow in Military Service and Training continued their activism, Secretary of Defense James Forrestal and the National Urban League's Lester Granger decided to form what they called a National Defense Conference on Negro Affairs. It was designed to allow representatives from civil rights organizations to advise the military on how to deal with racial problems.[59] The conference held a meeting on April 26, 1948. As a precursor to the committee formed by Truman's executive order later that summer, the meeting is

---

[55] Randolph even seemed willing to settle for the Republican version of the postwar FEPC, which lacked enforcement power (notably, Randolph had talked with Senator Taft about promoting the desegregation of the military). The recently formed NAACP-CIO coalition pressured other civil rights groups to allow the NAACP to take over the FEPC fight in light of Randolph's stance. See Baylor, "First to the Party," 126.

[56] Cornelius L. Bynum, *A. Philip Randolph and the Struggle for Civil Rights*, (Urbana: University of Illinois Press, 2010), 186, 194.

[57] Ibid., 86–187.

[58] L. D. Reddick, "The Negro Policy of the American Army Since World War II," *Journal of Negro History* 38(2), 1953, 201.

[59] Berman, *The Politics of Civil Rights in the Truman Administration*, 99.

illustrative of the tensions between the military establishment and civil rights advocates.

Kenneth Royall – the last Secretary of War and by then the first Secretary of the Army – summed up the military's perspective. "We cannot, in particularly this stage, experiment," he told the conference. "We cannot use the Army either to promote or to oppose any cause. And I want to say parenthetically that I fully recognize not only the propriety but the necessity for the Negro race to insist on the abolition of segregation. I have no lack of sympathy with it personally or from the standpoint of the Army, but it is a question of timing, and I think we are blind to the facts if we don't face it that it's a question of timing."[60]

His comments were not well received by Channing Tobias and Sadie Alexander, the two black members of the PCCR who were also in attendance at the conference. Tobias interrogated Royall's notion of what was "in the interest of National defense," while Alexander stated that African Americans might be just as concerned with "the eyes of the world in that we cannot practice right here the kind of democracy that we demand of other people" as with "protection for ourselves." Civil rights advocates, she said, were "asking for protection of the American ideal." Royall dismissed their comments as "political."[61]

As Royall's time was coming to a close, Philadelphia civil rights activist Hobson Reynolds and Howard University President Mordecai Johnson pressed further on the question of segregation. Reynolds told Royall that he was "trying to make a better non-segregated Army and to do away with segregation within the Army" rather than "making or for helping to make a better segregated Army." Johnson followed up by telling Royall the Army "has taken the pattern that exists in Mississippi and North Carolina and imposed it upon Massachusetts, Illinois, and Pennsylvania." He asked Royall whether this choice was "well advised"

---

[60] Meeting transcript, April 26, 1948, Folder: National Defense Congress on Negro Affairs (1948), Box 26, Niles Papers, HSTL. This quote can be found on p. 24. Earlier, Royall also wavered on trying to distinguish between discrimination and segregation: "It is not the intention of the Army that there be any discrimination other than such as you may think is inherent in segregation itself, and I would not be other than frank if I didn't say that there is some element of, at least from a mental standpoint, discrimination inherent in segregation, but, with that exception, there is no intention of permitting any segregation – I mean discrimination – in the Army." Ibid., 19.

[61] Ibid., 25–26.

and whether the Army had "weighed that matter seriously." Royall replied that there were "obvious ways that it has been given the most careful sort of consideration." With that, he said he would "be back any time you want me" and left the conference.[62] While interesting for what these exchanges reveal about the military's perspective on integration, the conference was ultimately ineffectual in terms of actual policy changes.

Two months later, on July 26, 1948, Truman issued Executive Order 9981 declaring that that there would be "equality of treatment and opportunity for all persons in the armed services" and establishing a President's Committee on Equality of Treatment and Opportunity in the Armed Services.[63] The seven-member committee contained representatives from business, universities, religious organizations, and civil rights advocates. Among the last group, the committee contained Lester Granger, head of the National Urban League, as well as John Sengstacke, a prominent black newspaper publisher. Former Solicitor General Charles Fahy was also a member of the committee, which came to be popularly known as the Fahy Committee. In addition to the seven official members on the committee, E. W. Kenworthy – who later went on to be a Washington correspondent for the *New York Times* – served as executive director of the staff.[64]

The committee's influence came from its structural position as a civilian agency that reported to the White House rather than to the military. While lacking enforcement powers of its own, presidential support aided the committee in achieving its goals. "I want the job done and I want to get it done in a way so everybody will be happy to cooperate to get it done," Truman told them. "Unless it is necessary to knock somebody's

---

[62] Ibid., 35–36. Johnson was not the only observer to argue that military segregation was extending southern Jim Crow to new realms of American life. As Mershon and Schlossman write, "Blacks frequently complained that the armed forces during World War II, like some New Deal programs during the 1930s, were actually extending the extreme forms of compulsory racial segregation characteristic of the Deep South to other parts of the country that did not follow such practices." Mershon and Schlossman, *Foxholes and Color Lines*, 67. In 1944, a white soldier actually wrote in to the *Chicago Defender* to complain that a colonel from the South was "bringing hate and discrimination to this wonderful state of Massachusetts." Ibid.

[63] Harry S. Truman: "Executive Order 9981 – Establishing the President's Committee on Equality of Treatment and Opportunity in the Armed Services," July 26, 1948, online by Gerhard Peters and John T. Woolley, The American Presidency Project, www.presidency.ucsb.edu/ws/?pid=60737.

[64] The full membership was Charles Fahy, Charles Luckman, Lester Granger, John H. Sengstacke, William E. Stevenson, Dwight Palmer, and Alphonsus J. Donahue.

ears down, I don't want to have to do that, but, if it becomes necessary, it can be done."[65]

The committee met over several months in early 1949. A major point of contention was whether the president's language about "equality of treatment and opportunity" meant an end to segregation, or whether these concepts might exist in a "separate but equal" framework.[66] According to Kenworthy's oral history interview, "[t]here was very little trouble with the Air Force or the Navy," but the Army proved to be a substantial challenge. The Army "entered objections every step of the way," Kenworthy remembered. When asked by the interviewer whether they were "difficult to work with," Kenworthy replied in the affirmative. "They were impossible!," he replied. "You had to cram it down their throat."[67]

The meeting records are consistent with Kenworthy's recollections.[68] At the January 13 meeting, for example, Granger pressed Major General John E. Dahlquist on the Army's justification of segregation. When Granger asked why black soldiers should be expected to follow the orders of white generals but not vice versa, Dahlquist stated, "We had a job of winning a war; and whether or not White troops would have followed them, we are not sure. Our first job was to whip the Germans." Granger was not satisfied by this answer. "I have never discovered any record about the Army being concerned about the morale of Negro troops who are forced to serve under a White officer," he said. "Their concern seemed to be about the morale of White troops who might be assigned to Negro officers. There is an inequality. The concern is for the morale of Whites rather than for the morale of Negroes." Dahlquist disagreed. "It is not a question of the concern of the morale of either," he said. "It's a question,

---

[65] Mershon and Schlossman, *Foxholes & Color Lines*, 190–191; Meeting transcript, January 12, 1949, Folder: Transcripts of Committee Meetings – Volumes I–III, Box 10, Fahy Committee Records, HSTL.

[66] Although I focus here on the military establishment's resistance, even Fahy raised the question himself at a February 21 meeting. "Could you tell me why the word 'segregation' is not used in the Executive Order?" he asked the other members. "If it is true that that is the purpose and it is the President's intent, why was the word not used? Why is it left to construction and ambiguity." Meeting transcript, February 21, 1949, Folder: Transcripts of Committee Meetings – Volumes IV–V, Box 10, Fahy Committee Records, HSTL. This quote can be found on p. 14.

[67] Oral History Interview with E. W. Kenworthy, January 26, 1971, Washington, DC, www.trumanlibrary.org/oralhist/kenwrhye.htm, 22.

[68] For further analysis of how different parts of the military were approaching the question of potentially integrating the armed forces in the immediate postwar period, see Mershon and Schlossman, *Foxholes & Color Lines*, 135–157.

in our best judgment, of how we can produce an Army that could defeat the enemy." When interrogated further, he suggested there was evidence that white soldiers would refuse black leadership, but black soldiers were willing to serve under the command of whites.[69]

At the March 17 meeting, former Assistant Secretary of War John McCloy described the strategic importance of the South during World War II (which, for McCloy, justified the placation of white southerners at the expense of black soldiers). For "climatic reasons," McCloy said, most training camps were placed in the South. When Granger later quipped that the military might "put a quota on southern enlistments," rather than focusing on black soldiers as the problem, McCloy pointed to the importance of white southern manpower. "Well, southerners make good soldiers, and when the country is in danger that is where they rush to the colors most rapidly," he said. "Enlistments from Texas and around always keep ahead of the rest of the country, and I don't know if you put quotas down whether you would get enough people in the Army. Again that is a statistical problem that I am not qualified to testify about."[70]

Army Secretary Kenneth Royall, who had spoken at the National Defense Congress on Negro Affairs the year before, appeared before the committee on March 28. The Army, he said, "is not an instrument for social evolution." He told the committee that it was "not the Army's job either to favor or to impede social doctrines, no matter how progressive they may be – it is not for us to lead or to lag behind the civilian procession exception to the extent that the national defense is affected." Regarding the specific issue of segregation, he said "the criteria must be what produces the greatest and most effective use of all our manpower –

---

[69] Meeting transcript, January 13, 1949, Folder: Transcripts of Committee Meetings – Volumes I–III, Box 10, Fahy Committee Records, HSTL. See pp. 50–51 for these quotes. Granger also asked Dahlquist about "a law which will protect men in uniform against civilian abuse, by making such attacks a Federal misdemeanor susceptible to the penalties of Federal law." Dahlquist deferred. "I think you're beyond me on that," he replied. "I would have to see the law. I think you are getting into the realm not of the soldier but of the sociologist and the lawyer on that." Ibid., 43–44.

[70] Meeting transcript, March 17, 1949, Folder: Transcripts of Committee Meetings – Volumes VI–VII, Box 11, Fahy Committee Records, HSTL. For the quotes, see p. 37 and p. 59. While the location of training camps seems more related to climate, the disproportionate number of southern whites in the military also played a more general role in setting the tone of debates around these issues. In a revealing phrase in their analysis of how the military approached the possibility of integration during this time period, Mershon and Schlossman write of "military – that is, southern – customs." Mershon and Schlossman, *Foxholes and Color Lines*, 68.

all Army manpower – including Negro manpower, and what builds up the best morale and spirit throughout the Army, so that we may place a winning Army on the battlefield. That has been and will continue to be our aim."[71]

Like McCloy at the March 17 meeting, Royall also discussed the problem of southern whites. First, he noted that soldiers in general are not blank slates. "We must remember that soldiers are not mere bodies that can be moved and handled as trucks and guns," he argued. "They are individuals who came from civilian life and often return thereto – plan to return thereto. They are subject to all the emotions, prejudices, ideals, ambitions and inhibitions that encumber our civil population throughout the country."[72]

Second, he pointed to the realities of space in military service. "Soldiers live and work closely together. They are not only on the same drill field but also in the same living and eating quarters. From the standpoint of both morale and of efficiency it is important in peace and in war that the barracks and the unit areas be so attractive to them that they will devote not only their duty time but a reasonable part of their optional time at the post – that they will not be watching the clock for a chance to get away." This, he suggested, made segregation unsurprising (and, presumably, unproblematic). "We must remember that in close personal relationships such as exist in an Army unit, that in civilian life voluntary segregation is the normal thing. And this is true even in those localities where no type of segregation is required by law."[73]

Finally, he turned to the problem of white southerners in particular. "We must also remember that a large part of the volunteers in the Army are Southerners – usually a larger proportion than from any other part of the country. Whether properly or not – we don't have to argue that – it is a well-known fact that close personal association with Negroes is distasteful to a large percentage of Southern whites." This,

---

[71] Meeting transcript, March 28, 1949, Folder: Transcripts of Committee Meetings – Volumes VI–VII, Box 11, Fahy Committee Records, HSTL. See pp. 3–4.

[72] Ibid., 6. In some ways, Royall's account of white soldiers is similar to that of Krebs's account in *Fighting for Rights*, in which he describes soldiers' identities as "highly contextual," arguing " one should not be surprised to see soldiers adopting regional, class, gendered, religious, or ethnic perspectives." Krebs, *Fighting for Rights*, 9. See Chapter 3 for a discussion of Krebs and the contact hypothesis.

[73] Meeting transcript, March 28, 1949, Folder: Transcripts of Committee Meetings – Volumes VI–VII, Box 11, Fahy Committee Records, HSTL. See pp. 6–7. Note the similarity between Royall's language ("Soldiers live and work closely together") and the wording of the 1948 military integration survey question.

he suggested, might create problems for enlistment. "A total abandonment of – or a substantial and sudden change in – the Army's partial segregation policy would in my opinion adversely affect enlistments and reenlistments not only from the South but from many other parts of the country, probably making peacetime selective service again necessary," Royall argued. "And a change in our policy would adversely affect the morale of many Southern soldiers as well as other soldiers who are now serving."[74]

Royall also mentioned, briefly at least, black soldiers. "On the other side of the question the point is made that the morale of the Negro soldier is adversely affected by the Army's partial segregation policies," Royall said. "Some have inferred that as a result of segregation the Negro is not treated equitably and justly and does not have the same opportunity for service and advancement as do white troops. I do not believe that there is any real substance in this inference."[75] When asked by Sengstacke whether it is "your thinking that you can have equality of opportunity within a segregated setup," Royall replied that he did. "As I said there is no doubt about the fact that segregation is conducive to discrimination unless it is constantly policed," he said. "I do not think it necessarily denies equality of opportunity. We have made a determined effort in the Army to see that it does not deny equality of opportunity. I don't know of any single thing to which I have given more attention personally."[76]

The comments of Royall, McCloy, and Dahlquist are indicative of the institutional challenges facing advocates of military integration. Unlike in the Roosevelt years, however, this time the challenge was overcome. Truman's support for the committee was a key factor in helping it achieve its goals, allowing a civilian committee to gradually begin to reshape military policy. Royall, for instance, was eventually pressured into resigning as a result of his opposition to integrating the Army.[77] On May 22, 1950, the committee released its report, *Freedom to Serve*.[78] That same year, the Army finally abolished its racial quota system and began integrating

---

[74] Ibid., 7.
[75] Ibid., 8.
[76] Ibid., 51.
[77] Ronald R. Krebs, "Rights and Gun Sights: Military Service and the Politics of Citizenship," (PhD dissertation, Columbia University, 2003), 444–448.
[78] *Freedom to Serve: Equality of Treatment and Opportunity in the Armed Serves: A Report by the President's Committee*, (Washington: United States Government Printing Office, 1950), www.trumanlibrary.org/civilrights/freeserv.htm.

at least some training camps, although ultimately it was the Korean War that would be "the coup de grâce for segregation in the Army," with the realities of combat this time leading to battlefield integration even ahead of formal commands to do so.[79]

The influence of views like those of Royall, McCloy, and Dahlquist likely had the inadvertent effect of slowing down the pace of the trend toward greater white racial liberalism that would begin to emerge by the 1950s and 1960s. During the Korean War, for example, whites who served alongside black soldiers seem to have been less racially prejudiced as a result.[80] Had this integration happened during World War II, however, it quite possible that such attitudes would have even more liberalized, since the enemy could be accurately portrayed as an extremist defender of racial hierarchies. The Korean War experience indicates that the concerns the War Department raised about efficiency and white morale would likely have been overcome by the exigencies of combat, when the difference between life and death for many white soldiers might well have depended on their ability to cooperate with black soldiers.[81]

Why had civil rights advocates accomplished under Truman what Roosevelt had refused to go along with? There were, of course, important electoral pressures. The executive order was announced just twelve days after the close of the 1948 Democratic National Convention – where Hubert Humphrey and other liberals affiliated with Americans for Democratic Action had successfully strengthened the civil rights plank of the party platform to include, among other things, "the right of equal treatment in the service and defense of our nation" – in an election year when many political observers assumed Truman would have a difficult time beating the Republican presidential candidate, Thomas Dewey.[82]

---

[79] Charles C. Moskos, Jr., "Racial Integration in the Armed Forces," *American Journal of Sociology* 72(2), 1966, 135. Providing a living representation of the connection between racial integration of the armed forces and allowing LGBT members to serve, Moskos would be the person to propose a "don't ask, don't tell policy" for LGBT service members during the Clinton administration.

[80] Ibid., 139–141. For the limitations to this, however, see Ibid., 142.

[81] See the penultimate section of Chapter 3 for a more in-depth articulation of his counterfactual.

[82] For an analysis of the 1948 Convention, see Frederickson, *The Dixiecrat Revolt*. For an analysis of the role played by the ADA, see Gillon, *Politics and Vision*. See also Harvard Sitkoff, "Harry Truman and the Election of 1948: The Coming of Age of Civil Rights in American Politics," *Journal of Southern History* 37(4), 1971, 596–616.

There were also the protest movements calling directly for military desegregation. Berman argues this was a central factor. "In all probability, Executive Order 9981 was also designed to reduce the possibility of an immediate confrontation between the administration and A. Philip Randolph," he writes.[83] There is evidence that some executive branch figures supported this interpretation. On September 9, 1948, White House aide Donald Dawson sent a memorandum to Truman with three bullet points: (1) "[s]ince your executive order was issued all important opposition to the draft on the basis of the Army's race policy has disappeared. Philip Randolph and Grant Reynolds have withdrawn from their Committee Against Jim Crow, and only a few C.O.'s and other war resisters remain in the movement."; (2) "Negro leaders and their white friends have been universal in the praise of the order and in their support of the proposed committee."; and (3) "[t]he Committee will have complete minority press support. The Negro press, which had been conducting a vigorous campaign against the Army's racial policy has now abandoned it."[84]

While it is true that the executive order coincided with these electoral and protest pressures, the committee's hearings did not begin until 1949, which meant that the process of integrating the armed services actually proceeded during Truman's final term. And, as stated earlier, while electoral and protest pressures can help explain why something happened rather than nothing, the military-centric nature of the advances suggests that the wartime context had something to do with the outcome. Indeed, some leaders of advocacy organizations who testified before the Fahy committee suggested the same. Harold Riegelman of the American Jewish Committee was among them. "If we ask, and rightly so, that every citizen of the United States be prepared to sacrifice his life to save American freedom, we cannot in any way justify inequality of treatment or opportunity in our citizens' army," Riegelman said. "Particularly now, with a war against racism so recently won, it is important for us to root out any vestiges of that doctrine in our own lives."[85]

For advocates like Randolph, Walter White, and others, the effort to integrate the armed forces could be directly connected back to their

---

[83] Berman, *The Politics of Civil Rights in the Truman Administration*, 117. Kenworthy suggests electoral incentives as well in his oral history interview.
[84] Ibid., 123.
[85] Meeting transcript, April 25, 1949, Folder: Transcripts of Committee Meetings – Volumes XV–XVI, Box 11, Fahy Committee Records, HSTL. See pp. 49–50 for the quote.

wartime appeals to Roosevelt.[86] While a combination of political pressure and Truman's beliefs about military service ultimately pressured the president to establish the bureaucratic framework making military integration possible, it was decisions made by civil rights activists during World War II that forced the integration of the armed forces onto the agenda in the first place. The actual implementation of this policy goal – the fact that it came via executive order rather than congressional legislation – is also consistent with the pattern of the 1940s wartime civil rights agenda, which tended to view unilateral executive action in the context of wartime as a way of getting around congressional roadblocks and an unsympathetic white mass public. Indeed, the committee seems to have had the same understanding. In an 1971 oral history interview, Kenworthy told the interviewer that had the issue gone to Congress, "with all of the Southern members and their having to impress their constituencies at home, there would be trouble. But if things were done quietly, you probably could get around the problem."[87]

The Fahy committee hearings also contained elements of the "Cold War civil rights" logic that would define the next stage of mainstream civil rights advocacy.[88] Conceptions of a "world audience" to

---

[86] It is interesting to note that rights advocates initially viewed Truman as less, rather than more, amenable to their claims than Roosevelt. As William Berman describes it, Truman "inherited the unresolved civil rights conflict from the Roosevelt administration, without at the same time inheriting the good will and affection that most Negroes felt for his predecessor." Berman, *The Politics of Civil Rights in the Truman Administration*, x. In 1944, nomination as vice president "was tantamount to election" as the new president, given Roosevelt's poor health. Robert H. Ferrell, *Choosing Truman: The Democratic Convention of 1944*, (Columbia: University of Missouri Press, 1994), 1. The *Pittsburgh Courier* called his vice presidential nomination an "appeasement of the South which must rank in cowardice and shortsightedness with the ineptitude shown by Chamberlain at Munich." Truman, they argued, was "a long way from being a Henry Wallace." Berman, *The Politics of Civil Rights in the Truman Administration*, 19. "I think the South has won a substantial victory in securing the defeat of Vice President Wallace," Alabama Governor Chauncey Sparks said. "I find him safe on states rights and the right of the state to control qualifications of its electors. In the matter of race relations Senator Truman told me he is the son of an unreconstructed rebel mother. I think the South has won a victory." Ibid., 21.

[87] Oral History Interview with E. W. Kenworthy, January 26, 1971, Washington, DC, 17.

[88] This approach was centered on the strategic logic of how appealing to the "third world" was hindered by often all-too-accurate claims by the Soviet Union about white supremacy in America. Mary L. Dudziak, *Cold War Civil Rights: Race and the Image of American Democracy*, (Princeton: Princeton University Press, 2000). For another analysis of the link between the Cold War and the civil rights movement, see also John David

be swayed – particularly in a "world where the dark peoples outnumber the white," as Riegelman told the Fahy committee on behalf of the American Jewish Committee – became more common as a matter of rhetorical strategy.[89] There is likewise evidence this was perceived by some of the committee members. On July 25, 1950, Kenworthy wrote to Fahy. "I do not believe that the prime motivation for adopting policies of equality of treatment and opportunity in the services should be to make an impression abroad," he wrote. "The fact remains, nevertheless, that the country now is engaged in war in the Orient where the whole color question is an extremely sensitive one. I can not believe that it is wise, when so much is at stake, for the Army to continue to discriminate against qualified Negro soldiers and to maintain its traditional policy of segregation."[90]

With a somewhat different international focus, Meyer Bernstein of the CIO talked at the Fahy Committee hearings about the European audience. The CIO's first interest in civil rights, Bernstein said, "is in respect to the GI's who have come from the labor movement or who will leave the labor movement in the future to join the armed forces." The second reason, however, was more internationalist in nature. "Our second interest in this matter is one of the general problem of strengthening the democratic processes here and at the same time giving encouragement, lending sustenance to democratic forces abroad," Bernstein said. "I think that whatever we do here in the United States must be done in part, at least, by keeping in mind the effect such action will have upon our friends in the rest of the world." Bernstein described talking with "union men" from various European countries, "and one of the first things these people ask about is how completely do we practice what we preach about equality of treatment, how thoroughly do we implement our democracy."[91]

Skrentny, "The Effect of the Cold War on African-American Civil Rights: American and the World Audience, 1945–1968," *Theory and Society* 27(2), 1998, 237–285.

[89] Meeting transcript, April 25, 1949, Folder: Transcripts of Committee Meetings – Volumes XV–XVI, Box 11, Fahy Committee Records, HSTL. The quote can be found on p. 50.

[90] Letter, E. W. Kenworthy to Charles Fahy, July 25, 1950, Folder: Correspondence, Box 31, Staff Member and Office Files: Philleo Nash Files, Truman Papers, HSTL.

[91] Meeting transcript, April 25, 1949, Folder: Transcripts of Committee Meetings – Volumes XV–XVI, Box 11, Fahy Committee Records, HSTL. See pp. 2–3. For a longer-term look at tensions between the strategies of labor unions and civil rights groups, see Paul Frymer, *Black and Blue: African Americans, the Labor Movement, and the Decline of the Democratic Party*, (Princeton: Princeton University Press, 2007).

CONCLUSION

When Truman left the White House on January 20, 1953, he retired to Independence, Missouri, to work on his memoirs and build a presidential library. By the end of the decade, he was speaking quite differently about civil rights. In the lead-up to the 1960 presidential election, some national Democrats actually saw Truman's outspokenness as a potential liability. "If anyone came into my store and tried to stop business I'd throw him out," he had told reporters. "The Negro should behave himself and show he's a good citizen. Common sense and good will can solve this thing." When the Detroit branch of the NAACP sent him a telegram asking about the quote, Truman stood by it. "Your telegram regarding the statement which I made about sit downs in the restaurant is correct," Truman replied. "I would do just what I said I would."[92]

"Truman strongly disapproved of the methods of the civil rights movement, the sit-ins and marches," McCullough writes. "The leaders of the movement, it seemed to him, were flouting the law, resorting to mob rule, which was not his idea of the right way to bring about progress. He also appeared to take seriously the view of J. Edgar Hoover that much of the movement was Communist-inspired." Fearful that Truman might say something that would prove detrimental to the 1960 presidential campaign of John F. Kennedy, Dean Acheson, his former Secretary of State, actually wrote Truman a letter to set him straight.[93] This is similarly reflected in Truman's unease with the 1963 March on Washington, where Martin Luther King, Jr., gave his famous "I Have a Dream Speech." "I think it's silly," Truman said of the march.[94]

Such statements do not mean that Truman retreated from his advocacy of certain civil rights programs during his presidential tenure. In a 1957 statement he prepared commemorating the tenth anniversary of the President's Committee on Civil Rights, he praised the committee for having "pinpointed the danger points where freedom was lagging," including segregation in the District of Columbia; employment, housing, and educational discrimination; and "infringements of the right to vote, to serve

---

[92] Telegram, Edward Turner and Arthur Johnson to Harry Truman, March 22, 1960, Folder: Civil Rights, Box 14, Post-Presidential Papers, Truman Papers, HSTL; Telegram, Harry Truman to Edward Turner and Arthur Johnson, March 24, 1960; Folder: Civil Rights, Box 14, Post-Presidential Papers, Truman Papers, HSTL.
[93] McCullough, *Truman*, 971.
[94] "March Silly, Says Truman," *Eureka Humboldt Times*, August 24, 1963. Accessed via http://newspaperarchive.com.

in the armed forces, to enjoy equal justice under the law."⁹⁵ Indeed, Truman seemed to remain proud of his civil rights accomplishments as president. Truman had not changed. Rather, he viewed the 1960s civil rights movement as something less legitimate than the demands in the context of World War II and its aftermath.

Truman was committed to what he understood to be decent treatment. Black men who wore the uniform of the US military deserved better than many, like Isaac Woodard, had received at the hands of white mobs upon their return. Yet what they "deserved," in Truman's mind, was limited. Truman's military republicanism led him to be sympathetic to certain civil rights policy outcomes. In an era of growing political pressures on the Democratic Party to address civil rights, advocates presented Truman with evidence of violence against black veterans, and Truman responded by appointing a committee to study the issue and eventually signing an executive order that began the integration of the armed forces. Yet as civil rights activists increasingly came to focus their efforts on bringing an end to all segregation – including private businesses – Truman's civil rights liberalism began to reach its limits.

Taken together with the analysis of the Roosevelt administration in the previous chapter, then, the best theoretical assessment of the consequences of World War II for the executive branch's response to civil rights advocacy should consider both the compelling aspects of the war (pressures for something to happen rather than nothing) as well as the constraining aspects (narrowing the realm of the agenda to war-specific issues and an emphasis on not hindering the president's foreign policy goals). In a sense, this period was a precursor to the form of "Cold War civil rights" that would emerge in the 1950s. As Mary Dudziak demonstrates, the Cold War would "simultaneously constrain and enhance civil rights reform" as well as "frame and thereby limit the nation's civil rights commitment."⁹⁶ This tendency has clear roots in World War II and its immediate aftermath, and this earlier period also has similarly restrictive aspects complementing the more liberating ones.

---

⁹⁵ Letter Draft, Harry Truman, December 11, 1957, Folder: Civil Rights, Box 14, Post-Presidential Papers, Truman Papers, HSTL. He was, however, a bit too optimistic about the speed of progress on civil rights: "Given the facts, the American people soon moved into action. Civic and religious organizations, veterans groups, labor unions and business associations, women's clubs, youth council – men and women in every walk of life and in every section of our land joined to close the gap between our ideals and our practices. Given the facts, the American people will always lead the way."

⁹⁶ Dudziak, *Cold War Civil Rights*, 11, 13.

6

War, Race, and American Political Development

America, Gunnar Myrdal wrote in 1944, "is again in a life-and-death struggle for liberty and equality, and the American Negro is again watching for signs of what war and victory will mean in terms of opportunity and rights for him in his native land." For white Americans, Myrdal argued, what he called "the Negro problem" had "taken on a significance greater than it has ever had since the Civil War." Myrdal was convinced that he was living in a time of change. "There is bound to be a redefinition of the Negro's status in America as a result of this War," he concluded.[1] Yet despite this seeming optimism, Myrdal also admitted a certain amount of uncertainty about the future trajectory of American racial politics. "The exact nature of this structural change in American society cannot yet be foreseen," he acknowledged. "History is not the result of a predetermined Fate. Nothing is irredeemable until it is past."[2]

Based on an extensive analysis of the available survey evidence and a range of archival sources, this book has offered an empirically grounded assessment of the consequences of World War II for race and American political development. In this concluding chapter, I begin by offering a brief summary of the preceding chapters, framed around the extent to which the findings presented here help to refine the more general theoretical relationship between war and the inclusion of marginalized groups. I then describe several potential avenues for future research that build on the arguments presented here, particularly possibilities offered by

---

[1] Gunnar Myrdal, *An American Dilemma: The Negro Problem and Modern Democracy*, (New York: Harper & Brothers Publishers, 1944), 997.
[2] Ibid.

extending the scope to other political institutions and other groups. I conclude by emphasizing the importance of taking war seriously in accounts of domestic political change more broadly.

THE WAR LIBERALIZATION THEORY REFINED

Can war provide a mechanism for the incorporation of marginalized groups in democratic societies? For the case of World War II and the response to black civil rights advocacy, this book argues that war's effects can be much more heterogeneous than that, and accounting for the ways in which war can both compel and constrain the politics of racial inclusion is a more helpful way to think about the question.

From some perspectives, World War II seems like the critical juncture that wasn't.[3] While containing the ingredients for a growth in racial liberalism, my analysis of survey evidence from the time period indicates that the war was less effective in shifting white attitudes than Myrdal expected and many have since assumed.[4] While there are exceptions to this trend – there is some evidence of declines in aggregate white racial prejudice, and some evidence of moderation among white veterans on a limited set of issues – the conservative aggregate trends for policy issues like antilynching legislation offer both an important empirical corrective and a key piece of a theoretical framework for explaining why the racial politics of the era proceeded as it did.

While World War II did not lead to aggregate shifts in white racial policy attitudes, from other vantage points the war clearly did shift the trajectory of racial politics over the course of the twentieth century, albeit in often contradictory ways.[5] The war's limited effects on white racial attitudes help make sense of this. Mass white racial attitudes provided

---

[3] On the concept of critical junctures, see Giovanni Capoccia and R. Daniel Kelemen, "The Study of Critical Junctures: Theory, Narrative, and Counterfactuals in Historical Institutionalism," *World Politics* 59(3), 2007, 341–369.

[4] Critics of Myrdal would not be surprised. "Myrdal was wrong," Charles Silberman argued in 1964. "White Americans are not torn and tortured by the conflict between their devotion to the American creed and their actual behavior," he continued. Charles Silberman, *Crisis in Black and White*, (New York: Random House, 1964), 10. See also Carol A. Horton, *Race and the Making of American Liberalism*, (New York: Oxford University Press, 2005), 161.

[5] It is possible that the war's effects on attitudes were simply limited, but it is also possible that it instead created push and pull factors, but ones that mostly balanced out in the aggregate.

an important constraint on congressional decision making, which left Congress an unlikely venue for progress on civil rights. Advocates strategically emphasized the possibly of unilateral executive action, as this was less constrained by majoritarian sentiments and presidents are often given more leeway in a time of war. In doing so, advocates emphasized new, war-specific issues like discrimination *in the defense industry* and segregation *in the armed forces*, which were rhetorically convenient sites in the context of World War II. Doing so led to some of the most important civil rights accomplishments of the first half of the twentieth century. Yet as advocates attempted to move beyond these war-specific advances – advocating for protections against discriminations in private industries beyond war production and integration beyond the confines of the armed forces – they found a much harder road.

In relating this study to broader inquiries, one takeaway point is that as a conceptual variable, "war" contains multitudes. World War II was a large-scale war, which shaped not just the lives of soldiers involved in fighting it, but also civilians on the home front through changes like rations and war production work. To the extent that a war is experienced in a meaningful way by ordinary citizens, it is more plausible that it will have domestic political consequences. Beyond scale, though, other aspects of wars must also matter. One particular aspect of war emphasized in this book is the ideological justification of the war. World War I, like World War II, also was a large-scale war, but its ideological justification was vague compared to World War II, and it was certainly harder to connect to the goals of domestic rights advocates.

But even in the case of a large-scale war where the ideological justification could be tied fairly directly to the rights claims of marginalized groups, the case of World War II also highlights how other features of war can be more constraining. In particular, many in the executive branch and military viewed domestic advocacy as a distraction from the more pressing concern of executing the war in an effective manner. Although advocates argued that integration, for example, would actually aid in military effectiveness, the elites in charge of such decisions mostly disagreed, believing instead that any disruption from the status quo would be harmful to group cohesion and morale, particularly of white troops. No matter how compelling many found the ideological logic of the war, the extent to which the War Department simply refused to budge – and President Roosevelt refused to order them to do so – prevented larger changes from happening during the war itself.

Finally, to the extent that large-scale wars fought in the name of inclusionary principles can offer at least some avenues for rights claims, such wars still privilege some rights claims more than others. This is especially true when rights claims are tied to military service, which limits the accessibility of those rights to those who could not – or would not – serve in the military. In World War II and its aftermath, this was true for black women, as well as those black men who would eventually grow unwilling to support the Truman administration's foreign policy decisions in the early Cold War era. In this way, the relationship between war and rights claims can sometimes privilege a framework that is not simply liberal or conservative, but is rather a mode of incorporation that benefits some actors more directly than others. War has long been related to the inclusion of marginalized groups, but this relationship is often far more heterogeneous than some accounts suggest.

NEXT STEPS

While this book provides an empirical corrective to common claims about white racial attitudes and a new assessment of the executive branch's response to wartime civil rights advocacy, several lines of inquiry remain open, both for the study of World War II and black civil rights, as well as the study of other wars and other marginalized groups. In this section, I highlight a few possibilities for such future research.

Extending the Scope

This book has analyzed World War II and American racial politics through the lens of white public opinion and the executive branch's response to civil rights advocacy, but the effects of World War II on other features of American politics also merit reappraisal.

At the national level, consider the war's effects on Supreme Court decision making. It is often taken for granted, for example, that the 1944 *Smith* v. *Allwright* case outlawing the white primary was motivated, at least in part, by the ideological logic of World War II. Yet the evidence for this claim is surprisingly lacking. The legal scholar Michael Klarman is perhaps the clearest example. While Klarman gives some credit to "Roosevelt's virtually complete recomposition of the Court," he argues this explanation is "missing something more fundamental – the significance of World War II." His argument, however, is surprisingly vague.

"This is necessarily a point of speculation," he acknowledges, "because nothing in the *Smith* opinion or the surviving conference notes refers to the significance of the war. Still, the justices cannot have failed to observe the tension between a purportedly democratic war fought against the Nazis, with their theories of Aryan supremacy, and the pervasive disenfranchisement of Southern blacks."[6]

Klinkner and Smith make a similar argument. "The Court's decision in *Smith* reflected its emerging stress on the protection of civil and political rights, an emphasis influenced by the changing global context," they write. Although they acknowledge that Justice Stanley Reed, who wrote the *Smith* majority opinion, "made no mention of the war," they point to two sources: a *New York Times* journalist, who declared in his opinion column that the "real reason" for the Court's move against the white primary was "that the common sacrifices of wartime have turned public opinion and the Court against previously sustained devices to exclude minorities"; and a 1979 book by the historian Darlene Clark Hine, which argues that "[t]he white primary was one of the casualties of World War II."[7] Neither source, however, provides direct evidence that the justices were directly affected by the war – these sources contain arguments along those lines, but not direct evidence substantiating them – yet they are treated as though they do.[8] A more systematic interrogation of World

---

[6] Michael J. Klarman, "The White Primary Rulings: A Case Study in the Consequences of Supreme Court Decisionmaking," *Florida State University Law Review* 29, 2001, 64. Klarman's discussion of how increases in southern legal challenges were partly a result of "the greater black militancy spawned by World War II" is more convincing. Ibid., 76. Such a claim fits with Christopher S. Parker, *Fighting for Democracy: Black Veterans and the Struggle Against White Supremacy in the Postwar South*, (Princeton: Princeton University Press, 2009).

[7] Philip A. Klinkner and Rogers M. Smith, *The Unsteady March: The Rise and Decline of Racial Equality in America*, (Chicago: University of Chicago Press, 2002), 193. For the original sources, see Arthur Krock, "In The Nation: Self-Reexamination Continues in the Supreme Court," *New York Times*, April 4, 1944; and Darlene Clark Hine, *Black Victory: The Rise and Fall of the White Primary in Texas*, (Millwood, NY: KTO Press, 1979).

[8] As Ian Lustick writes, "[T]o the extent social scientists use the work of historians (historiography) as a vehicle for access to the past, it is not access to the variety of possible behaviors and patterns that historiography offers, but access to the variety of behaviors and patterns that historians, governed by their own implicit theories, commitments, and access to evidence, have identified... What is required, though, is recognition that background narratives are constructed, not discovered." Ian S. Lustick, "History, Historiography, and Political Science: Multiple Historical Records and the Problem of Selection Bias," *American Political Science Review* 90(3), 1996, 613.

War II–era Supreme Court decision making could offer additional insight into how the war did or did not shape national political institutions and their response to rights advocacy.[9]

An alternative approach would be to focus instead on variation in subnational politics in this era. Even in a cursory scan of the archival evidence, state and local political actors appear. New York City mayor Fiorello La Guardia, for example, corresponded with the Roosevelt White House on issues related to civil rights, including the threatened March on Washington and Roosevelt's eventual decision to issue an executive order on employment in the defense industry.[10] To what extent did wartime advocacy shape the legislative, mayoral, and gubernatorial responses to civil rights demands in other cities and states across the country?

The work of Margaret Weir highlights how an examination of state politics complicates traditional depictions of a singular "New Deal order," with the United States instead appearing as "a layered polity in which federal initiatives were overlaid on state political systems that operated with different administrative capacities and political logics." Such state systems, she argues, were "congenial political homes for the opponents of liberalism" during the New Deal and its aftermath.[11] How, if at all, does a subnational focus allow a different story to emerge about the war's effects on racial politics? Did the war allow local activists to reframe the rights claims they presented to politicians, or did the war instead merely marginalize them until the conflict's aftermath?

Assessing Legacies of the Wartime Civil Rights Agenda

This book has focused mostly on the war's short-term consequences, with some analysis of the racial attitudes of white veterans into the early

---

[9] For a detailed examination of judicial speech off the bench in a slightly later era (1953–1969), see Robert A. Whitaker, "Freedom of Speech: The Speeches of the Warren Court Justices and the Legitimacy of the Supreme Court" (PhD dissertation, University at Albany, State University of New York, 2016). Although Whitaker does not study the 1944 *Smith* v. *Allwright* decision, he does provide some interesting language that is relevant for scholars of the Cold War civil rights linkage. See especially ibid., 205–206. Whitaker's study could provide a good model for an analysis of earlier Court decisions if similar archival evidence exists for that period.

[10] See Chapter 4.

[11] Margaret Weir, "States, Race, and the Decline of New Deal Liberalism," *Studies in American Political Development* 19, 2005, 158, 160.

1960s. The medium- and long-term institutional legacies of the war, however, might likewise merit some attention. The military desegregation debate in particular had the effect of further strengthening the link, forged during World War II, between the domestic policy aspirations of civil rights activists and the foreign policy goals of the executive branch. This was relatively uncontested during the war against Nazi Germany, led to growing tensions during the Cold War, and reached a boiling point by the Vietnam era.[12]

Tensions between moderates and radicals became especially salient during the Vietnam War. By the 1960s, military service itself had come under interrogation by younger activists. In 1969, the historian Richard Dalfiume published an article about the World War II–era military desegregation debate. But as he noted, in the midst of the Vietnam war, the relationship between US foreign policy and the civil rights movement was starting to look very different. "Today the militant segment of the civil rights movement deplores the use of colored troops in a war against the colored people of Asia," he wrote. As Dalfiume knew, this was a substantial change from the old – and much derided – quota system, which had kept the number of black soldiers below population levels in general, but especially in combat units. "Ironically," he wrote, "it was only a generation ago that the most militant Negroes were fighting to overcome discriminatory restrictions on their service in the armed forces. Then the cry was 'the right to fight'."[13]

Newer organizations like the Student Nonviolent Coordinating Committee (SNCC) came to view sending black men to fight people of color in Vietnam as being itself part of white supremacy – rather than a tool to break it down.[14] Organizations like the NAACP, by contrast, were

---

[12] Mary L. Dudziak, *Cold War Civil Rights: Race and the Image of American Democracy*, (Princeton: Princeton University Press, 2000). Carol Anderson acknowledges this "half-hearted, but necessary, response to black inequality," but argues that it also "systematically eliminated human rights as a viable option for mainstream African American leadership." Carol Anderson, *Eyes Off the Prize: The United Nations and the African American Struggle for Human Rights, 1944–1955*, (New York: Cambridge University Press, 2003), 5. While I focus in this discussion on the Vietnam era, anti-communism was dividing the movement much earlier. For one illustrative example, see the split between the NAACP and Du Bois. Gerald Horne, *Black & Red: W.E.B. Du Bois and the Afro-American Response to the Cold War, 1944–1963*, (Albany: State University of New York Press, 1986).

[13] Richard M. Dalfiume, "Military Segregation and the 1940 Presidential Election," *Phylon* 30(1), 1969, 42.

[14] On January 6, 1966, the executive committee of SNCC issued a "blanket denunciation of the war in Vietnam," which bluntly labeled the war as "racist and imperialist,"

reluctant to oppose Lyndon Johnson's war in Vietnam for fear it might weaken their relationship with the greatest presidential ally the group had seen.[15] Not unlike President Truman's comments in his later years, both Johnson and the NAACP "shared a mutual antipathy to those who acted outside the channels of the political system."[16]

To what extent had the civil rights politics of the World War II era linked civil rights activism to the foreign policy goals of the executive branch in the late 1940s and early 1950s? By the time the Vietnam War came around, did this World War II–era linkage make it more difficult for groups like the NAACP to oppose the foreign policy of a president whose work on domestic civil rights they so valued? To what extent did this make a rupture more likely with a new generation of more radical activists – not as tamed by the imperatives of the Cold War, and without a direct experience with Truman's executive orders – for whom supporting civil rights meant also opposing what they viewed as an imperialistic war against other people of color in Vietnam? Tracing the processes through which these outcomes did – or did not – follow directly from choices civil rights advocates made in the 1940s would be an interesting place for future researchers to look.

and further stated that their role "was not to fight in Vietnam, but here in this country for freedoms that are denied here at home." A few months later, the Congress of Racial Equality (CORE) followed SNCC's example and denounced the war as well. Daniel Seth Lucks, "The Vietnam War and Its Tragic Impact on the Civil Rights Movement and African Americans" (PhD dissertation, University of California, Berkeley, 2009), 2. Stokely Carmichael appeared on CBS's Face the Nation in June 1966 and said he opposed the draft. "My own feeling is that there is no reason why black people should be fighting for free elections in Vietnam for some other people to get free elections when they don't have it in their own country," he told the national TV audience. Ibid., 215.

[15] Patricia Sullivan, "Movement Building During the World War II Era: The NAACP's Legal Insurgency in the South." In *Fog of War: The Second World War and the Civil Rights Movement*, ed. Kevin M. Kruse and Stephen Tuck, (New York: Oxford University Press, 2012). Whitney Young of the Urban League viewed it as a matter of practical politics. "If we are not with Lyndon Johnson on Vietnam," he declared, "then he is not going to be with us on civil rights." Lucks, "The Vietnam War and Its Tragic Impact on the Civil Rights Movement and African Americans," 340. Just a few days after Martin Luther King Jr.'s antiwar speech at Riverside Church, the NAACP's Roy Wilkins spoke at Yale University and said, "If I am going to cry about something, I am going to cry about the murder of Wharlest Jackson in Natchez, Mississippi, rather than about civilians in Vietnam." Ibid., 360. See also Daniel S. Lucks, *Selma to Saigon: The Civil Rights Movement and the Vietnam War*, (Lexington: University Press of Kentucky, 2016).

[16] Ibid., 357. Black newspapers, too, were clear in criticizing the antiwar civil rights left.

Other Wars and Other Marginalized Groups

This book has focused on white attitudes and executive branch behavior related to the rights claims of African Americans during World War II, but this analysis can also help inform more general questions about the relationship between war and the incorporation of marginalized groups. While there are multiple ways of extending the framework, here I focus primarily on how expectations about the relationship between war and rights claims look different if the war is held constant but the group is altered. In particular, how might this study of the response to black civil rights advocacy during World War II relate to questions about Japanese-American and Mexican-American advocacy during that same war? I also briefly describe how this book's framework might suggest ways of approaching other wars and other groups, although this is necessarily far more speculative.

This book has focused on World War II as a war the United States waged against Nazi Germany, but it was also a war waged against Japan. While the ideological logic of the war against Nazism allowed African-American rights advocates to link the war to their domestic goals, the war against Japan was more easily utilized in pursuit of racial exclusion rather than inclusion. With their loyalty to the United States viewed as suspect by the federal government (and a large number of ordinary citizens), Americans of Japanese ancestry were forcibly placed into internment camps, a decision that the Supreme Court actually upheld as constitutional in 1944.[17]

Ironically, in the war's aftermath, Japanese-American rights advocacy was ultimately more successful than that of African Americans. One reason for this, according to Krebs, is that Japanese Americans "regularly highlighted the valor they had displayed during the war," while black civil rights activists generally did not. Because of this, "[o]pponents of equal rights for African Americans thus had rhetorical options that the opponents of Japanese Americans did not."[18] Despite widespread wartime suspicions of disloyalty, Japanese Americans

---

[17] For a contemporaneous discussion of this issue, see Eugene V. Rostow, "The Japanese American Cases – A Disaster," *Yale Law Journal* 54, 1945, 489–535. For historical overviews, see Wendy L. Ng, *Japanese American Internment During World War II: A History and Reference Guide*, (Westport, CT: Greenwood Press, 2002); and Greg Robinson, *A Tragedy of Democracy: Japanese Confinement in North America*, (New York: Columbia University Press, 2010).

[18] Ronald R. Krebs, *Fighting for Rights: Military Service and the Politics of Citizenship*, (Ithaca: Cornell University Press, 2006), 167–168.

"overcame these obstacles by cultivating a reputation for unusual civic virtue"; "[t]he centerpiece of this strategy was military service as proof of loyalty."[19]

This is articulated in more detail by the historian Ellen Wu, who emphasizes the more problematic trade-offs involved in this strategy. The Japanese American Citizens League (JACL) put forth a "carefully constructed representation of Japanese Americans as cooperative, loyal, and patriotic," she writes. Through the "figure of the Nisei soldier," the organization created "an intentionally crafted archetype of Japanese American manhood that foregrounded the notion of martial patriotism – unwavering loyalty to the United States demonstrated through the sacrifice of military service."[20] While partly in agreement with Krebs – she describes JACL's strategy as "providing a persuasive basis for making claims on society and the state" – Wu writes with a more critical tone, taking stock of the way in which these decisions marginalized radical voices and led, more broadly, to a construction of Asian-American politics that defined Asian Americans as "definitely not-black," which had the effect of undermining the rights claims of African Americans.[21]

One way to build on the work of Wu, Krebs, and others would be to offer an analysis of trends in American public opinion toward Japanese Americans, similar to the trends in attitudes toward African Americans presented in Chapters 2 and 3 of this book. In December 1942, for example, only a third of Americans said those in internment camps should be allowed to return to their homes after the war.[22] When and why did such negative attitudes begin to shift? Were white veterans distinguishable from nonveterans in such attitudes? If so, it is possible that the moderating trend in racial attitudes related to African Americans presented in Chapter 3 might not extend to Japanese Americans, whom white veterans might have perceived as being similar to the enemy, a comparison that was not made for African Americans.

The difference in the wartime experience of African Americans and Japanese Americans suggests that a variety of factors might be relevant in explaining outcomes of interest. The extent to which the

---

[19] Ibid., 169.
[20] Ellen Wu, *The Color of Success: Asian Americans and the Origins of the Model Minority*, (Princeton: Princeton University Press, 2014), 73.
[21] Ibid., 74.
[22] This survey is available from iPoll.

war served to reinforce or challenge a group's prewar social position seems like an especially key variable. African Americans were marginalized before the war, but the war offered an opportunity for rights advocates to link their goals to the broader goals of the war effort. Japanese Americans were also marginalized, but the war led many Americans to further view them as disloyal, a fate that did not apply nearly as much to African Americans. This did not prevent postwar gains from being made – Japanese-American rights advocates adapted their strategies to this context – but the context made accommodationist strategies more likely to succeed, while silencing more radical voices.

One way to further refine this would be to look to other groups less commonly studied during the World War II era. For example, studying Mexican-American rights advocacy during this period, especially in comparison to that of African Americans and Japanese Americans, might further clarify how a marginalized group's prewar social position interacted with the ways in which the war could be used strategically by those advocating greater rights for the group.[23]

Extending this framework to other wars would require a clear articulation of similarities and differences. Other large-scale wars might be assessed with respect to differences in their ideological logic, the specifics of the material undertaking necessitated by mobilization, and the willingness or unwillingness of political elites to deal with domestic issues while undertaking the war effort. For wars that are smaller in scale, by contrast, while this tripartite distinction might still prove useful, it is likely that size itself will lead to a smaller role for these wars generally, although they might have particularly important implications for certain groups.[24]

---

[23] On World War II–era Mexican-American civil rights advocacy in Texas, see Thomas A. Guglielmo, "Fighting for Caucasian Rights: Mexicans, Mexican Americans, and the Transnational Struggle for Civil Rights in World War II Texas," *Journal of American History* 92(4), 2006, 1212–1237. The 1943 "Zoot Suit Riots" in Los Angeles also highlighted racial tensions between Mexican Americans and whites in California. See Eduardo Obregón Pagán, *Murder at the Sleepy Lagoon: Zoot Suits, Race, and Riot in Wartime L.A.*, (Chapel Hill: The University of North Carolina Press, 2003).

[24] For example, the wars in Afghanistan and Iraq are more likely to have implications for Muslim Americans than African Americans. The relationship between war and military service and LGBT rights claims also merits further examination. For a historical approach that considers military service in addition to other institutional settings, see Margot Canaday, *The Straight State Sexuality and Citizenship in Twentieth-Century America*, (Princeton: Princeton University Press, 2011).

Public Opinion and the Study of American Political Development

Methodologically, this book demonstrates the benefits of better integrating the study of public opinion with the historical study of political institutions, two approaches that have traditionally been largely separate in the study of American politics.[25] To a large degree, this is a result of the institutional development of the discipline itself. Modern historical institutionalism developed in part as a critique of behavioralism (exemplified by studies of opinion and voting behavior). Yet, while understandable from this perspective, this distinction between mass opinion and political institutions has little intellectual merit, and in some cases serves to limit our understanding of important historical developments. In this book, for example, I have shown how original analysis of survey data from this era can offer a more accurate assessment of the nature of white racial attitudes than prior accounts, which in turn provides important contextual information for making sense of why certain political arenas were more plausible locations for policy victories than others during this time period.

While the concept of "public opinion" dates back well before the emergence of survey research, surveys are the most common tool used by political scientists to measure what ordinary people think about politics.[26] Considering the attention APD scholarship has given to the New Deal era, it is notable that modern political opinion polling emerged during Roosevelt's second term, a historical coincidence that opens up significant opportunities for research that emphasizes the role of mass attitudes in making sense of political development during the New Deal, World War II, and early Cold War era.

In recent years, these early surveys have become more accessible than ever before, and scholars are beginning to use them to answer a growing number of interesting questions. Eric Schickler, for example, has used surveys from this era to demonstrate a mass-level relationship between economic liberalism, Democratic voting behavior, and racial liberalism

---

[25] For an argument in favor of better integrating them, see Robert Y. Shapiro, "Public Opinion," in *The Oxford Handbook of American Political Development*, ed. Richard Valelly, Suzanne Mettler, and Robert Lieberman, (New York: Oxford University Press, 2016), 516–534.

[26] Susan Herbst, *Numbered Voices: How Opinion Polling Has Shaped American Politics*, (Chicago: University of Chicago Press, 1993); Amy Fried, *Pathways to Polling: Crisis, Cooperation and the Making of Public Opinion Professions*, (New York: Routledge, 2012).

at a much earlier era than many might expect.[27] In work coauthored with Devin Caughey, he has also used early survey evidence to assess the public's response to labor unions in the New Deal and World War II eras, which provides a helpful vantage point from which to assess long-standing counterfactual debates about labor strategy and influence in the US context.[28] Others have started examining topics including the individual-level factors correlated with attitudes toward Jews during the Nazi era and support for a peacetime draft in the immediate aftermath of World War II.[29] Future studies building on these early efforts, particularly those that tie trends in mass attitudes to broader historical institutionalist accounts of American politics, will likely prove to be fruitful for our understanding of American political development.

WAR, RACE, AND AMERICAN POLITICAL DEVELOPMENT

Political scientists in general – and scholars of American politics in particular – ought to take more seriously the role of war in restructuring domestic American politics.[30] While scholars of comparative politics and international relations have followed the lead of Charles Tilly, Peter Gourevitch, and others in examining the impact of war on state-building, the impact of the international system on domestic politics, and so on, this is much less true of the American politics subfield, which has tended to emphasize domestic factors.[31]

---

[27] Eric Schickler, *Racial Realignment The Transformation of American Liberalism, 1932–1965*, (Princeton: Princeton University Press, 2016).

[28] Eric Schickler and Devin Caughey, "Public Opinion, Organized Labor, and the Limits of New Deal Liberalism, 1936–1945," *Studies in American Political Development* 25(2), 2011, 162–189.

[29] Susan Welch, "American Opinion Toward Jews During the Nazi Era: Results from Quota Sample Polling During the 1930s and 1940s," *Social Science Quarterly* 95(3), 2014, 615–635; Benjamin O. Fordham, "Historical Perspective on Public Support for the Draft: War Costs and Military Service," *Journal of Global Security Studies* 1(4), 2016, 302–322.

[30] For more general advocacy of these goals, see Ira Katznelson and Martin Shefter, ed., *Shaped by War and Trade: International Influences on American Political Development*, (Princeton: Princeton University Press, 2002); David R. Mayhew, "Wars and American Politics," *Perspectives on Politics* 3(3), 2005, 473–493; Elizabeth Kier and Ronald R. Krebs, ed., *In War's Wake: International Conflict and the Fate of Liberal Democracy*, (New York: Cambridge University Press, 2010).

[31] "War made the state and the state made war" was Tilly's famous phrasing. See Charles Tilly, "Reflections on the History of European State-Making," in Charles Tilly (ed.), *The Formation of National States in Western Europe*, (Princeton: Princeton University

In part, this is reflective of the influence of early researchers like Anthony Downs who set the framework for much political science scholarship about American politics. "In essence, we are assuming that citizens' political tastes are fixed," Downs wrote in his influential 1957 book *An Economic Theory of Democracy*, and many political scientists studying not just behavior but also institutions have followed suit. In the very next sentence, however, Downs pointed to exceptions from this general rule. "Even though these tastes often change radically in the long run," he wrote, "we believe our assumption is plausible in the short run, *barring wars or other social upheavals.*"[32]

Although not always easy to model parsimoniously, scholars of American politics should take more seriously the social upheaval of wartime. This is not without its difficulties. To the extent that wars are contingent events, studying their consequences can be challenging for conventional approaches to understanding domestic political outcomes.[33] If the goal is to explain important outcomes in American political development, though, it might be necessary to simply accept this. "In general, it is probably a mistake to invest in grand schematic explanations of American history that underplay contingency," David Mayhew argues, "and wars are hard to beat as bearers of contingency."[34]

This is especially true for scholars of race and American political development because of the variety of ways in which war-making has been tied to the incorporation of marginalized groups through history. A focus on war need not downplay the variety of domestic factors – including economic depression, a growing federal government, and a burgeoning linkage between civil rights organizations and labor unions – that shaped

---

Press, 1975), 42. Tarrow refines this somewhat by noting that "making war also created the space and incentives for social movements." Sidney Tarrow, *Power in Movement: Social Movements and Contentious Politics*, Second Edition, (New York: Cambridge University Press, 1998), 60. For a more developed perspective on state-building by Tilly, however, see Charles Tilly, *Coercion, Capital and European States, A.D. 990–1992*, (Malden, MA: Wiley-Blackwell, 1992). For a discussion of how international politics can shape domestic politics from an international relations perspective, see Peter Gourevitch, "The Second Image Reversed: The International Sources of Domestic Politics," *International Organization* 32(4), 1978, 881–912.

[32] Anthony Downs, *An Economic Theory of Democracy*, (Boston: Addison-Wesley), 47. Emphasis added.

[33] Ian Shapiro and Sonu Bedi, "Introduction: Contingency's Challenge to Political Science," in *Political Contingency: Studying the Unexpected, the Accidental, and the Unforeseen*, ed. Ian Shapiro and Sonu Bedi, (New York: New York University Press, 2007), 1.

[34] Mayhew, "Wars and American Politics," 482.

the trajectory of American racial politics. Rather, a focus on war can complement such accounts by helping to make sense of the specific form that important outcomes took, such as the particularly military-centric nature of 1940s civil rights victories. As this book has shown, war can be deeply intertwined with the rights of marginalized groups, but its effects can be uneven and often surprising, its consequences both compelling and constraining.

Appendix

ARCHIVAL SOURCES

Franklin D. Roosevelt Presidential Library, Hyde Park, NY

- Papers as President, Official File
- Francis Biddle Papers

Library of Congress, Washington, DC

- Harold L. Ickes Papers
- Truman K. Gibson Papers
- A. Philip Randolph Papers

Harry S. Truman Presidential Library, Independence, MO

- Harry S. Truman Papers, White House Central Files, Official File
- Harry S. Truman Papers, Post-Presidential Papers
- Harry S. Truman Papers, Staff Member and Office Files, Philleo Nash Files
- Philleo Nash Papers
- David K. Niles Papers
- George M. Elsey Papers
- RG 220: Records of the President's Committee on Equality of Treatment and Opportunity in the Armed Services

Methodological Appendix for Chapter 2

In this section, I provide complete question wordings, demographic information regarding the sample for each study, and information about the weighting protocol used to correct for the known biases of each sample.

Racial prejudice

The analysis of racial prejudice questions is based on the 1944 "Attitudes Toward Negroes" survey (NORC survey #1944-0225), which interviewed 2,521 national adults face to face in May 1944. All respondents to this survey were white. The 2,521 respondents included 1,180 men and 1,341 women. To at least partially correct for any biases introduced by the quota sampling procedure, I utilize Berinsky and Schickler's "eduWhites" weight, which divides the sample into 32 possible gender/region/education combinations and weights each respondent more or less depending on the extent to which their demographic subgroup is under- or oversampled in this particular study. Doing this creates a more accurate estimate of aggregate white opinion.

I use the following questions:

1. Good living: "Do you think Negroes have the same chance as white people to make a good living in this country?"
2. Fair treatment: "Do you think most Negroes in the United States are being treated fairly or unfairly?"
3. Jobs: "Do you think Negroes should have as good a chance as white people to get any kind of job, or do you think white people should have the first chance at any kind of job?"
4. Blood: "As far as you know, is Negro blood the same as white blood, or is it different in some way?"
5. Intelligence: "In general, do you think Negroes are as intelligent as white people – that is, can they learn just as well if they are given the same education?"
6. Nurse: "If you were sick in a hospital, would it be all right with you if you had a Negro nurse, or wouldn't you like it?"

For comparisons, I first use the 1943 "Postwar Problems, Old Age Pension, Public Schools and Free Speech" survey (NORC Survey #1943-0217), which interviewed 2,560 national adults face to face in November

1943. Of the 2,560 total respondents, 2,317 were white, including 1,080 white men and 1,237 white women. I again calculate a 32-category "eduWhites" weight for this dataset. This study first asked the good living question that would later be used in the 1944 "Attitudes Toward Negroes" survey, using identical question wording.

I then use the 1946 "Minorities; United Nations" survey (NORC survey #1946-0241), which interviewed 2,589 national adults face to face from May 4–25, 1946. Of the 2,589 total respondents, 2,360 were white, including 1,125 white men and 1,235 white women. I am only able to calculate a 24-category variation of the "eduWhites" weight for this dataset, since I am unable to distinguish between whites who attended high school and whites who actually graduated (these two groups are thus lumped together in the dataset). This study repeated the fair treatment, jobs, blood, intelligence, and nurse questions from the 1944 "Attitudes Toward Negroes" survey using identical question wordings.

Antilynching Legislation

The "eduWhites" weight is ideal for my purposes, but it requires knowing the educational attainment of respondents, which was generally not asked in the earliest surveys. For the prewar lynching questions, I use Berinsky and Schickler's already-created weighting variables, which are available from iPoll. In cases where occupational status is available (measured dichotomously by Berinsky and Schickler as professional/semi-professional and other), I use a 16-category "profWhites" weight, which is the same as "eduWhites," but using a 2-category occupational categorization instead of a 4-category educational one. In cases where occupation was also not asked, the best proxy for class is phone ownership. In such cases, I use a 16-category "phoneBlack" weight, also calculated by Berinsky and Schickler (but note that I am looking at whites only, so it is similar to the other two weights in that regard). For the postwar questions, I create my own "eduWhites" weights following Berinsky and Schickler's approach.

The analysis of attitudes toward antilynching legislation uses the questions and datasets listed below:

1. Gallup Poll # 63 (January 7–12, 1937): "Should Congress enact a law which would make lynching a federal crime?"

Methodological Appendix for Chapter 2 175

- This study interviewed 3,019 national adults face to face. Of the 3,019 total respondents, 2,956 were white, including 1,891 white men and 1,065 white women. For the January 1937 study, I present estimates of white opinion using the "profWhites" weight.

2. Gallup Poll # 1937-0096: Poverty/WPA/Control of Banks/Politics (August 18–23, 1937): "Should Congress pass a law making lynching a federal crime?"

    - This study interviewed 2,998 national adults face to face. Of the 2,998 total respondents, 2,927 were white, including 1,917 white men and 1,010 white women. For the August 1937 study, I present estimates of white opinion using the "phoneBlack" weight.

3. Gallup Poll # 1937-0102: "Roosevelt Administration/Minimum Wage/Presidential Election" (October 30–November 4, 1937): "Should Congress pass a law which would make lynching a federal crime?"

    - This study interviewed 2,972 national adults face to face. Of the 2,972 total respondents, 2,906 were white, including 1,899 white men and 1,007 white women. For the October/November 1937 study, I present estimates of white opinion using the "phoneBlack" weight.

4. Gallup Poll # 1937-0104: "Employment/College Football/Politics" (November 21–26, 1937): "If a local peace officer is negligent in protecting a prisoner from a lynch mob, should the federal government have the right to punish this peaces officer?"

    - This study interviewed 2,780 national adults face to face. Of the 2,780 total respondents, 2,713 were white, including 1,740 white men and 973 white women. For the November 1937 study, I present estimates of white opinion using the "profWhites" weight.

5. Gallup Poll # 1937-0106: "China and Japan/Automobiles/Finances" (December 15–20, 1937): "Congress is now considering a lynching bill which would give the Federal government power to: Fine and imprison local policemen who are negligent in protecting a prisoner from a lynch mob, and also to Make a county in which a lynching occurs pay a fine up to $10,000 to the victim of his family. Do you approve of this bill?"

- This study interviewed 2,858 national adults face to face. Of the 2,858 total respondents, 2,786 were white, including 1,760 white men and 1,026 white women. For the December 1937 study, I present estimates of white opinion using the "phoneBlack" weight.

6. Gallup Poll # 181(January 13–18, 1940): "Congress is now considering a bill against lynching which would punish lynching these two ways: (HAND CARD TO RESPONDENT) Will you please read this card and tell me whether you approve or disapprove of this bill against lynching. [CARD SAYS: '1. Fine and imprison local police officers who fail to protect a prisoner from a lynch mob/2. Make a county in which a lynching occurs pay a fine up to $10,000 to the victim or his family']"
   - This study interviewed 3,133 national adults face to face (note that iPoll lists 3,134 on the website, but the dataset contains one fewer than that). Of the 3,133 total respondents, 3,033 were white, including 2,028 white men and 1,005 white women. For the January 1940 study, I present estimates of white opinion using the "profWhites" weight.

7. Gallup Poll # 1947-0398: "Politics/Peace Treaty" (June 6–11, 1947): "At present, state governments deal with most crime committed in their own state. In the case of a lynching, do you think the United States (federal) Government should have the right to step in and deal with the crime if the State Government doesn't deal with it justly?"
   - This study interviewed 3,171 national adults face to face. Of the 3,171 total respondents, 2,944 were white, including 1,459 white men and 1,482 white women. For the June 1947 study, I present estimates of white opinion using the "eduWhites" weight.

8. Gallup Poll # 1948-0413: "Inflation/Business/Presidential Election" (February 20–25, 1948): "At present, state governments deal with most crimes committed in their own state. In the case of a lynching, do you think the United States (Federal) Government should have the right to step in and deal with the crime – or do you think this should be left entirely to the state government?"
   - This study interviewed 3,168 national adults face to face. Of the 3,168 total respondents, 2,986 were white, including 1,520 white men and 1,459 white women. For the February

1948 study, I present estimates of white opinion using the "eduWhites" weight.

9. Gallup Poll # 1948-0414: "Foreign Policy/States/Civil Rights/Presidential Election" (March 5–10, 1948): "At present, state governments deal with most crimes committed in their own state. In the case of a lynching, do you think the U.S. (Federal) Government should have the right to step in and deal with the crime – or do you think this should be left entirely to the state government?"

  - This study interviewed 3,040 national adults face to face. Of the 3,040 total respondents, 2,872 were white, including 1,443 white men and 1,427 white women. For the March 1948 study, I present estimates of white opinion using the "eduWhites" weight.

10. Gallup Poll # 1948-0433: "Rationing and Price Control/Neighbors/Business Depression/Taft-Hartley Law/Politics" (November 26–December 1, 1948): "At present, state governments deal with most crimes committed in their own state. In the case of a lynching, do you think the U.S. (Federal) Government should have the right to step in and deal with the crime – or do you think this should be left entirely to the state government?"

  - This study interviewed 3,034 national adults face to face. Of the 3,034 total respondents, 2,745 were white, including 1,377 white men and 1,368 white women. For the November/December 1948 study, I present estimates of white opinion using the "eduWhites" weight.

11. Gallup Poll # 1949-0439: "Pyramid Clubs/Lobbyists/Taxes/Japan/Truman" (March 19–24, 1949): "At present, state governments deal with most crimes committed in their own state. In the case of a lynching, do you think the U.S. (Federal) Government should have the right to step in and deal with the crime – or do you think this should be left entirely to the state government?"

  - This study interviewed 2,193 national adults face to face. Of the 2,193 total respondents, 1,998 were white, including 983 white men and 1,015 white women. For the March 1949 study, I present estimates of white opinion using the "eduWhites" weight.

12. Gallup Poll # 1950-0451: "Government/Politics" (January 8–13, 1950): "At present, state governments deal with most crimes

committed in their own state. In the case of a lynching, do you think the U.S. (federal) government should have the right to step in and deal with the crime – or do you think this should be left entirely to the state and local governments?"

- This study interviewed 1,498 national adults face to face. Of the 1,498 total respondents, 1,322 were white, including 682 white men and 640 white women. For the January 1950 study, I present estimates of white opinion using the "eduWhites" weight.

A footnote in Chapter 2 describes versions of the graphs where the different question types are marked accordingly, which are presented here as Figures A1–A2.

Abolition of the Poll Tax

The analysis of attitudes toward abolishing the poll tax uses the following questions and datasets:

1. Gallup Poll # 1940-0226: World War II/Defense Programs (December 18–23, 1940): "Some Southern states require every voter to pay a poll tax amounting to about a dollar a year before they can vote. Do you think these poll taxes should be abolished?"
   - This study interviewed 3,008 national adults face to face (note that the iPoll documentation lists 3,012). Of the 3,008 total respondents, 2,894 were white, including 2,008 white men and 885 white women. For the December 1940 study, I present estimates of white opinion using the "profWhites" weight.

2. Gallup Poll # 1948-0414: Foreign Policy/States/Civil Rights/Presidential Election (March 5–10, 1948): "Some Southern states require every voter to pay a poll tax amounting to about a dollar a year before they can vote. Do you think these poll taxes should be abolished?"
   - See lynching section.

3. Gallup Poll # 1948-0433: Rationing and Price Control/Neighbors/Business Depression/Taft-Hartley Law/Politics (November 26–December 1, 1948): "Some Southern States require every voter to pay a poll tax amounting to about a dollar a year before they can vote. Do you think these poll taxes should be abolished (done away with)?"
   - See lynching section.

Methodological Appendix for Chapter 2 179

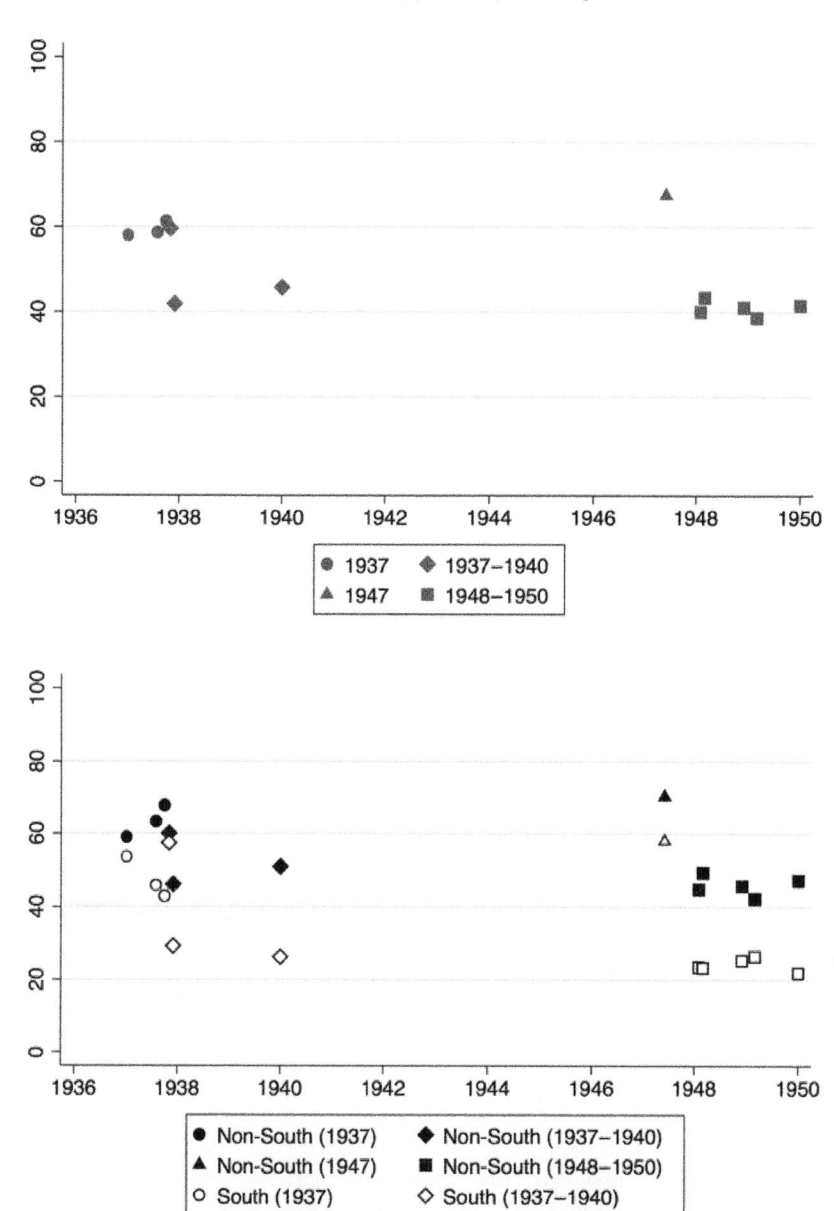

FIGURE A1: Support for federal antilynching legislation by question wording

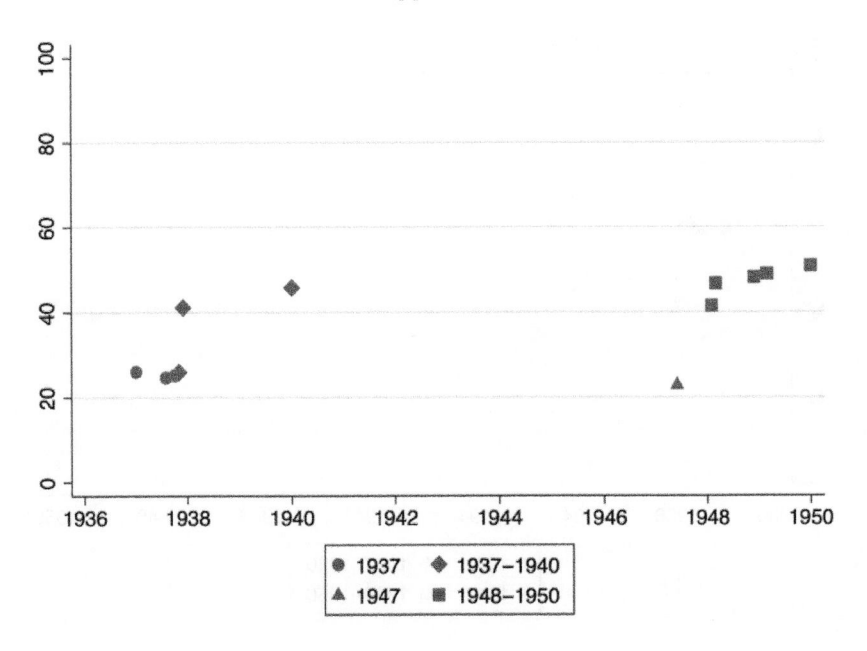

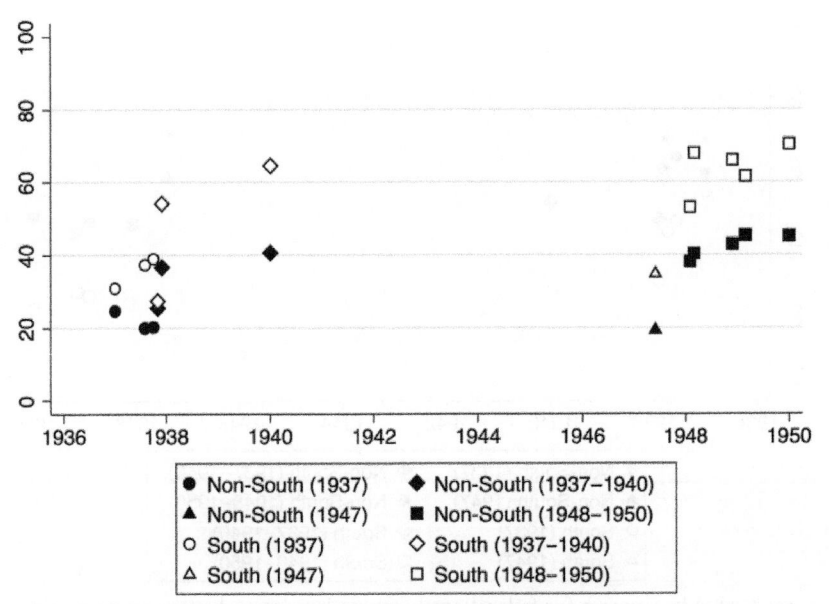

FIGURE A2: Opposition to federal antilynching legislation by question wording

4. Gallup Poll # 1949-0439: Pyramid Clubs/Lobbyists/Taxes/Japan/ Truman (March 19–24, 1949): "Some Southern states require every vote to pay a poll tax amounting to about a dollar a year before they can vote. Do you think these poll taxes should be abolished (done away with)?"
   - See lynching section.
5. Gallup Poll # 450 (November 27–December 1, 1949): "Some Southern states require every voter to pay a poll tax amounting to about a dollar a year before they can vote. Do you think these poll taxes should or should not be abolished (done away with)?"
   - This study interviewed 2,810 national adults face to face, but only those receiving Form K were asked about the poll tax. Of the 1,497 total Form K respondents, 1,358 were white, including 667 white men and 667 white women. For the December 1949 study, I present estimates of white opinion using the "eduWhites" weight.

Wartime Civil Rights Issues

The analysis of attitudes toward military integration uses two surveys. I first use Gallup Poll #270 (June 11–16, 1942), which interviewed 2,932 national adults face to face. This included 2,732 white respondents, with 1,797 white men and 935 white women. I present estimates of white opinion using the "profWhites" weight.

I use the following question:

1. "Should negro and white soldiers serve together in all branches of the armed forces?"

The second dataset for military integration is Gallup Poll # 419 (May 28–June 2, 1948), which interviewed 3,172 national adults face to face. Of the 3,172 total respondents, 2,994 were white, including 1,482 white men and 1,511 white women. I present estimates of white opinion using the "eduWhites" weight. This survey asked two variants of a question about integrating the military:

1. Live and work: "Would you favor or oppose having Negro and white troops throughout the U.S. Armed Services live and work together – or should they be separated as they are now?"
2. Serve: "It has been suggested that white and colored men serve together throughout the U.S. Armed Services – that is, live and

work in the same units. Do you think this is a good idea or a poor idea?"

The analysis of attitudes toward state fair employment laws uses Gallup Poll # 349 (June 14–20, 1945), which interviewed 3,135 national adults, including 2,692 whites, with 1,267 white men and 1,422 white women. I present estimates of white opinion using the "eduWhites" weight. The survey asked two variants of a question about such laws:

1. "Do you favor or oppose a law in this state which would require employers to hire a person if he is qualified for the job, regardless of his race or color?"
2. "Would you favor or oppose a state law which would require employees to work alongside persons of any race or color?"

The analysis of attitudes toward soldier voting uses the 1944 "Soldier's Vote" survey (NORC survey #1944-0222), which interviewed 485 national adults face to face from December 31, 1943, to January 4, 1944. Of the 485 total respondents, 395 were white, including 200 white men and 194 white women. I present estimates of white opinion using a variant of the "eduWhites" weight using a dichotomous South/non-South regional variable. The survey asked the following question:

1. "Do you think Negroes over 21 in the armed forces should be allowed to vote or not?"

METHODOLOGICAL APPENDIX FOR CHAPTER 3

In addition to using the 1946 NORC survey #1946-0241, 1948 Gallup Poll #419, and 1948 Gallup Poll #1948-0413 studies previously used in Chapter 2, the analysis of white attitudes in the 1960s uses the "Negro Political Participation Study, 1961–1962" (ICPSR 7255), which interviewed 694 white adults in the former Confederate states. The researchers also interviewed 618 black adults in the former Confederate states, and an additional 264 black college students. (These samples are not used in this book, but interested readers should consult Christopher Parker's *Fighting for Democracy*.) The study uses the more modern

Methodological Appendix for Chapter 3

ANES sampling procedure, so the concerns about biases in quota sampling are not applicable to this dataset.

I use the following questions:

1. Segregation: "What about you? Are you in favor of integration, strict segregation, or something in between?"
2. Black voting: "Now, I'd like to read some of the kinds of things people tell me when I interview them and ask you whether you agree or disagree with them. I'll read them one at a time and you just tell me the letter in front of the answer that's closest to how you feel... Colored people ought to be allowed to vote."
3. Sit-ins: "What is your feeling about this?" Asked of those who answered yes to "Have you ever heard of the sit-in movement – that is, some of the colored people going into stores, and sitting down at lunch counters, and refusing to leave until they are served?"
4. Anti-integration protests: "Now, I'd like to read some of the kinds of things people tell me when I interview them and ask you whether you agree or disagree with them. I'll read them one at a time and you just tell me the letter in front of the answer that's closest to how you feel... Demonstrations to protest integration of schools are a good idea, even if a few people have to get hurt."
5. Black friend: "Have you ever known a colored person well enough that you would talk to him as a friend?"

Education – necessarily controlled for because of sampling concerns in the 1940s datasets – takes on additional importance when studying veterans, especially in the later time period, as Berinsky suggests using the weighting variables as explanatory variables in regression models.[1] The 1961 cross-tabs are suggestive. In the white sample used here, 26 percent of respondents had some college experience, including 27 percent of men and 25 percent of women. Among men, 35 percent had served in the military during the years appropriate for this study. Among these veterans, 31 percent had some college experience, compared to 25 percent of men overall (and just 10 percent of men in the appropriate age range who had not served in the military).[2] This is likely largely due to the effects of the

---

[1] Berinsky, "American Public Opinion in the 1930s and 1940s," 518.
[2] The latter difference is statistically significant.

1944's Servicemen's Readjustment Act – the GI Bill – which substantially aided white veterans in attending college.[3]

Controlling for education in the 1961 sample might raise concerns about posttreatment bias. The veterans hypothesis is assessed with regression analysis, where a statistically significant coefficient for the veteran variable in a multivariate model (controlling for other factors correlated with racial attitudes) is understood as support for the hypothesis. Educational attainment is part of the model. By 1961 in particular, it is possible that for many respondents educational attainment might actually be partially a result of the "treatment" of military service due to the effects of the GI Bill. In an experimental framework, including posttreatment variables in a model can introduce bias.[4]

Table B1 of this appendix replicates the analysis using a model specification that does not include the educational attainment indicator variables as controls. The results for the voting rights question are robust. For the other three, the coefficients for the veteran variables remain in the same direction, but are now larger and somewhat closer to statistical significance (although the p-values range from 0.14 to 0.18, which still do not meet standard thresholds for significance). These models are more suggestive of a potential relationship between veteran status and

---

[3] While the GI Bill was vastly beneficial for whites, empirical analysis demonstrates its differential effects on educational attainment between northern and southern black veterans, with little effect on collegiate outcomes for black veterans in the South. Sarah Turner and John Bound, "Closing the Gap or Widening the Divide: The Effects of the G.I. Bill and World War II on the Educational Outcomes of Black Americans," *Journal of Economic History* 63(1), March 2003, 145–177. This was not entirely unexpected in the immediate aftermath of the GI Bill's passage. Writing for the American Council on Race Relations at the end of the war, William Caudill predicted that "the white GI will be considered first a veteran, second and incidentally a white man; the Negro GI will often be considered first a Negro, second and incidentally a veteran." Quoted in David H. Onkst, "'First a Negro...Incidentally a Veteran': Black World War Two Veterans and the G. I. Bill of Rights in the Deep South, 1944–1948," *Journal of Social History*, 31(3), 1998, 533. More generally, see the debate between Katznelson and Mettler regarding the GI Bill's potentially differential impact by race: Ira Katznelson, *When Affirmative Action Was White: An Untold History of Racial Inequality in Twentieth-Century America*, (New York: W. W. Norton & Company, 2005); Suzanne Mettler, *Soldiers to Citizens: The G.I. Bill and the Making of the Greatest Generation*, (New York: Oxford University Press, 2007); Ira Katznelson and Suzanne Mettler, "On Race and Policy History: A Dialogue About the G.I. Bill," *Perspectives on Politics* 6(3), 2008, 519–537.

[4] It is important not to use causal language too strongly. Although the draft was semi-random, reasons the military used to refuse service included illiteracy and poor health, which might correlate with racial attitudes and would be hard to control for.

TABLE B1: *1961 veterans analysis (OLS, no education controls)*

	Black Voting	Segregation	Sit-ins	Protest Integration
Veteran	−0.54***	−0.14	−0.22	−0.24
	(0.13)	(0.10)	(0.15)	(0.17)
Age	−0.01	0.00	−0.01	−0.00
	(0.01)	(0.01)	(0.01)	(0.01)
Constant	2.13***	2.63***	4.27***	1.76***
	(0.38)	(0.29)	(0.42)	(0.49)
R^2	0.08	0.01	0.01	0.01
N	198	197	191	192

Standard errors in parentheses. *** $p < 0.001$

TABLE B2: *1961 veterans analysis (ordered probit models)*

	Black Voting	Segregation	Sit-ins	Protest Integration
Veteran	−0.80***	−0.07	−0.15	−0.11
	(0.22)	(0.21)	(0.18)	(0.21)
Grammar	0.29	0.36	0.15	0.43
	(0.32)	(0.30)	(0.27)	(0.31)
HS Grad	0.27	0.03	0.15	0.11
	(0.33)	(0.30)	(0.27)	(0.32)
College	−0.32	−0.71*	−0.45	−0.48
	(0.39)	(0.31)	(0.29)	(0.37)
Age	−0.02	−0.00	−0.00	−0.01
	(0.01)	(0.01)	(0.01)	(0.01)
Cut 1	−0.36	−1.74**	−2.43***	0.28
	(0.65)	(0.64)	(0.60)	(0.66)
Cut 2	0.31	−0.63	−1.67**	0.71
	(0.64)	(0.63)	(0.57)	(0.66)
Cut 3	0.54		−1.15*	0.96
	(0.65)		(0.56)	(0.66)
Cut 4			0.45	
			(0.56)	
Pseudo R^2	0.07	0.07	0.02	0.04
Log Likelihood	−152.83	−154.12	−219.99	−173.66
N	198	197	191	192

Standard errors in parentheses. * $p < 0.05$, ** $p < 0.01$, *** $p < 0.001$

the other measures of racial attitudes, but the evidence for statistical significance is still lacking. It is possible that more significant relationships would be found in a larger dataset, but the nature of historical work

TABLE B3: *Black friend, 1961 (veterans vs. nonveterans)*

	Friend	Friend
Veteran	0.82*	0.90**
	(0.35)	(0.34)
Grammar	−0.20	
	(0.50)	
HS Grad	−0.18	
	(0.52)	
College	0.23	
	(0.58)	
Age	0.01	0.01
	(0.02)	(0.02)
Constant	−0.19	−0.31
	(1.07)	(0.97)
Pseudo R^2	0.03	0.03
Log Likelihood	−124.03	−124.58
N	199	199

Standard errors in parentheses. $^*p < 0.05$, $^{**}p < 0.01$

means that it is likely impossible ever to know for sure. In the spirit of transparency, though, these models are presented here, which will enable readers to make their own interpretive judgments.

In the main text, I use OLS regression for the 1961 dataset. I also provide ordered probit models in Table B2. The results are substantively similar, so I use the easier-to-interpret OLS models in the main text. The chapter also refers to an analysis of the relationship between military service and having a black friend. These results are shown in Table B3 of this appendix.

Bibliography

Alwin, Duane F., Ronald L. Cohen, and Theodore M. Newcomb. 1991. *Political Attitudes Over the Life Span: The Bennington Women After Fifty Years*. Madison: University of Wisconsin Press.

Alwin, Duane F. and Jon A. Krosnick. 1991. "Aging, Cohorts, and the Stability of Sociopolitical Orientations Over the Life Span." *American Journal of Sociology* 97(1). 169–195.

Anderson, Carol. 2003. *Eyes Off the Prize: The United Nations and the African American Struggle for Human Rights, 1944–1955*. New York: Cambridge University Press.

Arsenault, Raymond. 2009. *The Sound of Freedom: Marian Anderson, the Lincoln Memorial, and the Concert That Awakened America*. New York: Bloomsbury Press.

Bateman, David A. 2018. *Disenfranchising Democracy Constructing the Electorate in the United States, the United Kingdom, and France*. New York: Cambridge University Press.

Bateman, David A., Ira Katznelson, and John Lapinski. 2015. "Southern Politics Revisited: On V. O. Key's 'South in the House.'" *Studies in American Political Development* 29(2). 154–184.

Bates, Beth Topkins. 1997. "A New Crowd Challenges the Agenda of the Old Guard in the NAACP, 1933–1941." *American Historical Review* 102(2). 340–377.

Baum, Matthew A. and Samuel Kernell. 2001. "Economic Class and Popular Support for Franklin Roosevelt in War and Peace." *Public Opinion Quarterly* 65. 198–229.

Baylor, Christopher A. 2013. "First to the Party: The Group Origins of the Partisan Transformation on Civil Rights." *Studies in American Political Development* 27(2). 111–141.

Baylor, Christopher A. 2017. *First to the Party: The Group Origins of Political Transformation*. Philadelphia: University of Pennsylvania Press.

Berinsky, Adam J. 2006. "American Public Opinion in the 1930s and 1940s: The Analysis of Quota-Controlled Sample Survey Data." *Public Opinion Quarterly* 70(4). 499–529.

Berinsky, Adam J. 2009. *In Time of War: Understanding American Public Opinion from World War II to Iraq.* Chicago: University of Chicago Press.

Berinsky, Adam and Eric Schickler. 2011. "Gallup Data, 1936–1945: Guide to Coding & Weighting." Unpublished Manuscript, Massachusetts Institute of Technology and University of California, Berkeley.

Berman, William C. 1970. *The Politics of Civil Rights in the Truman Administration.* Columbus: Ohio State University Press.

Black, Earl and Merle Black. 1987. *Politics and Society in the South.* Cambridge: Harvard University Press.

Blair, Sara. 2007. *Harlem Crossroads: Black Writers and the Photograph in the Twentieth Century.* Princeton: Princeton University Press.

Bloom, Joshua. 2015. "The Dynamics of Opportunity and Insurgent Practice: How Black Anti-Colonialists Compelled Truman to Advocate Civil Rights." *American Sociological Review* 80(2). 391–415.

Brinkley, Alan. 1995. *The End of Reform: New Deal Liberalism in Recession and War.* New York: Vintage Books.

Brooks, Jennifer E. 2004. *Defining the Peace: World War II Veterans, Race, and the Remaking of Southern Political Tradition.* Chapel Hill: The University of North Carolina Press.

Brophy, Ira N. 1945–46. "The Luxury of Anti-Negro Prejudice." *Public Opinion Quarterly* 9(4). 456–466.

Butler, John Sibley and Kenneth L. Wilson. 1978. "*The American Soldier* Revisited: Race Relations and the Military." *Social Science Quarterly* 59(3). 451–467.

Bynum, Cornelius L. 2010. *A. Philip Randolph and the Struggle for Civil Rights.* Urbana: University of Illinois Press.

Caldeira, Gregory A. 1987. "Public Opinion and the U.S. Supreme Court: FDR's Court-Packing Plan." *American Political Science Review* 81(4). 139–153.

Campbell, Angus, Philip Converse, Warren Miller, and Donald Stokes. 1960. *The American Voter.* New York: Wiley.

Canaday, Margot. 2009. *The Straight State: Sexuality and Citizenship in Twentieth Century America.* Princeton: Princeton University Press.

Cantril, Hadley and Mildred Strunk. 1951. *Public Opinion 1935–1946.* Princeton: Princeton University Press.

Capoccia, Giovanni and R. Daniel Kelemen. 2007. "The Study of Critical Junctures: Theory, Narrative, and Counterfactuals in Historical Institutionalism." *World Politics* 59(3). 341–369.

Carey, Jr., Tony E., Regina P. Branton, and Valeria Martinez-Ebers. 2014. "The Influence of Social Protests on Issue Salience Among Latinos." *Political Research Quarterly* 67(3). 615–627.

Carrell, Scott E., Mark Hoekstra, and James E. West. 2015. "The Impact of Intergroup Contact on Racial Attitudes and Revealed Preferences." NBER Working Paper No. 20940.

Carroll, Fred. 2017. *Race News: Black Journalists and the Fight for Racial Justice in the Twentieth Century.* Urbana, Chicago, and Springfield: University of Illinois Press.

Carter, Michael. 1942. "U.S. Must Give Vote and Equal Pay to Everyone – Mrs. FDR." *Afro-American*. July 18.

Carter, Michael. 1942. "America Will Lose the Peace unless It Gives Equal Duties and Opportunities to Everyone." *Afro-American*. August 15.

Carter, Michael. 1942. "U.S. Not Using Enough Colored War Workers, Warns Paul V. McNutt." *Afro-American*. December 12.

Carter, Michael. 1943. "Race Hate Choking All of Nation – Dewey." *Afro-American*. October 24.

Carter, Michael. 1943. "I Have Done Everything to Abolish Discrimination." *Afro-American*. June 5.

Carter, Michael. 1943. "An Interview With: Truman K. Gibson Civilian Aide to Secretary of War." *Afro-American*. July 17.

Carter, Michael. 1943. "No Freedom Here for Colored People, says V-President Wallace: 'We Haven't Solved Problem Anywhere.'" *Afro-American*. October 23.

Caughey, Devin. 2018. *The Unsolid South: Mass Politics and National Representation in a One-Party Enclave*. Princeton: Princeton University Press.

Chen, Anthony S. 2009. *The Fifth Freedom: Jobs, Politics, and Civil Rights in the United States, 1941–1972*. Princeton: Princeton University Press.

Cobb, James C. 1997. "World War II and the Mind of the Modern South." In *Remaking Dixie: The Impact of World War II on the American South*, ed. Neil McMillen. Jackson: University Press of Mississippi.

Collins, Charles Wallace. 1947. *Whither Solid South? A Study in Politics and Race Relations*. New Orleans: Pelican Publishing Company.

Collins, William J. 2001. "Race, Roosevelt, and Wartime Production: Fair Employment in World War II Labor Markets." *American Economic Review* 91(1). 272–286.

Converse, Jean. 1987. *Survey Research in the United States: Roots and Emergence 1890–1960*. Berkeley: University of California Press.

Crespi, Leo P. 1945. "Is Gunnar Myrdal on the Right Track?" *Public Opinion Quarterly* 9(2). 201–212.

Dahmer, Claude, Jr. and Elliott McGinnies. 1949. "Shifting Sentiments Toward Civil Rights in a Southern University." *Public Opinion Quarterly* 13(2). 241–251.

Dalfiume, Richard M. 1968. "The 'Forgotten Years' of the Negro Revolution." *The Journal of American History* 55(1). 90–106.

Dalfiume, Richard M. 1969. "Military Segregation and the 1940 Presidential Election." *Phylon* 30(1). 42–55.

Daniel, Pete. 1990. "Going Among Strangers: Southern Reactions to World War II." *The Journal of American History* 77(3). 242–258.

David, Thomas J. 1989. "Emancipation Rhetoric, Natural Rights, and Revolutionary New England: A Note on Four Black Petitions in Massachusetts, 1773–1777." *New England Quarterly* 62(2). 248–263.

"Defeat at Detroit." 1943. *The Nation*. July 3.

Downs, Anthony. 1957. *An Economic Theory of Democracy*. Boston: Addison-Wesley.

Doyle, William. 1999. *Inside the Oval Office: The White House Tapes from FDR to Clinton.* New York: Kodansha International.
Du Bois, W. E. B. 1918. "Close Ranks." *The Crisis.* July.
Du Bois, W. E. B. 1935. *Black Reconstruction in America.* New York: Harcourt, Brace and Company.
Du Bois, W. E. B. 1944. "My Evolving Program for Negro Freedom." In *What the Negro Wants,* ed. Rayford W. Logan. Chapel Hill: University of North Carolina Press.
Dudziak, Mary L. 2000. *Cold War Civil Rights: Race and the Image of American Democracy.* Princeton: Princeton University Press.
Dudziak, Mary L. 2012. *War Time: An Idea, Its History, Its Consequences.* New York: Oxford University Press.
Eisinger, Robert M. 2003. *The Evolution of Presidential Polling.* New York: Cambridge University Press.
Ellison, Ralph. 1995. *Shadow and Act.* New York: Vintage Books.
Emery, Michael, Edwin Emery, and Nancy L. Roberts. 2000. *The Press and America: An Interpretive History of the Mass Media.* Boston: Allyn & Bacon.
Epstein, Lee and Jeffrey A. Segal. 2000. "Measuring Issue Salience." *American Journal of Political Science* 44(1). 66–83.
Erikson, Robert S. 1976. "The Relationship Between Public Opinion and State Policy: A New Look Based on Some Forgotten Data." *American Journal of Political Science* 20(1). 25–36.
Ewald, Alec C. 2009. *The Way We Vote: The Local Dimension of American Suffrage.* Nashville: Vanderbilt University Press.
Farhang, Sean and Ira Katznelson. 2005. "The Southern Imposition: Congress and Labor in the New Deal and Fair Deal." *Studies in American Political Development* 19. 1–30.
Ferrell, Robert H. 1994. *Choosing Truman: The Democratic Convention of 1944.* Columbia: University of Missouri Press.
Finkle, Lee. 1973. "The Conservative Aims of Militant Rhetoric: Black Protest During World War II." *The Journal of American History* 60(3). 692–713.
Foner, Eric. 1988. *Reconstruction: America's Unfinished Revolution, 1863–1877.* New York: Harper & Row.
Fordham, Benjamin O. 2016. "Historical Perspective on Public Support for the Draft: War Costs and Military Service." *Journal of Global Security Studies* 1(4). 302–322.
Francis, Megan Ming. 2014. *Civil Rights and the Making of the Modern American State.* New York: Cambridge University Press.
Fraser, Nancy and Linda Gordon. 1994. "Civil Citizenship Against Social Citizenship? On the Ideology of Contract-Versus-Charity." In *The Condition of Citizenship,* eds. Bart van Steenbergen. Thousand Oaks: SAGE.
Frederickson, Kari. 2001. *The Dixiecrat Revolt and the End of the Solid South, 1936–1968.* Chapel Hill: The University of North Carolina Press.
Fried, Amy. 2012. *Pathways to Polling: Crisis, Cooperation and the Making of Public Opinion.* New York: Routledge.
Frymer, Paul. 2007. *Black and Blue: African Americans, the Labor Movement, and the Decline of the Democratic Party.* Princeton: Princeton University Press.

Garfinkel, Herbert. 1973. *When Negroes March: The March on Washington Movement in the Organizational Politics for FEPC.* New York: Atheneum.

Gibson, Campbell and Kay Jung. 2002. "Historical Census Statistics on Population Totals by Race, 1870 to 1990, and by Hispanic Origin, 1970 to 1990, for the United States, Regions, Divisions, and States." Unpublished Manuscript, Population Division, U.S. Census Bureau.

Gillon, Steven M. 1987. *Politics and Vision: The ADA and American Liberalism, 1947–1985.* New York: Oxford University Press.

Glenn, Evelyn Nakano. 2004. *Unequal Freedom: How Race and Gender Shaped American Citizenship and Labor.* Cambridge: Harvard University Press.

Goodwin, Doris Kearns. 1994. *No Ordinary Time: Franklin and Eleanor Roosevelt: The Home Front in World War II.* New York: Simon & Schuster Paperbacks.

Gourevitch, Peter. 1978. "The Second Image Reversed: The International Sources of Domestic Politics." *International Organization* 32(4). 881–912.

Graves, John Temple. 1942. "The Southern Negro and the War Crisis." *Virginia Quarterly Review* 18(4). 500–517.

Green, Thomas Lee. 1981. "Black Cabinet Members in the Franklin Delano Roosevelt Administration." PhD dissertation, University of Colorado.

Greenberg, David. 2008. "The Idea of 'the Liberal Media' and Its Roots in the Civil Rights Movement." *The Sixties: A Journal of History, Politics and Culture* 1(2). 167–186.

Guglielmo, Thomas A. 2006. "Fighting for Caucasian Rights: Mexicans, Mexican Americans, and the Transnational Struggle for Civil Rights in World War II Texas." *The Journal of American History* 92(4). 1212–1237.

Guglielmo, Thomas A. 2010. "'Red Cross, Double Cross': Race and America's World War II-Era Blood Donor Service." *Journal of American History* 91(1). 63–90.

Haas, Francis J. and G. James Fleming. 1946. "Personnel Practices and Wartime Changes." *Annals of the American Academy of Political and Social Science* 244. 48–56.

Hall, Jacquelyn Dowd. 2005. "The Long Civil Rights Movement and the Political Uses of the Past." *Journal of American History* 91(4). 1233–1263.

Hamby, Alonzo L. 1976. *Beyond the New Deal: Harry S. Truman and American Liberalism.* New York: Columbia University Press.

Hamby, Alonzo L. 1991. "An American Democrat: A Reevaluation of the Personality of Harry S. Truman." *Political Science Quarterly* 106(1). 33–55.

Hassall, Mark. 2000. "The Army." In *The Cambridge Ancient History*, ed. Alan K. Bowman, Peter Garnsey, and Dominic Rathbone. Vol. 11. New York: Cambridge University Press.

Hastie, William G. and Thurgood Marshall. 1942. "Negro Discrimination and the Need for Federal Action." *Law Guild Review.* 21–23.

Henderson, Alexa B. "FEPC and the Southern Railway Case: An Investigation into the Discriminatory Practice of Railroads During World War II." *Journal of Negro History* 61(2). 173–187.

Herbst, Susan. 1993. *Numbered Voices: How Opinion Polling Has Shaped American Politics.* Chicago: University of Chicago Press.

Hine, Darlene Clark. 1979. *Black Victory: The Rise and Fall of the White Primary in Texas*. Millwood, NY: KTO Press.

Hintze, Otto. 1994. "Military Organization and the Organization of the State." In *The State: Critical Concepts*, ed. John A. Hall. New York: Routledge.

Hirsch, Arnold. 1998. *Making the Second Ghetto: Race and Housing in Chicago, 1940–1960*. Chicago: University of Chicago Press.

Hohn, Maria. 2008. "'We Will Never Go Back to the Old Way Again': Germany in the African-American Debate on Civil Rights." *Central European History* 41(4). 605–637.

Horne, Gerald. 1986. *Black & Red: W.E.B. Du Bois and the Afro-American Response to the Cold War, 1944–1963*. Albany: State University of New York Press.

Horton, Carol A. 2005. *Race and the Making of American Liberalism*. New York: Oxford University Press.

Horton, James Oliver and Lois E. Horton. 1998. *In Hope of Liberty: Culture, Community and Protest Among Northern Free Blacks, 1700–1860*. New York: Oxford University Press.

Horton, Lois E. 1999. "From Class to Race in Early America: Northern Post-Emancipation Racial Reconstruction." *Journal of the Early Republic* 19(4). 629–649.

Howell, William, Saul Jackman, and Jon Rogowski. 2013. *The Wartime President*. Chicago: The University of Chicago Press.

Jacobs, Lawrence R. and Robert Y. Shapiro. 1989. "Public Opinion and the New Social History: Some Lessons for the Study of Public Opinion and Democratic Policy Making." *Social Science History* 13. 1–24.

Janken, Kenneth Robert. 2003. *White: The Biography of Walter White, Mr. NAACP*. New York: The New Press.

Jenkins, Jeffrey A. and Justin Peck. 2013. "Building Toward Major Policy Change: Congressional Action on Civil Rights, 1941–1950." *Law and History Review* 31(1). 139–198.

Johnson, Charles S. and Associates. 1943. *To Stem This Tide: A Survey of Racial Tension Areas in the United States*. New York: AMS Press.

Johnson, Kimberley. 2010. *Reforming Jim Crow: Southern Politics and State in the Age Before Brown*. New York: Oxford University Press.

Jordan, William. 1995. "'The Damnable Dilemma': African-American Accommodation and Protest During World War I." *Journal of American History* 81(4). 1562–1583.

Juhnke, William E. 1974. "Creating a New Charter of Freedom: The Organization and Operation of the President's Committee on Civil Rights, 1946–48." PhD dissertation, University of Kansas.

Juhnke, William E. 1989. "President Truman's Committee on Civil Rights: The Interaction of Politics, Protest, and Presidential Advisory Commission." *Presidential Studies Quarterly* 19. 593–610.

Kastellec, Jonathan P. and Eduardo L. Leoni. 2007. "Using Graphs Instead of Tables in Political Science." *Perspectives on Politics* 5(4). 755–771.

Katz, Michael B. 2008. *The Price of Citizenship: Redefining the American Welfare State: Updated Edition*. Philadelphia: University of Pennsylvania Press.

Katznelson, Ira. 1999. "*Review of Civic Ideals: Conflicting Visions of Citizenship in U.S. History. Political Theory* 27(4). 565–570.
Katznelson, Ira. 2005. *When Affirmative Action Was White: An Untold History of Racial Inequality in Twentieth-Century America.* New York: W. W. Norton & Company.
Katznelson, Ira. 2013. *Fear Itself: The New Deal and the Origins of Our Time.* New York: Liveright Publishing Corporation.
Katznelson, Ira, Kim Geiger, and Danial Kryder. 1993. "Limiting Liberalism: The Southern Veto in Congress, 1933–1950." *Political Science Quarterly* 108(2). 283–306.
Katznelson, Ira and Suzanne Mettler. 2008. "On Race and Policy History: A Dialogue About the G.I. Bill." *Perspectives on Politics* 6(3). 519–537.
Katznelson, Ira and Martin Shefter, ed. 2002. *Shaped by War and Trade: International Influences on American Political Development.* Princeton: Princeton University Press.
Kellstedt, Paul M. 2003. *The Mass Media and the Dynamics of American Racial Attitudes.* New York: Cambridge University Press.
Kelly, Alfred H. 1987 [1962]. "The School Desegregation Case." In *Quarrels That Have Shaped the Constitution*, ed. John A. Garraty. New York: Harper & Row Publishers.
Kerber, Linda K. 1998. *No Constitutional Right to Be Ladies: Women and the Obligations of Citizenship.* New York: Hill and Wang.
Key, V. O., Jr. 2006 [1949]. *Southern Politics in State and Nation.* Knoxville: University of Tennessee Press.
Keyssar, Alexander. 2000. *The Right to Vote: The Contested History of Democracy in the United States.* New York: Basic Books.
Kier, Elizabeth and Ronald R. Krebs, ed. 2010. *In War's Wake: International Conflict and the Fate of Liberal Democracy.* New York: Cambridge University Press.
Kier, Elizabeth and Ronald R. Krebs. 2010. "Introduction: War and Democracy in Comparative Perspective." In *In War's Wake: International Conflict and the Fate of Liberal Democracy*, ed. Elizabeth Kier and Ronald R. Krebs. New York: Cambridge University Press.
Kirby, John B. 1980. *Black Americans in the Roosevelt Era: Liberalism and Race.* Knoxville: University of Tennessee Press.
Klarman, Michael J. 2001. "The White Primary Rulings: A Case Study in the Consequences of Supreme Court Decisionmaking." *Florida State University Law Review* 29(1). 55–107.
Klinkner, Philip A. 2001. Review of *Divided Arsenal: Race and the American State During World War II. American Political Science Review* 95(3). 735.
Klinkner, Philip A. and Rogers M. Smith. 2002. *The Unsteady March: The Rise and Decline of Racial Equality in America.* Chicago: University of Chicago Press.
Koistinen, Paul A. C. 2004. *Arsenal of World War II: The Political Economy of American Warfare, 1949–1945.* Lawrence: University Press of Kansas.
Koppes, Clayton R. and Gregory D. Black. 1986. "Blacks, Loyalty, and Motion-Picture Propaganda in World War II." *Journal of American History* 73(2). 383–406.

Krebs, Ronald R. 2003. "Rights and Gun Sights: Military Service and the Politics of Citizenship." PhD dissertation, Columbia University.

Krebs, Ronald R. 2006. *Fighting for Rights: Military Service and the Politics of Citizenship*. Ithaca: Cornell University Press.

Krock, Arthur. 1944. "In the Nation: Self-Reexamination Continues in This Supreme Court." *New York Times*. April 4.

Kruse, Kevin M. and Stephen Tuck. 2012. "Introduction: The Second World War and the Civil Rights Movement." In *Fog of War: The Second World War and the Civil Rights Movement*, ed. Kevin M. Kruse and Stephen Tuck. New York: Oxford University Press.

Kryder, Daniel. 2000. *Divided Arsenal: Race and the American State During World War II*. New York: Cambridge University Press.

Ladd, Jonathan M. 2011. *Why Americans Hate the Media and How It Matters*. Princeton: Princeton University Press.

Lawrence, George H. and Thomas D. Kane. 1995. "Military Service and Racial Attitudes of White Veterans." *Armed Forces & Society* 22(2). 235–255.

Lawson, Steven F. 1976. *Black Ballots: Voting Rights in the South, 1944–1969*. New York: Columbia University Press.

Lazarsfeld, Paul F. 1950–1951. "The Obligations of the 1950 Pollster to the 1984 Historian." *Public Opinion Quarterly* 14(4). 617–638.

Lee, Taeku. 2002. *Mobilizing Public Opinion: Black Insurgency and Racial Attitudes in the Civil Rights Era*. Chicago: University of Chicago Press.

Leff, Mark H. 1991. "The Politics of Sacrifice on the American Home Front in World War II." *Journal of American History* 77(4), 1296–1318.

Levy, Yahil. 2013. "Convertible Sacrifice – A Conceptual Proposition." *Sociological Perspectives* 56(3). 439–463.

Lichtenstein, Nelson and Robert Korstad. 1988. "Opportunities Found and Lost: Labor, Radicals, and the Early Civil Rights Movement." *Journal of American History* 75(3). 786–811.

Lieberman, Robert C. 1998. *Shifting the Color Line: Race and the American Welfare State*. Cambridge: Harvard University Press.

Logan, Rayford W., ed. 1944. *What the Negro Wants*. Chapel Hill: University of North Carolina Press.

Lovell, George I. 2012. *This is Not Civil Rights: Discovering Rights Talk in 1939 America*. Chicago: University of Chicago Press.

Lucks, Daniel S. 2009. "The Vietnam War and Its Tragic Impact on the Civil Rights Movement and African Americans." PhD dissertation, University of California, Berkeley.

Lucks, Daniel S. 2016. *Selma to Saigon: The Civil Rights Movement and the Vietnam War*. Lexington: University Press of Kentucky.

Lustick, Ian S. 1996. "History, Historiography, and Political Science: Multiple Historical Records and the Problem of Selection Bias." *American Political Science Review* 90(3). 605–618.

Marshall, T. H. 1950. *Citizenship and Social Class: And Other Essays*. New York: Cambridge University Press.

Martin, John Frederick. 1979. *Civil Rights and the Crisis of Liberalism: The Democratic Party 1945–1975*. Boulder: Westview Press.

Marwick, Arthur. 1974. *War and Social Change in the Twentieth Century: A Comparative Study of Britain, France, Germany, Russia, and the United States.* London: Macmillan.

Marwick, Arthur, ed. 1988. *Total War and Social Change.* New York: St. Martin's Press.

Masaharu, Sato and Barak Kushner. 1999. "'Negro Propaganda Operations': Japan's Short-Wave Radio Broadcasts for World War II Black Americans." *Historical Journal of Film, Radio, and Television* 19(1). 5–26.

Maslow, Will. 1946. "FEPC: A Case Study in Parliamentary Maneuver." *University of Chicago Law Review* 13(4). 407–444.

Matthews, Donald R. and James W. Prothro. 1966. *Negroes and the New Southern Politics.* New York: Harcourt, Brace & World.

Mayhew, David R. 2005. "Wars and American Politics." *Perspectives on Politics* 3(3). 473–493.

McAdam, Doug. 1999 [1982]. *Political Process and the Development of Black Insurgency 1930–1970: Second Edition.* Chicago: The University of Chicago Press.

McCulloch, Margaret C. 1943. "What Should the American Negro Reasonably Expect as the Outcome of a Real Peace?" *The Journal of Negro Education* 12(3). 557–567.

McCullough, David. 1992. *Truman.* New York: Simon & Schuster.

McMahon, Kevin J. 2004. *Reconsidering Roosevelt on Race: How the Presidency Paved the Road to Brown.* Chicago: University of Chicago Press.

McMillen, Neil R. 1997. "Fighting for What We Didn't Have: How Mississippi's Black Veterans Remember World War II." In *Remaking Dixie: The Impact of World War II on the American South*, ed. Neil R. McMillen. Jackson: University Press of Mississippi.

Melish, Joanne Pope. 2000. *Disowning Slavery: Gradual Emancipation and ? Race? in New England, 1780–1860.* Ithaca: Cornell University Press.

Mershon, Sherie and Steven Schlossman. 1998. *Foxholes & Color Lines: Desegregating the U.S. Armed Forces.* Baltimore: Johns Hopkins University Press.

Mettler, Suzanne. 2007. *Soldiers to Citizens: The G.I. Bill and the Making of the Greatest Generation.* New York: Oxford University Press.

Mickey, Robert. 2015. *Paths Out of Dixie: The Democratization of Authoritarian Enclaves in America's Deep South, 1944–1972.* Princeton: Princeton University Press.

Modell, John, Marc Goulden, and Sigurdur Magnusson. 1989. "World War II in the Lives of Black Americans: Some Findings and Interpretations." *The Journal of American History* 76(3). 838–848.

Moon, Henry Lee. 1948. *The Balance of Power: The Negro Vote.* Garden City, NY: Doubleday.

Moskos, Charles C. 1966. "Racial Integration in the Armed Forces." *American Journal of Sociology* 72(2). 132–148.

Motz, Jane R. 1964. "The Black Cabinet: Negroes in the Administration of Franklin D. Roosevelt." Master's thesis, University of Delaware.

Myrdal, Gunnar. 1944. *An American Dilemma: The Negro Problem and Modern Democracy.* New York: Harper & Brothers Publishers.

National Opinion Research Center. 1944. *Should Soldiers Vote! A Special Report Based on a Spot-Check Survey.*
National Opinion Research Center. 2011. *Social Science Research in Action.*
Ng, Wendy L. 2002. *Japanese American Internment During World War II: A History and Reference Guide.* Westport, CT: Greenwood Press.
Nteta, Tatishe M. and Melinda R. Tarsi. 2016. "Self-Selection Versus Socialization Revisited: Military Service, Racial Resentment, and Generational Membership." *Armed Forces & Society* 42(2). 362–385.
Odum, Howard W. 1948. "Social Change in the South." *Journal of Politics* 10(2). 242–258.
O'Kelly, Charlotte G. 1982. "Black Newspapers and the Black Protest Movement: Their Historical Relationship, 1827–1945." *Phylon* 43(1). 1–14.
Onkst, David H. 1998. "'First a Negro…Incidentally a Veteran': Black World War Two Veterans and the G. I. Bill of Rights in the Deep South, 1944–1948." *Journal of Social History* 31(3). 517–543.
Pagán, Eduardo Obregón. 2003. *Murder at the Sleepy Lagoon: Zoot Suits, Race, and Riot in Wartime L.A..* Chapel Hill: The University of North Carolina Press.
Page, Benjamin I. and Robert Y. Shapiro. 1992. *The Rational Public: Fifty Years of Trends in Americans' Policy Preferences.* Chicago: The University of Chicago Press.
Parker, Christopher S. 2009. "When Politics Becomes Protest: Black Veterans and Political Activism in the Postwar South." *Journal of Politics* 71. 113–131.
Parker, Christopher S. 2009. *Fighting for Democracy: Black Veterans and the Struggle Against White Supremacy in the Postwar South.* Princeton: Princeton University Press.
President's Committee on Civil Rights. 1947. *To Secure These Rights: The Report of the President's Committee on Civil Rights.* Washington, DC: U.S. Government Printing Office.
President's Committee on Equality of Treatment and Opportunity in the Armed Services. 1950. *Freedom to Serve: Equality of Treatment and Opportunity in the Armed Services: A Report by the President's Committee.* Washington, DC: U.S. Government Printing Office.
Prior, Markus. 2007. *Post-Broadcast Democracy: How Media Choice Increases Inequality in Political Involvement and Polarizes Elections.* New York: Cambridge University Press.
Rable, George C. 1958. "The South and the Politics of Antilynching Legislation, 1920–1940." *Journal of Southern History* 51. 201–220.
Reddick, L. D. 1953. "The Negro Policy of the American Army Since World War II." *The Journal of Negro History* 38(2). 194–215.
Riehm, Edith S. 2002. "Forging the Civil Rights Frontier: How Truman's Committee Set the Liberal Agenda for Reform 1947–1965." PhD dissertation, Georgia State University.
Roberts, Gene and Hank Klibanoff. 2006. *The Race Beat: The Press, the Civil Rights Struggle, and the Awakening of a Nation.* New York: Alfred A. Knopf.
Robinson, Greg. 2010. *A Tragedy of Democracy: Japanese Confinement in North America.* New York: Columbia University Press.

Roosevelt, Franklin D. 1943. "Excerpts from the Press Conference," December 28, 1943. Online by Gerhard Peters and John T. Woolley, The American Presidency Project. www.presidency.ucsb.edu/ws/?pid=16358.
Rosenberg, Jonathan. 2005. *How Far the Promised Land?: World Affairs and the American Civil Rights Movement from the First World War to Vietnam*. Princeton: Princeton University Press.
Rostow, Eugene V. 1945. "The Japanese American Cases – A Disaster." *Yale Law Journal* 54. 489–535.
Rotnem, Victor W. 1943. "The Federal Civil Right 'Not to Be Lynched.'" *Washington University Law Review* 28(2). 57–73.
Ryan, Joseph W. 2010. "What Were They Thinking? Samuel A. Stouffer and *The American Soldier*." PhD dissertation, University of Kansas.
Saldin, Robert P. 2010. *War, the American State, and Politics Since 1898*. New York: Cambridge University Press.
Schickler, Eric. 2013. "New Deal Liberalism and Racial Liberalism in the Mass Public, 1937–1968." *Perspectives on Politics* 11(1). 75–98.
Schickler, Eric. 2016. *Racial Realignment: The Transformation of American Liberalism, 1932–1965*. Princeton: Princeton University Press.
Schickler, Eric and Devin Caughey. 2011. "Public Opinion, Organized Labor, and the Limits of New Deal Liberalism." *Studies in American Political Development* 25(2). 162–189.
Schickler, Eric, Kathryn Pearson, and Brian D. Feinstein. 2010. "Congressional Parties and Civil Rights Politics from 1933 to 1972." *Journal of Politics* 72(3). 672–689.
Schultz, Kevin M. 2008. "The FEPC and the Legacy of the Labor-Based Civil Rights Movement of the 1940s." *Labor History* 49(1). 71–92.
Schuman, Howard, Charlotte Steeh, Lawrence Bobo, and Maria Krysan. 1997. *Racial Attitudes in America: Trends and Interpretations: Revised Edition*. Cambridge: Harvard University Press.
Shapiro, Ian and Sonu Bedi. 2007. "Introduction: Contingency's Challenge to Political Science." In *Political Contingency: Studying the Unexpected, the Accidental, and the Unforeseen*, ed. Ian Shapiro and Sonu Bedi. New York: New York University Press.
Shapiro, Robert Y. 2016. "Public Opinion." In *The Oxford Handbook of American Political Development*, ed. Richard Valelly, Suzanne Mettler, and Robert Lieberman. New York: Oxford University Press.
Shklar, Judith N. 1991. *American Citizenship: The Quest for Inclusion*. Cambridge: Harvard University Press.
Silberman, Charles. 1964. *Crisis in Black and White*. New York: Random House.
Sitkoff, Harvard. 1971. "Racial Militancy and Interracial Violence in the Second World War." *The Journal of American History* 58(3). 661–681.
Sitkoff, Harvard. 1971. "Harry Truman and the Election of 1948: The Coming of Age of Civil Rights in American Politics." *The Journal of Southern History* 37(4). 597–616.
Sitkoff, Harvard. 2010. *Toward Freedom Land: The Long Struggle for Racial Equality in America*. Lexington: The University Press of Kentucky.
Skowronek, Stephen. 1995. "Order and Change." *Polity* 28(1). 91–96.

Skrenty, John David. 1998. "The Effect of the Cold War on African-American Civil Rights: America and the World Audience, 1945–1968." *Theory and Society* 27(2). 237–285.
Smith, Rogers M. 1999. *Civic Ideals: Conflicting Visions of Citizenship in U.S. History*. New Haven: Yale University Press.
Sokol, Jason. 2006. *There Goes My Everything: White Southerners in the Age of Civil Rights, 1945–1975*. New York: Alfred A. Knopf.
Sosna, Morton. 1997. "Introduction." In *Remaking Dixie: The Impact of World War II on the American South*, ed. Neil McMillen. Jackson: University Press of Mississippi.
Southern, David W. 1987. *Gunnar Myrdal and Black-White Relations: The Use and Abuse of an American Dilemma*. Baton Rouge: Louisiana State University Press.
Springer, Melanie J. "Defining 'the South' (Is Not a Straightforward Matter)." Paper presented at the 2011 meeting of the State Politics and Policy Conference, Hanover, NH.
Springer, Melanie J. and Seth C. McKee. 2015. "A Tale of 'Two Souths': White Voting Behavior in Contemporary Southern Elections." *Social Science Quarterly* 96(2). 588–607.
Stimson, James A., Michael B. MacKuen, and Robert S. Erikson. 1995. "Dynamic Representation." *American Political Science Review* 89(3). 543–565.
Stouffer, Samuel A., Arthur A. Lumsdaine, Marion Harper Lumsdaine, Robin M. Williams, Jr., M. Brewster Smith, Irving L. Janis, Shirley A. Star, and Leonard S. Cottrell, Jr. 1949. *The American Soldier: Combat and Its Aftermath*. Princeton: Princeton University Press.
Stouffer, Samuel A., Edward A. Suchman, Leland C. DeVinney, Shirely A. Star, and Robin M. Williams, Jr. 1949. *The American Soldier: Adjustment During Army Life*. Princeton: Princeton University Press.
Sullivan, Patricia. 2012. "Movement Building During the World War II Era: The NAACP's Legal Insurgency in the South." In *Fog of War: The Second World War and the Civil Rights Movement*, ed. Kevin M. Kruse and Stephen Tuck. New York: Oxford University Press.
Tarrow, Sidney. 1998. *Power in Movement: Social Movements and Contentious Politics: Second Edition*. New York: Cambridge University Press.
Tilly, Charles. 1975. "Reflections on the History of European State-Making." In *The Formation of National States in Western Europe*, ed. Charles Tilly. Princeton: Princeton University Press.
Tilly, Charles. 1992. *Coercion, Capital, and European States, AD 990–1992*. Malden, MA: Wiley-Blackwell.
Topping, Simon. 2004. "'Supporting Our Friends and Defeating Our Enemies': Militancy and Nonpartisanship in the NAACP, 1936–1948." *Journal of African American History* 89(1). 17–35.
Turner, Sarah and John Bound. 2003. "Closing the Gap or Widening the Divide: The Effects of the G.I. Bill on the Educational Outcomes of Black Americans." *The Journal of Economic History* 63(1). 145–177.

Ward, Jason Morgan. 2011. *Defending White Democracy: The Making of a Segregationist Movement & the Remaking of Racial Politics, 1936–1965*. Chapel Hill: University of North Carolina Press.

Ward, Jason Morgan. 2012. "'A War for States' Rights': The White Supremacist Vision of Double Victory." In *Fog of War: The Second World War and the Civil Rights Movement*, ed. Kevin M. Kruse and Stephen Tuck. New York: Oxford University Press.

Weatherford, Stephen M. and Boris Sergeyev. 2003. "Thinking About Economic Interests: Class and Recession in the New Deal." *Political Behavior* 22(4). 311–339.

Weir, Margaret. 2005. "States, Race, and the Decline of New Deal Liberalism." *Studies in American Political Development* 19. 157–172.

Weiss, Nancy J. 1983. *Farewell to the Party of Lincoln: Black Politics in the Age of FDR*. Princeton: Princeton University Press.

Welch, Susan. 2014. "American Opinion Toward Jews During the Nazi Era: Results from Quota Sample Polling During the 1930s and 1940s." *Social Science Quarterly* 95(3). 615–635.

West, Darrell. 2001. *The Rise and Fall of the Media Establishment*. Boston: Bedford/St. Martin's.

Whitaker, Robert A. 2016. "Freedom of Speech: The Speeches of the Warren Court Justices and the Legitimacy of the Supreme Court." PhD dissertation, University at Albany, State University of New York.

White, Steven. 2014. "The Heterogeneity of Southern White Distinctiveness." *American Politics Research* 42(4). 551–578.

White, Walter. 1945. *A Rising Wind*. Garden City, NY: Doubleday, Doran and Company, Inc.

White, Walter. 1948. *A Man Called White: The Autobiography of Walter White*. New York: The Viking Press.

Williams, Chad L. 2010. *Torchbearers of Democracy: African American Soldiers in the World War I Era*. Chapel Hill: University of North Carolina Press.

Williams, Chad L. 2018. "World War I in the Historical Imagination of W. E. B. Du Bois." *Modern American History* 1(1). 3–22.

Winter, James P. and Chaim H. Eyal. 1981. "Agenda Setting for the Civil Rights Issue." *Public Opinion Quarterly* 45(3). 376–383.

Woodward, C. Vann. 1955. *The Strange Career of Jim Crow*. New York: Oxford University Press.

Wu, Ellen. 2014. *The Color of Success: Asian Americans and the Origins of the Model Minority*. Princeton: Princeton University Press.

Wynn, Neil A. 1993 [1976]. *The Afro-American and the Second World War: Revised Edition*. New York: Holmes & Meier.

Zangrando, Robert L. 1980. *The NAACP Crusade Against Lynching, 1909–1950*. Philadelphia: Temple University Press.

Zelizer, Julian E. 2012. "Confronting the Roadblock: Congress, Civil Rights, and World War II." In *Fog of War: The Second World War and the Civil Rights Movement*, ed. Kevin M. Kruse and Stephen Tuck. New York: Oxford University Press.

Index

A Rising Wind, see White, Walter
Acheson, Dean, 155
Advisory Committee on Negro Troop Policies, 118
African Americans
  as the "balance of power", 130
  in the military, 110–112
    Army, 111
    Marine Corps, 111
    Navy, 111–112
    quota, 111
  migration, 129–130
Aiken, SC, 134
Alabama, 64, 153
Alexander, Sadie, 137, 145
American Civil Liberties Union (ACLU), 137
American Council on Race Relations, 42
American Federation of Labor (AFL), 135
American Jewish Committee, 152, 154
American National Election Studies (ANES), 33
The American Soldier, 75, 90–92
Americans for Democratic Action (ADA), 130, 151
An American Dilemma, see Myrdal, Gunnar
Anderson, Carol, 163
Anderson, Marian, 11, 32
Anti-Semitism, 99, 109, 169
Axis powers, 2, 20, 23, 103

Baltimore Afro-American, 102–106
Barfoot, Van T., 67
Baylor, Christopher, 13
Berinsky, Adam, 34
Berman, William C., 152
Bernstein, Meyer, 154
Bethune, Mary McLeod, 117, 126
Biddle, Francis, 99–101, 109
Bilbo, Theodore, 67, 133, 141
Birmingham, AL, 141
Black Cabinet, 11–12
Black Worker, 120–121
Black, Hugo, 31
Brinkley, Alan, 3
Brooks, Jennifer, 69
Brotherhood of Sleeping Car Porters, 3, 117
Brown v. Board of Education, 39
Brown, Jeanette Welch, 117
Burge, Wendell, 101
Butler, John Sibley, 71
Byrd, Harry, 141

California, 63
Camp Gordon, 134
Canaday, Margot, 15
Cantril, Hadley, 32
Capoccia, Giovanni, 24
Carey, James B., 137
Carmichael, Stokely, 164
Carr, Robert K., 137

Carter, Michael, 102–106
Carthage, MS, 67
Charlotte, NC, 141
Chen, Anthony, 125
Chicago Defender, 120, 134, 140
Chicago, IL, 63
Churchill, Winston, 124
Civil Rights Congress, 107
Civil Rights Section (Justice Department), 100, 101, 124
Civil War, 9, 95
Clark, Tom, 136
Cold War, 18, 126, 153–154, 163
Columbia, TN, 107
Committee Against Jim Crow in Military Service and Training, 144
Congress, 4, 25, 95, 140–142, 144, 153
Congress of Industrial Organizations (CIO), 12, 130, 137, 154
Congress of Racial Equality (CORE), 164
contact hypothesis, 71, 88–93
contingency, 170
Costigan, Edward, 108
Cramer, Lawrence, 99
The Crisis, 110
critical junctures, 24, 158

Dahlquist, John E., 147–148
Dalfiume, Richard, 163
Daniel, Pete, 5
Daniels, Jonathan, 42, 100–101, 117
Dartmouth College, 137
Daughters of the American Revolution, 32
Dawson, Donald, 152
Democratic National Convention (1948), 130, 151
Democratic Party, *see* Democratic National Convention (1948), *see* Humphrey, Hubert, *see* Lucas, Scott, *see* Mitchell, Arthur, *see* Roosevelt, Franklin, *see* Truman, Harry
Department of Justice, 100, 101, 124
Des Moines, IA, 115
desegregation, military, *see* segregation, military
Detroit race riot, 1, 67, 103
Detroit, MI, 1–2, 67, 101, 103
Dewey, Thomas, 103, 151
Dickey, John S., 137
Dies Committee, 102
discrimination
  against black soldiers and veterans, 138–139
  in employment, 119–120
Dixiecrats, 130
Donahue, Alphonsus J., 146
Double-V campaign, 3, 4
Downs, Anthony, 170
Du Bois, W. E. B., 10–12
Dudziak, Mary, 18, 20–21, 156
dynamic representation, 25

Early, Stephen, 113, 124
Eastland, James, 4, 67
Eisenhower, Dwight, 69
elections
  1936, 11, 31
  1944, 99, 153
  1948, 130, 151
  1960, 155
Embree, Edwin, 107
Ernst, Morris L., 137
Ethridge, Mark, 96, 124
Evansville, IN, 68
executive branch
  growth in executive power during wartime, 25–26, 66
  justification of focus, 25–26
  scholarly debate about Roosevelt and Truman administrations' actions on civil rights, 17–20
  unilateral executive action, *see* executive orders
executive orders
  8802, 123, 135
  9808, 136
  9981, 146, 152

Fahy Committee, *see* President's Committee on Equality of Treatment and Opportunity in the Armed Services
Fahy, Charles, 146–147
fair employment
  as part of PCCR legislative recommendations, 138
  as part of wartime civil rights agenda, 14
  background, 119–120
  in comparison to totalitarianism in Europe, 121
  March on Washington Movement and, 120–123

202 Index

public opinion toward, 60–61
   southern white attitudes, 61
   unilateral executive action and, 125
Fair Employment Practices Committee
   (FEPC), 101, 123–125, 135
Federal Council of Churches, 135
Federal Writers' Project, 103
Field, Marshall, 107
filibuster, 11, 25, 140
First World War, *see* World War I
Foner, Eric, 9, 71
Forrestal, James, 123, 144
Fort Sill, 115
Fortune, 32
France, 73, 99, 112
Frederickson, Kari, 135
Freedom to Serve: Equality of Treatment and Opportunity in the Armed Serves: A Report by the President's Committee, 150

Gallup, 31–32
Gallup, George, 31
General Social Survey (GSS), 32, 33
Georgia, 69, 134, 136, 141
Germany, 9, 21, 99
Gibson, Truman, 106, 114, 142–144
Gittelsohn, Roland B., 137
Goe, Robert, 136
Goodwin, Doris Kearns, 117
Gourevitch, Peter, 169
Graham, Frank P., 137
Grand Rapids, MI, 137
Granger, Lester, 144, 146–148
Graves, John Temple, 3, 40
Greenberg, David, 38

Haas, Francis J., 137
Hamby, Alonzo, 131
Hassett, William, 100
Hastie, William, 47, 114
Hine, Darlene Clark, 161
Hintze, Otto, 8
Hobby, Oveta, 115
Hoover, J. Edgar, 155
Howard University, 145
Humphrey, Hubert, 151

Ickes, Harold
   Baltimore Afro-American interview, 104–105

civil rights sympathies, 11
column, 107
correspondence regarding Southern Regional Council, 107
correspondence with *Negro Digest* editor, 105
refusal to join Civil Rights Congress petition, 107
Illinois, 63, 130, 140, 145
impressionable years hypothesis, 70
Independence, MO, 128, 155
Indiana, 68
Iowa, 115
Iraq War, 167
Ives, Irving, 140

Jackson, Wharlest, 164
Japan, 101–102
Japanese American Citizens League (JACL), 166
Japanese American internment, 165–166
Japanese Americans, 165–167
Johnson, Charles S., 68, 107
Johnson, John H., 105, 105
Johnson, Kimberley, 12, 57, 109
Johnson, Lyndon, 164
Johnson, Mordecai, 145–146

Kansas City, MO, 130
Katznelson, Ira, 41, 47, 64
Kelemen, R. Daniel, 24
Kellstedt, Paul, 35–36, 39–40
Kelly, Alfred H., 39
Kennedy, John F., 155
Kenworthy, E. W., 146–147, 153–154
Key, V. O., Jr., 41
Keyssar, Alexander, 64
King, Jr., Marin Luther, 164
Klarman, Michael, 160–161
Klinkner, Philip, 4–5, 16–19, 161–162
Knox, Frank, 112, 122
Knox, Ralph, 95–97
Korean War, 151
Korematsu v. United States, 165
Krebs, Ronald, 5, 19, 91, 165–166
Krock, Arthur, 161
Kruse, Kevin, 5
Kryder, Daniel, 5, 17–19, 39
Ku Klux Klan (KKK), 31, 130

La Guardia, Fiorello, 122, 124, 162

labor unions, *see* American Federation of Labor (AFL), *see* Brotherhood of Sleeping Car Porters, *see* Congress of Industrial Organizations (CIO), *see* Randolph, A. Philip
Landon, Alf, 31
LGBT rights, 167, 167
Literary Digest, 31
Locke, Alain, 99
long civil rights movement, 10
Los Angeles Times, 140
Los Angeles, CA, 167
Louisiana, 63, 64
Lucas, Scott, 140
Luckman, Charles, 137, 146
lynching
    as a national political issue, 47–48
    as part of PCCR legislative recommendations, 138
    as part of wartime civil rights agenda, 14
    attitudes of white veterans, 81–82
    southern veterans, 82
    congressional legislation to address, 108
    declining incidence of, 4, 53
    early NAACP advocacy against, 11
    in comparison to totalitarianism in Europe, 108–109
    public opinion toward federal investigations of, 49–54
    and issues of federalism, 53–54
    southern white attitudes, 49–52
    Roosevelt's reluctance to take public stand against, 108–109
    survey questions about, 48–49
    wartime investigations of, 109

March on Washington (1963), 155
March on Washington Movement, 120–123, 135
Marshall, T. H., 14–15
Marshall, Thurgood, 47
mass media, 35–38
Massachusetts, 145, 146
Matthews, Donald, 74
Matthews, Francis P., 137
Mayhew, David, 170
McAdam, Doug, 18
McCloy, John, 143, 148
McCullough, David, 132, 136
McIntyre, Marvin, 95–97, 99, 104, 108, 121

McNutt, Paul, 106, 124–125
Mexican Americans, 167
Michigan, 1–2, 130
"Michigan School", 35
military segregation, *see* segregation, military
military service, 8, 15–16, 70–72
Mississippi
    demographic characteristics, 6
    politicians from, 4, 67, 140–141
    racial violence in, 109, 128, 164
    segregation in, 145
    survey respondents, 64
    white soldiers from, 67
Missouri, 101, 128, 132, 155
Mitchell, Arthur, 57
Moore v. Dempsey, 11
Moskos, Charles, 91, 151
Murphy, Carl, 108–109
Muslim Americans, 167
Myrdal, Gunnar, 2, 29–30, 42, 66, 157

Nash, Philleo, 42, 133
Natchez, MS, 164
The Nation, 2
National Annenberg Election Survey (NAES), 33
National Association for the Advancement of Colored People (NAACP)
    A. Philip Randolph and, 13–14
    as civil rights organization, 3
    CIO and, 12
    Detroit branch of, 155
    founding of, 11
    Issac Woodard case and, 135
    membership growth, 13–14
    National Emergency Committee Against Mob Violence and, 135
    press release in response to 1940 White House meeting, 113
    support for Vietnam war, 163–164
National Colored Democratic Association, 133
National Council of Negro Women, 117
National Defense Conference on Negro Affairs, 144–146
National Emergency Committee Against Mob Violence, 135
National Opinion Research Center (NORC), 32, 41
National Urban League, 135, 144, 164

National Youth Administration, 122
Negro Digest, 105
Negro Newspaper Publishers Association, 100, 116
Negro Political Participation Study, 74
New Deal, 11, 31, 47, 108, 162
New York, 4, 69, 130, 140
New York City, 63, 68, 122, 162
New York Times, 140, 146, 161
Newsweek, 36
Niagara Movement, 11
Niles, David, 113, 136
North Carolina, 128, 134, 145

Odum, Howard, 68
Office of Production Management (OPM), 124
Office of War Information (OWI), 32, 101–102
Ohio, 130
Oklahoma, 115

Page, Benjamin, 36
Palmer, Dwight, 146
Parker, Christopher, 71–73, 75, 82
Patterson, Robert, 112–113, 122–123
Pearl Harbor, 20, 21, 96, 114
Pendergast, Tom, 130
Pennsylvania, 63, 130, 145
Perkins, Frances, 106–107
Philadelphia, PA, 95
Pittsburgh Courier, 140, 153
poll tax
  as a racial issue, 56–57
  as part of PCCR legislative recommendations, 138
  as part of wartime civil rights agenda, 14
  in comparison to totalitarianism in Europe, 109
  public opinion toward abolition of, 55–57
    southern white attitudes, 55–56
  survey questions about, 54–55
presidency, *see* executive branch
President's Committee on Civil Rights (PCCR), 136–141, 155–156
President's Committee on Equality of Treatment and Opportunity in the Armed Services, 146–154
propaganda (Axis), 101–103
protests
  anti-integration (1960s), 87–88
Prothro, James, 74
public opinion
  American political development and, 7, 168–169
  as a concept, 168
  emergence of survey research and, 31

racial prejudice, 41–47, 76–79
Randolph, A. Philip
  1940 White House meeting, 112–114
  as civil rights leader, 3
  as organizer of Committee Against Jim Crow in Military Service and Training, 144, 152
  as organizer of March on Washington Movement, 120–123
  correspondence with Mary McLeod Bethune, 126–127
  importance of desegregating the military, 144
  leadership style of, 13
  speaking invitation to Eleanor Roosevelt, 117
  views on implementation of FEPC order, 124
  views on PCCR report, 140
rationing, 22
Reconstruction, 9, 111
Red Cross, 118
Red Summer (1919), 10
Republican Party, *see* Dewey, Thomas, *see* Ives, Irving, *see* La Guardia, Fiorello, *see* Landon, Alf, *see* Taft, Robert, *see* Willkie, Wendell
republicanism (political theory), 8, 15, 24, 71
Revolutionary War, 8
Reynolds, Grant, 144, 152
Reynolds, Hobson, 145
Riegelman, Harold, 152, 154
rights of citizenship, 8, 14–16
Riverside Church, 164
Roman Empire, 8
Roosevelt, Eleanor, 105–106, 117–118, 122
Roosevelt, Franklin
  "Dr. Win-the-War", 98
  efforts to downplay civil rights issues during the war, 96

efforts to maintain coalition with
  southern Democrats, 108
meeting with Randolph and White, 112
opposition to March on Washington,
  121
scholarly assessments of civil rights
  actions of, 17, 97–98
use of polling data, 32
views on poll tax, 56
Roosevelt, Jr., Franklin, 137
Roper Center, 32, 33, 62
Rotnem, Victor, 101
Rowe, James, 130
Royall, Kenneth, 145–146, 148–150, 150
Russell, William, 141

Saldin, Robert, 17
Schickler, Eric, 34, 168–169
Schultz, Kevin, 125
Schuman, Howard, 35
Second World War, *see* World War II
segregation
  blood donations, 43, 118
  in the southern states, 4, 36, 86–87, 132, 140
segregation, military
  1940 White House meeting, 112–114
  A. Philip Randolph and, 144
  Advisor Committee on Negro Troop Policies and, 118
  advocacy during Roosevelt presidency, 110–125
  advocacy during Truman presidency, 141–154
  as part of PCCR legislative recommendations, 138
  as part of wartime civil rights agenda, 14
  attitudes of white veterans, 79–80
  Committee Against Jim Crow in Military Service and Training and, 144
  Executive Order 9981, 146
  Fahy Committee and, 146–154
  in practice, 110–111
  integration experiments and, 89–91
  National Defense Congress on Negro Affairs and, 144–146
  public opinion, 57–60
    southern whites, 58–59
  quota system and, 95–97, 111
  training of officer candidates and, 114–115

Truman Gibson and, 142–143
World War I and, 110
Sengstacke, John, 146, 150
Shapiro, Robert, 36
Sheridan, John E., 95–97
Sherrill, Henry Knox, 137
Shishkin, Boris, 137
Shklar, Judith, 65
Sikeston, MO, 101
Silberman, Charles, 158
sit-in movement, 84–86, 155, 155
Skowronek, Stephen, 24
slavery, 9
Smith v. Allwright, 42, 160–162
Smith, Rogers, 4–5, 16–19, 161–162
Sokol, Jason, 68–69, 73
soldier voting legislation, 62–64
Sommers, Davidson, 143
South Carolina, 133–134, 136
Southern Regional Council, 107
southern states
  definition, 41
  military training locations and, 73, 148
  white southern attitudes
    anti-integration protests, 87–88
    fair employment, 61
    lynching, 49–52, 82
    poll tax, 55–56
    racial prejudice, 44–46
    rural areas, 46, 52, 59
    segregation, 86–87
    segregation, military, 58–59
    sit-in movement, 84–86
    soldier voting, 62–64
    voting rights, 84
Sparks, Chauncey, 153
Stage Door Canteen, 68
Stengstacke, John, 116
Stennis, John, 141
Stevenson, William E., 146
Stimson, Henry, 112, 115, 117–118, 122
Stouffer, Samuel, *see The American Soldier*
Strunk, Mildred, 32
Student Nonviolent Coordinating
  Committee (SNCC), 163
Supreme Court, 31, 42, 160–162
Survey Graphic, 99
survey research
  as an elite construct, 60
  development, 31–32
  quota sampling, 33–35

weighting protocol, 34–35

Taft, Robert, 144
Tarrow, Sidney, 170
Tennessee, 63, 107
Texas, 6, 148
Tilly, Charles, 169
Tilly, Dorothy, 137
To Secure These Rights: The Report of the President's Committee on Civil Rights, 90, 137–141
Tobias, Channing, 137, 145
total war, 22
Trotter, William Monroe, 11
Truman, Bess, 128
Truman, Harry
  1948 message to Congress, 142
  expectations for PCCR report, 139
  military service in World War I, 131–132
  Missouri upbringing, 128–129
  personality, 132
  prejudiced views, 128–129
  response to violence against black veterans, 128, 132, 135–136
  support for Fahy committee, 146–147
  support from civil rights organizations, 129
  views on civil rights, 131–132
  postpresidency, 155–156
Truman, Margaret, 128
Truman, Mary Jane, 128
Tuck, Stephen, 5
Tully, Grace, 96, 99

University of Chicago, 32
University of Denver, 32
University of North Carolina, 68, 74, 137

Vermont, 9
veterans
  historical research on white veterans, 68–69
  identifying veteran status in surveys, 74–76, 83–84
  racial attitudes of white veterans, 76–82, 84–88
  violence against black veterans, 128, 133–136
Vietnam war, 163–164
Virginia, 141
voting rights
  as part of PCCR legislative recommendations, 138
  attitudes of white veterans, 84
  democratic citizenship and, 65
  in the nineteenth century, 9
  soldier voting legislation, *see* soldier voting legislation

Wallace, Henry, 106
Walsh, Howard, 109
War Department, 112–113, 123, 142–143
War in Afghanistan, 167
War Manpower Commission, 124
Washington Post, 140
Washington, Booker T., 11
Washington, DC, 121
Weir, Margaret, 162
What the Negro Wants, 12
Whitaker, Robert A., 162
White, Walter
  1940 White House meeting, 112–114
  as author of *A Rising Wind*, 67–69
  as civil rights leader, 3
  as visitor to training facilities and bases, 68, 114–116
  criticism of Dies Committee, 102
  leadership style of, 13
  March on Washington Movement and, 122–123
  meeting with Advisory Committee on Negro Troop Policies, 118
  suggestions to Roosevelt, 114, 116
  understanding of differences between Roosevelt and Truman, 135
  views on implementation of FEPC order, 125
  views on PCCR report, 140
Wilkins, Roy, 110, 129, 164
Williams, Aubrey, 122
Williston, F. O., 121–122
Willkie, Wendell, 103
Wilson, Charles E., 137
Wilson, Kenneth, 71
Wilson, Woodrow, 112
Wolfe, Oscar, 140
Women's Army Auxiliary Corps (WAAC), 115
Woodard, Isaac, 133–136
Woodring, Harry, 110
World War I, 9, 110, 112
World War II

"postwar" shorthand and, 18
as a variable, 22–24, 158–160
temporal boundaries of, 20–22
Wu, Ellen, 166

Yale University, 164
Young, Whitney, 164

Zelizer, Julian, 25